THOMAS MANN

A CHRONICLE OF HIS LIFE

THOMAS MANN
A CHRONICLE OF HIS LIFE

Hans Bürgin and Hans-Otto Mayer

English translation by
Eugene Dobson

UNIVERSITY OF ALABAMA PRESS
University, Alabama

Photographs reproduced by permission of
Hans-Otto Mayer

Standard Book Number: 8173–8061–2
Library of Congress Catalog Card Number: 68–10989
Manufactured in the United States of America

TABLE OF CONTENTS

TRANSLATOR'S PREFACE

A great many books about Thomas Mann are currently available in English, and a number of them deal with a part of his life or touch on his life at one stage or another. Arthur Eloesser's biography of Mann, published in 1925, and Erika Mann's account of the last year of her father's life, are especially noteworthy. However, no full biography of Thomas Mann has been published in English to date, and it seems quite possible that the lack will continue to exist for some years to come; certainly no definitive account of Mann's creative life can be written until biographers have had an opportunity to consult his notebooks, and these are to remain sealed in the Thomas Mann Archive in Zürich until 1975. The present work, a "chronicle," does not purport to be a biography in the full sense of the term, but it does have the great merit of taking into account all stages of Mann's life, and the further merit of doing so in rather circumstantial terms.

Its value as a concise work of reference is undeniable, and in this respect, at least, it is likely to be of permanent use no matter how many full biographies may eventually be written—indeed, it is probable that the authors of many such works will turn to the Bürgin/Mayer chronicle more than once in the course of their research.

The marginal bibliography accompanying the chronicle, though a pain in the neck for the translator, the editor, and the compositor alike, should be of considerable assistance to the reader. It includes, in addition to the data given in the German edition, bibliographical information concerning English translations of the works cited. In each case the additional information has been inserted chronologically according to the publication date of the original German work, rather than in terms of the publication date of the English translation itself. Entries for English language collections of short stories, essays, or "selections" from Mann's writings have been placed according to the publication date of the first work in the collection. Where a chapter from a novel is listed as having been published separately, I have given the chapter title in English.

With the gracious permission of the Alfred A. Knopf Publishing Company, the copyright holder, I have quoted from published translations of Mann's works when such were available. (In so doing I have come to appreciate, even more fully than I had before, the remarkable skill of Helen T. Lowe-Porter!) In giving the source of a quoted passage used in the text, I have used the English title when the passage has been extracted from a published translation, the German title when the translation is my own. Of the many collections of Mann's letters, only one has been translated into English to date: *Letters to Paul Amann*. Most of the many quotations from

Mann's letters in the chronicle are from the collected letters, which I have abbreviated as *Briefe I, II,* or *III.**

Thanks are due the compilers Hans Bürgin and Hans-Otto Mayer, for their exemplary cooperation in making this translation possible and in furthering its accomplishment. Among other things, they made available to me a large number of corrections that were subsequently to be incorporated in a new printing of the chronicle in German. I should also like to thank those with whom I had occasion to consult in regard to translation and bibliographical problems, and especially the following individuals: Ernest Seemann, Morgan L. Walters, Francis Squibb, Mary Gray Porter, J. C. Hayes, Jerry Lewis Warren, Harry Ainsworth, and Axel Claesges. I must also acknowledge the encouragement of my wife, Frances Tucker Dobson, as well as her indefatigable assistance at several stages of the work.

University, Alabama EUGENE DOBSON
January, 1969

**Briefe I* = *Thomas Mann, Briefe 1889–1936,* edited by Erika Mann. Frankfurt on Main: S. Fischer Verlag, 1961.

Briefe II = *Thomas Mann, Briefe 1937–1947,* edited by Erika Mann. Frankfurt on Main: S. Fischer Verlag, 1963.

Briefe III = *Thomas Mann, Briefe 1948–1955* und Nachlese, edited by Erika Mann. Frankfurt on Main: S. Fischer Verlag, 1965.

Amann = *Thomas Mann: Letters to Paul Amann 1915–1952,* edited by Herbert Wegener, translated by Richard and Carla Winston. Middleton, Connecticut: Wesleyan University Press, 1960.

Bertram = *Thomas Mann an Ernst Bertram: Briefe aus den Jahren 1910–1955,* edited by Inge Jens. Pfullingen: Neske Verlag, 1960.

FROM THE PREFACE TO THE GERMAN EDITION

. . .

As it stands, this chronicle should give the reader a measure of insight into the character and work methods of a writer who became a major representative of German culture in the twentieth century. We have tried to portray that writer's life, one rich in public honors and yet also burdened with cares in great measure; to depict something of the world in which he lived; and to trace the main lines of development in his work and his close connections with the principal literary and political currents of his time. Through the use of quotations from Mann's writings, published and unpublished, we have tried to create a kind of concise "autobiography" of the man, illuminating his life and works in a way that will have some appeal not only for his already established reading public and scholars but also for those who know relatively little about him.

It is understandable that the different parts of the chronicle are unequal in weight and in what they comprehend. Mann's circle of influence was relatively limited in the early stages of his career, and sources of information for those years are correspondingly scanty. Subsequently the effect of his work spread throughout the whole civilized world, resulting in an overabundance of material on the later stages of his life, and forcing us to make a selection that may well be subject to criticism but which was necessary to attain a measure of unity. We alone are responsible for the selection of material to be included and for the writing of the narrative.

Especial thanks are due Frau Katja Mann, who permitted us to use quotations from her husband's works and letters, and Frau Erika Mann for her aid and counsel. Fräulein Ida Herz of London, for decades associated with Thomas Mann and his work, has read the manuscript and made numerous astute contributions. Dr. Hans Wysling, director of the Thomas Mann Archives in Zürich, gave us valuable information. Professor Klaus W. Jonas of Pittsburgh, Pennsylvania, Professor Herbert Lehnert of Houston, Texas, Erich Neumann, director of the Thomas Mann Archives of German Academy of Science in Berlin, Heinz Saueressig of Biberach on the Riss, and Dr. Georg Wenzel, founder and chairman of the Thomas Mann Circle in the German Cultural League, also contributed information for inclusion in this work. To all we extend our cordial thanks.

[*June, 1965*]

PREFACE TO THE AMERICAN EDITION

Thomas Mann spent some of his most important years in the United States. The American publisher Alfred A. Knopf made personal contact with him in Switzerland during the writer's first year of exile, and Mann made his first journey to the United States the following year. Subsequently he accepted a guest professorship at Princeton University and settled permanently on American soil, building a home in Pacific Palisades, California and, in 1944, becoming a citizen of the United States. "Well then," he would write later, "I have spent fifteen years in this mighty land, whose short history includes a war of liberation and which Goethe called a 'relief of mankind.' I owe this land great thanks, for it has accepted with hearty willingness this refugee from Hitler's Germany and accorded my work the most splendid honors."

Some of Mann's most important works date from the American period of his life. He finished *The Beloved Returns* at Princeton in 1939. His Indian novella, *The Transposed Heads*, followed early in August, 1939 and within that same year he began the fourth volume of the Joseph novel, which he finished at Pacific Palisades in January, 1943. Certain motifs of his *Joseph in Egypt* cannot be fully understood except by reference to the influence of America on Mann's outlook and his respect for President Franklin D. Roosevelt and his politics. The "book of sorrow," *Doctor Faustus*, was written in America during the years 1943–1947, and was followed—to mention only the major works—by *The Holy Sinner* and large sections of *The Memoirs of Felix Krull, Confidence Man*.

During all of his American years Mann occupied himself tirelessly with political questions. He delivered innumerable speeches and readings throughout the country in the 1930's and after, and in such political appearances he unswervingly championed the true Germany of Goethe, Nietzsche, and Schopenhauer as against the "Germany" of Adolf Hitler and his kind. During the crisis of World War II Mann grew far beyond the former evaluation of his critics into a representative of the "other Germany," the real Germany, and became one of the world's most respected exponents of humanity, civilization, and genuine democracy. He became a world citizen whose voice could not be ignored. His work can be called, in the true sense of the word, *world* literature.

Even now the phenomenon of Thomas Mann continues to have an effect in American literary criticism. In no other land are his novels, novellas, and essays so carefully and critically studied as in the United States. A great number of dissertations and works about Mann have come from American universities, and Yale and Princeton universities, to mention only two, maintain major collections of his manuscripts, letters, and editions of his works.

In its original form this chronicle was accorded a good deal of generous praise by American critics and a goodly measure of acceptance in American universities and among some American followers of Mann's work. It is hoped that Professor Dobson's admirable English translation will make the chronicle accessible to a wider circle of readers, and that it will further the understanding and appreciation of Thomas Mann's life and accomplishments.

HANS BÜRGIN HANS-OTTO MAYER

Kappeln/Schlei and Düsseldorf
December, 1968

THOMAS MANN

A CHRONICLE OF HIS LIFE

THE PARENTS

The father of T.M., Thomas Johann Heinrich Mann, was born August 22, 1840. He was the son of Johann Siegmund Mann (1797–1863) and his second wife, Elisabeth Marty (1811–1890), who were living in Lübeck at Mengstrasse 4 (the "Buddenbrook House"). After the death of his father, Thomas Johann Heinrich Mann became owner of the Johann Siegmund Mann firm, which dealt in the sale and transport of grain. He was made Royal Dutch Consul in 1864. "How often have I caught myself up, realizing with a smile that it is actually the personality of my dead father which, as my secret example, determines my actions and omissions. Perhaps there are those listening to me who have seen him living and working in the city in one of his many positions—those who remember his dignity and common sense, his energy and industry, his personal and spiritual elegance, his social grace and humor, and the bonhomie with which he could talk to the common folk, who depended on him in a genuinely filial way. He was not a simple man, not strong, but rather nervous and sensitive. He was a self-restrained, successful man, who early achieved respect and honor in this world, the world in which he built his beautiful house." [*Lübeck als geistige Lebensform*]
On June 4, 1869 Thomas Johann Heinrich Mann married Julia da Silva-Bruhns, born in Angra dos Reis, Brazil, on August 14, 1851. She was the daughter of the plantation owner, Johann Ludwig Bruhns from Lübeck (1821–1893) and his wife, Maria Luiza da Silva (1828–1856), "a Portugese-Creole Brazilian." Julia "was distinctly Latin in type, in her youth a much-admired beauty and extraordinarily musical. When I ask myself the hereditary origin of my characteristics I am fain to recall Goethe's famous little verse and say that I too have from my father 'des Lebens ernstes Führen,' but from my mother the 'Frohnatur'—the sensuous, artistic side, and, in the widest sense, the 'Lust zu fabulieren.' " [*A Sketch of My Life*]
After the early death of her mother, Julia had been brought to Lübeck in 1856 and educated in the boarding school (Vor dem Mühlentor) of Therese Bousset. She had grown up in the house (Auf der Parade) of her uncle Peter Eduard Bruhns.

In 1870, Consul Heinrich Mann and his wife rented an apartment at Breite Strasse 54. Luiz Heinrich Mann, T.M.'s brother, was born on March 27, 1871 and baptized on May 7 in the protestant Marienkirche by Pastor Trummer. A year later, Consul Mann bought the house at Breite Strasse 36 (destroyed in World War II).

CHILDHOOD AND YOUTH

June 6, 1875

Paul Thomas Mann is born. "I was born on Sunday, June 6, 1875 at twelve noon. The stars were favorable, as those adept at astrology later assured me, and promised, on the basis of my horoscope, a long and happy life as well as a quiet death." [*Lebenslauf,* 1936]

July 11, 1875

Thomas is baptized by Pastor Münzenberger in the Marienkirche. Godfathers are Consul Heinrich Marty, brother of T.M.'s grandmother Elisabeth Mann (née Marty), and his uncle Nikolaus Heinrich Stolterfoht, farm owner at Castorf [in Low German, Castorp—*trans.* note] and husband of Julia Mann's sister Maria.

February 19, 1877

Consul Heinrich Mann is elected to the Lübeck Senate. In the assembly of February 28, he is named purchasing agent for the Committee on Construction and for the Department of Indirect Taxes and also a member of the Central Committee on Poverty and of the Commission on Trade and Maritime Affairs. In 1885, he becomes chairman both of the last agency and of the Tariff Bureau.

August 23, 1877

T.M.'s sister Julia Elisabeth Therese ("Lula") is born and baptized on October 14, at St. Jakobi.

1881

Senator Mann buys the property at Beckergrube 52 from the estate of the merchant Alexander Grammann, and builds a house (destroyed during World War II)—in keeping with his position. "My childhood was sheltered and happy. We five children, three boys and two girls, grew up in a spacious and dignified house built by my father; but we had a second home in the old family dwelling beside St. Mary's, where my paternal grandmother lived alone, and which today is shown to the curious as 'the Buddenbrook House.'" [*A Sketch of My Life*]

September 23, 1881

T.M.'s sister Carla Augusta Olga Maria is born. She is baptized on December 1, in the Marienkirche.

Easter, 1882

T.M. enters school, and from 1882 to 1889 attends the three elementary and three pre-Gymnasium grades at the private school of Dr. Bussenius on Fleischhauerstrasse, which was commonly called the "*Kandidatenschule.*"

On his personal relationship with his mother: "I believe that I, her second child, was dearest to her heart." [Letter to Agnes E. Meyer, June 29, 1939, *Briefe II*]

She reads aloud from Hans Christian Andersen's fairy tales and Fritz Reuter's *Ut mine Stromtid,* sings songs by Schubert, Schumann, Brahms, and Liszt, and plays Chopin. ". . . often she would devote her free evenings to us when she would read Fritz Reuter's tales to us under the lamp at the table in the parlor. Her foreign accent made Reuter's Mecklenburger Low German sound even stranger, but she knew this dialect better than anyone else in the house . . . Of course, I preferred even more to hear my mother play and sing. Her Bechstein piano stood in the drawingroom, a bright corner room, . . . and here I would sit for hours and listen to her well-rehearsed, sensitive playing, which sounded best in the etudes and nocturnes of Chopin." [*Das Bild der Mutter*]

April 6, 1884

Emanuel Geibel, an honored citizen of Lübeck, dies. "As a child, I saw Emanuel von Geibel in Travemünde, with his white moustache and a shawl over his shoulders. Because of my parents he spoke to me, even in a friendly manner." [*Lübeck als geistige Lebensform*]

Easter, 1889

T.M. enters the Katharineum, a Gymnasium, in the department devoted primarily to scientific studies. He requires five years to finish the three grades, having to repeat two. "School I loathed, and to the end failed to satisfy its demands. I despised it as a milieu, I was critical of the manners of its masters, and I early espoused a sort of literary opposition to its spirit, its discipline, and its methods of training." [*A Sketch of My Life*]

His teacher during the last three years is Prof. Dr. Baethcke. "Five years ago I visited Lübeck, on the Free City's seven hundreth anniversary, and renewed acquaintance with the master of the lower second who also had taught Latin and German. I told the snowy-haired Emeritus that I knew he had always found me a thorough good-for-nothing, but that I had quietly taken in a good deal in his classes nonetheless." [*A Sketch of My Life*]

T.M.'s friendship with Otto Grautoff, son of a Lübeck book-dealer, who is later to become a writer and art historian, extends far into the years at Munich.

The summers, 1882–1891

Holidays in Travemünde. "There lies the *sea*, the Baltic, which a boy catches sight of first in Travemünde. The Travemünde of forty years ago had its old Kurhaus in the Biedermeier style, its Swiss-style chalets, and its concert pavilion, where the little long-haired, gypsy-like bandleader Hess used to concertize with his group. I would sit on the steps of the pavilion and smell the summer fragrance of the boxwood . . . At this place, in Travemünde, this vacation paradise, I spent undoubtedly the happiest days of my life. Those times of peace and satisfaction could never be forgotten or equalled by anything later." [*Lübeck als geistige Lebensform*]

During the years 1882–1891

First literary efforts. "I had begun with childish plays, which I and my younger brothers and sisters performed before our parents and aunts. Then there were poems, inscribed to a dear friend, the one who as Hans Hansen, in *Tonio Kröger*, has a sort of symbolic existence, though in real life he took to drink and made a melancholy end in Africa." [*A Sketch of My Life*] *GEDICHTE AN EINEN FREUND*

October 14, 1889

Earliest extant letter of T.M. (To Frieda Laurentine Hartenstein, probably one of the young ladies visiting in the Mann home) mentions a play "Aischa." T.M. signs the letter "lyric-dramatic poet." [*Briefe I*] *ROMANZE AUF DEN TOD DER ARRIA*

In his last year in secondary school: "A Romance on the

Heroic Death of Arria: '*Paete, non dolet . . .*' " [*A Sketch of My Life*]

Also known to exist is the title of "an anticlerical play 'The Priests.' "

DIE PRIESTER: EIN DRAMA

Winter, 1889

T.M. and his sister Julia take part in a private course in dancing under the supervision of Rudolf Knoll, Ballet Director of the Deutsches Schauspielhaus in Hamburg. "What became of the flaxen-haired dancing partner who later was the object of love lyrics, I cannot say." [*A Sketch of My Life*]

GEDICHT AN EINE TANZSTUNDEN-PARTNERIN

Easter, 1890

T.M. is confirmed in the Marienkirche.

April 12, 1890

His brother, Karl Viktor Mann, is born and is baptized June 5, at St. Jakobi.

May 23, 1890

The centennial day of the Johann Siegmund Mann firm. "I saw the lines of congratulants and representatives, the city and harbor decorated with flags, and I saw my father—the man of the day, admired and loved with great tenderness, wisely representing a century of middle-class diligence. My heart was full of anxiety . . . I knew then that I would not follow my father and my father's fathers, at least not as it was silently requested of me that day. I knew it would not be I who would help the old firm to continue." [*Hundert Jahre Reclam*]

December 6, 1890

Catherina Elisabeth Mann, née Marty, the last of T.M.'s grandparents, dies. The old family house on Mengstrasse is sold.

October 13, 1891

Senator Thomas Johann Heinrich Mann dies at fifty-one. "My father died a relatively young man, of blood-poisoning, when I was fifteen [sic]. Thanks to his intelligence and superior bearing, he had always been a highly respected, popular, and influential citizen. But his business for some time had not gone very well, and the hundred-year-old grain firm went into liquidation not long after a funeral which in size and pomp surpassed anything that had been seen in Lübeck for many years." [*A Sketch of My Life*]

1891

Julia Mann moves with her children outside the city gates (Roeckstrasse 9). Heinrich Mann is learning to be a book-dealer in Dresden. The house at Beckergrube 52 is sold.

1892

T.M. first hears the music of Richard Wagner when the tenor Emil Gerhäuser is engaged at the Lübeck Stadttheater. "My first encounter with the music of Richard Wagner, which the theater of my city made possible for me, was one of the great artistic experiences of my life . . . At that time young Emil Gerhäuser was the heroic tenor of the city opera. His voice at its prime, he sang from *Tannhäuser, Meistersinger*, and several arias from *Lohengrin*. Without being presumptious, I think I can safely say that the Stadttheater never gave shelter to a more receptive, entranced listener than I was on that delightful evening." [*Erinnerungen ans Lübecker Stadttheater*]

Easter, 1892

Julia Mann moves with the three youngest children to Munich. T.M. goes to boarding school, first under the instruction of Dr. Hupe and later under Dr. Timpe.

Easter, 1893

T.M.'s last year of school, under Dr. Hempel: "Of this period I have the most jovial memories. The 'institution' had given up all hope for me. It left me to my fate, and that was dark to me; but, feeling myself quite hearty and clever, I was not cast down. I sat away the hours. Outside school I lived very much as I liked, and stood well with my fellow boarders, in whose premature drinking bouts I gaily condescended to take part now and then." [*A Sketch of My Life*] The poem, *Zweimaliger Abschied*, is probably written about this time.

ZWEIMALIGER ABSCHIED (DER FRÜHLINGSSTURM, May, 1893)

May, 1893

Under the pseudonym "Paul Thomas," T.M. publishes the periodical *Frühlingssturm: Monatsschrift für Kunst, Litteratur und Philosophie* with his friend, Otto Grautoff, and several school colleagues. Two issues appear before the publication fails. "*Spring Storm*! As a spring storm blows through an oppressive landscape, we shall sweep with words and thoughts through the morass of musty brains and ignor-

DER FRÜHLINGSSTURM (May and June–July, 1893)

ance and narrow-mindedness, the pompous philistinism which oppresses us." [Preface to the *Frühlingssturm*]

March 16, 1894

T.M. leaves school with permission to be an officer for one year of voluntary military service. He goes to Munich.

1894–1896 Munich
LITERARY AND JOURNALISTIC EFFORTS

April, 1894

T.M. works as an apprentice without pay at the South German Fire Insurance Bank in Munich. He lives with his mother in an apartment at Rambergstrasse 2. He writes secretly on his short story *Gefallen* during his working hours: "I sat at my sloping desk surrounded by snuff-taking clerks and copied out accounts; but secretly I also wrote my first tale, a love story called *Gefallen*. It earned me my first literary success. . . . the story also brought me a warm-hearted and encouraging letter from Richard Dehmel and later even a visit from that much-admired poet." [*A Sketch of My Life*]

GEFALLEN (DIE GESELLSCHAFT, Leipzig, October, 1894)

Autumn, 1894

T.M. gives up his post with the insurance company and enrolls as an auditor at the Technische Hochschule in Munich, with the intention of becoming a journalist.

November 4, 1894

He enrolls for the following lectures: Professor Max Haushofer, The National Economy (four hours); Professor Felix Stieve, Culture and World History (four hours); Professor Wilhelm Hertz, German Mythology (two hours); Professor Franz von Reber, The Foundation of Aesthetics (one hour); and Professor Karl von Reinhardstöttner, Shakespeare's Tragedies. "I registered at the University and attended lectures which seemed fairly likely to forward me in the rather indefinite calling I proposed: courses in history, political economy, literature, and art. From time to time I attended these with fair regularity and not quite without profit." [*A Sketch of My Life*]

He becomes a member of the Academic-Dramatic Society. In the coffee houses of Munich, as the author of *Gefallen*, he makes the acquaintance of contemporary writers and poets: Otto Erich Hartleben, Oskar Panizza, Julius Schaumberger, Ludwig Scharf, Heinrich von Reder, and Erich Koch-Weser, who is later to become a statesman.

" . . . great and decisive impressions that came to me from my reading . . .": "Probably my earliest prose writings that saw the light of print betray clearly enough the intellectual and stylistic influence of Nietzsche . . . Certainly the contact with him was to a high degree decisive for an intellect still in its formative stage; . . . what I saw above all in Nietzsche was the victor over self. I took nothing literally; I *believed* him hardly at all; and this precisely made my love for him a passion on two planes—gave it, in other words, its depth." [*A Sketch of My Life*]

November 29, 1894

T.M. sends his next short story, *The Little Professor*, to Richard Dehmel who had agreed to accept it for the periodical *Pan*. Dehmel refuses it but writes the author a "quite charming letter."

DER KLEINE PROFESSOR (lost)

February, 1895

T.M. goes to Fasching celebrations, concerts, and the theater. He works occasionally on a fairy tale play in verse, *The Old King*, and on the short story, *Walter Weiler*. "Recently I have only managed to write some lyric poems. One does not have to possess either industriousness or perseverance to write poetry. I usually write it while going to sleep." [Unpublished letter to Otto Grautoff]

DER ALTE KÖNIG (lost)
WALTER WEILER (later entitled DER BAJAZZO)
POEMS, among them *SIEHST DU, KIND, ICH LIEBE DICH* (DIE GESELLSCHAFT, Leipzig, January, 1895)

April, 1895

Heinrich Mann becomes editor of the periodical, *Das Zwanzigste Jahrhundert: Blätter für deutsche Art und Wohlfahrt*, previously edited by Friedrich Lienhard.

May, 1895

At the beginning of the summer semester, T.M. enrolls as a student in the general polytechnical division of the Hochschule and hears the following series of lectures: Prof. Franz von Reber, Art History (German Architecture after Charlemagne); Prof. Felix Stieve, German History in the Nineteenth Century; Prof. Wilhelm Hertz, German Literature in the Middle Ages. "I was particularly enthusiastic over a course on the court epic by Wilhelm Hertz, the poet and translator from Middle High German." [*A Sketch of My Life*]

May 15, 1895
T.M. sends the short story *Walter Weiler* to Richard Dehmel: "I hope only that you will sooner or later find the leisure to look through the story and give me your opinion as to whether it is worth anything." [*Briefe I*]

June 15, 1895
In the German premiere of Ibsen's *The Wild Duck,* sponsored by the Academic-Dramatic Society and under the direction of Ernst von Wolzogen, T.M. plays the role of the businessman Werle.

He writes occasional book reviews and satirical comments for the periodical *Das Zwanzigste Jahrhundert.*

Articles in DAS ZWANZIGSTE JAHRHUNDERT (Berlin, 1895–96)

July–October, 1895
With his brother Heinrich, T.M. takes his first trip to Italy—Palestrina and Rome: "I spent the last year in Italy, in and around Rome. In the mountains I passed the warm months and at the end of September went back into the city . . ." [*Der Wille zum Glück*]

October, 1895
After his return to Munich, T.M. continues to write for *Das Zwanzigste Jahrhundert* with his brother Heinrich, who not long thereafter returns to Italy.

1896
T.M. begins the short story *Der Wille Zum Glück.*

DER WILLE ZUM GLÜCK (SIMPLICISSIMUS, August/September, 1896)

June, 1896
He takes his first trip to Vienna: "I went there when I was twenty-one, after I had received two hundred marks from an endowment policy, which matured at my coming of age. I had determined to throw all this money away in Vienna, and after three or four days this was accomplished, even though I stayed in the good old Hotel Klomser on the Herrengasse." [*Verhältnis zu Wien*]

1896–1898
THE ITALIAN SOJOURN

ENTTÄUSCHUNG (in DER KLEINE HERR FRIEDEMANN. Berlin: S. Fischer, 1898)

October, 1896
T.M. spends three weeks in Venice and then travels via Ancona and Rome to Naples.

November, 1896

He writes the short story *"Disillusionment."*

December, 1896

He lives in Rome at Via Torre Argentina 34 with his brother Heinrich. "My brother, who originally meant to be an artist, sketched a great deal, while I, in the reek of endless three-centesimi cigarettes, devoured Scandinavian and Russian literature and wrote." [*A Sketch of My Life*]

T.M. sends the short story *Little Herr Friedemann,* which he had written in Munich, to the *Neue deutsche Rundschau.* The editor, Oskar Bie, requests that T.M. send all his work. A collection of short stories is prepared to include *Little Herr Friedemann, Der Tod, The Dilettante, Tobias Mindernickel,* and *Little Lizzy.*

1897

T.M. and Heinrich Mann write the *Bilderbuch für artige Kinder* as a confirmation present for their sister Carla. It is a collection of satiric poems, caricatures, and fantasies.

Spring, 1897

Samuel Fischer, the publisher, writes T.M. suggesting a longer prose work. *Buddenbrooks* is first planned as a joint effort of Thomas and Heinrich.

Summer, 1897

Living in an apartment (Albergo Casa Bernardini) in Palestrina, T.M. prepares to write *Buddenbrooks* by making genealogical and chronological notes. He requests information from his sister Julia and his uncle Wilhelm Marty about matters of the family and its connection with the city of Lübeck.

Autumn, 1897

He returns to Rome.

October, 1897

He begins writing the novel. "When I began to write *Buddenbrooks*, I was sitting in Rome at Via Torre Argentina trenta quattro, four floors up. My home city had little reality for me, and I was not very convinced of its existence. It seemed to me with its inhabitants nothing essentially more than an earlier dream, both ludicrous and respectable, and in the most proper way my own. For three years I worked on the book with care and fidelity." [*Bilse und ich*]

DISILLUSIONMENT (STORIES OF THREE DECADES. New York: Alfred A. Knopf, 1936. 567 pp.)

DER KLEINE HERR FRIEDEMANN (NEUE DEUTSCHE RUNDSCHAU, May, 1897)

LITTLE HERR FRIEDEMANN (STORIES OF THREE DECADES)

DER TOD (SIMPLICISSIMUS, January, 1897)

DER BAJAZZO (NEUE DEUTSCHE RUNDSCHAU, September, 1897)

THE DILETTANTE (STORIES OF THREE DECADES)

TOBIAS MINDERNICKEL (NEUE DEUTSCHE RUNDSCHAU, January, 1898)

TOBIAS MINDERNICKEL (STORIES OF THREE DECADES)

The first page of the manuscript is dated, "End of October, 1897."

Spring, 1898

The first collection of stories, *Der Kleine Herr Friedemann*, appears. "While I was still in Rome my first book came out . . . I could 'see myself' in the Roman bookshops." [*A Sketch of My Life*]

End of April, 1898

T.M. returns to Munich.

LUISCHEN (DIE GESELLSCHAFT, Volume One, 1900) *LITTLE LIZZY* (STORIES OF THREE DECADES) *BILDERBUCH FÜR ARTIGE KINDER* (1933, lost) *DER KLEINE HERR FRIEDEMANN,* Novellen (Berlin: S. Fischer, 1898. 2,000 copies)

1898–1900
WITH *SIMPLICISSIMUS*

May 1, 1898

T.M. takes his first bachelor apartment at Theresienstrasse 82, first floor to the right, but he soon moves to Barerstrasse 69, a second floor apartment.

1898–1900

He becomes reader and copyreader for *Simplicissimus:* "Korfiz Holm was at that time a member of the publishing house of Langen, whose head, like Wedekind, was living abroad under a charge of *lèse-majesté*. Holm was Baltic by birth and a friend from Lübeck days, where he had been graduated from the first form. He met me on the street one day and offered me a position on *Simplicissimus* at a hundred marks a month. For about a year—until Langen, still in Paris, abolished the job I held—I worked as a reader and press reader in the fine offices on Schackstrasse. My particular task was to make the first selection from the incoming short-story manuscripts and to submit my suggestions to my superior, Dr. Geheeb, brother of the Landschule educationist. This occupation had some sense." [*A Sketch of My Life*]

November, 1898

T.M. takes an apartment in Schwabing [a section of Munich] at Markstrasse 5, fourth floor. He describes his apartment in the story, *The Wardrobe*, written between the 23rd and 29th of November. The story appears in the collection, *Tristan*, with the dedication "For Carla." [Thomas Mann's Notizbücher, Thomas Mann Archives, Zürich]

DER KLEIDERSCHRANK (NEUE DEUTSCHE RUNDSCHAU, June, 1899) THE WARDROBE (STORIES OF THREE DECADES)

1899

T.M. begins a close friendship with Kurt Martens, author of *Roman aus der Décadence* (1898). "I had close and sympathetic relations with Kurt Martens, the author of novels and short stories . . . He belonged to the few people—I could count them on the fingers of one hand—whom I ever addressed as '*du.*'" [*A Sketch of My Life*]

Other literary and artistic acquaintances of T.M. at this time are Markus Behmer, Arthur Holitscher, Alfred Kubin, and Hans von Weber.

June, 1899

T.M. moves to Feilitzstrasse 5, fourth floor: "I was such an impassioned bicycle rider at that time that I scarcely went a step on foot, but even in a pouring rain took my way, in cloak and galoshes, upon my machine. I carried it on my shoulder up the three flights of stairs to my flat, where it lived in the kitchen. Mornings, after my work, I used to stand it on its saddle and clean it." [*A Sketch of My Life*]

July, 1899

He continues to work on *Buddenbrooks*, interrupting this to write stories such as *Gerächt*. "Don't think badly of me for what is to appear next in *Simplicissimus*. It is of little value, but until the novel is finished I must in one way or another keep myself in the public eye. By the way, in the next weeks the *Gesellschaft* is to print something of mine [*Little Lizzy*] which is older and better, very melancholy and biting. [To Kurt Martens, *Briefe I*]

GERÄCHT, (SIMPLICISSIMUS, August, 1899)

The poem, *Monolog*, in terza rima, is written during this time.

MONOLOG, poem in *terza rima* (DIE GESELLSCHAFT, 1899, Volume 2)

September, 1899

T.M. spends his holidays in Denmark. He visits Lübeck and stays at the Hotel Stadt Hamburg. This is the time of the episode in which he is almost arrested for fraud in his home town. He spends nine days in Aalsgard on Sund, the narrow strip of land between Denmark and Sweden. Here he has the idea of writing *Tonio Kröger*.

Autumn, 1899

T.M. reads Schopenhauer: "My tall, narrow room in the suburbs seemed to sway before my eyes . . . Here for days I lay stretched out on a peculiarly shaped chaise or settee, reading *Die Welt als Wille und Vorstellung*. Lonely, irregular

youth, craving at the same time life and death—how it gulps the magic potion of these metaphysics, whose true essence is erotic and in which I recognize the spiritual source of the Tristan music. One reads in this way only once. It will not happen again. And what a fine thing it was that I did not have to keep locked within myself such an experience as this, that a beautiful opportunity presented itself to me to describe what I felt, to give thanks for it through immediate poetic expression! For only two steps from my settee lay the impossibly and impractically ponderous manuscript . . . which had progressed just to the point at which I had to bring about the death of Thomas Buddenbrook." [*Betrachtungen eines Unpolitischen: Einkehr*]
See *Buddenbrooks* (Part 10, Chapter 1).

November 24, 1899

The Royal Court Player, Otto König, reads *The Wardrobe* on the second lecture evening of the Munich Literary Society.

1900

T.M.'s sister Julia marries the banker Joseph Löhr, Jur. D., a native of Frankfurt (1862–1922). Part Three of *Buddenbrooks* is dedicated to Julia: "This part is sincerely dedicated to my sister in remembrance of our bay on the Baltic."
T.M. loses his post on the editorial staff of *Simplicissimus*. He works on the final chapters of *Buddenbrooks*.

August, 1900

". . . I have finished." [Letter to Kurt Martens, *Briefe I*]
"The manuscript went to Fischer, with whom, after the *Little Herr Friedemann* collection, I felt I have a connection. I still remember packing it; clumsily dropping the hot wax on my hand and making a big blister which was to hurt for days." [*A Sketch of My Life*]
He writes the story, *The Way to the Churchyard*, which ". . . was particularly liked by Ludwig Thoma." [*A Sketch of My Life*]
The dedication reads, "For Arthur Holitscher."

DER WEG ZUM FRIEDHOF (*Simplicissimus*, September 20, 1900) *THE WAY TO THE CHURCHYARD* (*Stories of Three Decades*)

October 1, 1900

T.M. serves as one-year volunteer with the Royal Bavarian Infantry in the Prince's Regiment. "I suffered tortures from the noise, the enforced idleness, the iron compulsion to be trim." [*A Sketch of My Life*]

He spends some time in hospital for an inflammation of his ankle tendon.

December, 1900

He is released from service as being unfit: "Only after a quarter of a year, even before Christmas, I was released from service with a simple dismissal. My feet did not want to fit themselves into that ideal masculine way of walking which is called parade drill." [*Im Spiegel*]

During this time in the infirmary, he writes an imploring letter to S. Fischer, who had requested that *Buddenbrooks* be shortened. "The letter, written and sent under the spur of strong feeling, did not fail in its effect. Fischer decided to publish . . ." [*A Sketch of My Life*]

1900–1905
TRISTAN, TONIO KRÖGER, FIORENZA

Autumn, 1900

During this time or perhaps earlier, T.M. conceives the idea of writing a drama of the renaissance—"Der König von Florenz" or "Savonarola." In December he visits an exhibition of copies of Florentine renaissance sculpture: ". . . for me, exceptionally interesting. Through these portrait busts one may become acquainted in such a pleasant way with the type of people of that time." [Letter to Heinrich Mann, *Briefe I*]

End of December, 1900

He works "on a new story with bitterly melancholy characters" [*Tristan*]. [Letter to Heinrich Mann, December 29, 1900, *Briefe I*]

January, 1901

"At present, I have surrendered myself with affection to the enjoyment of my new freedom and feel already perfectly at home in the art, music, theater, and literary life of Munich . . ." [Letter to Hilde Distel, *Briefe I*]

He attends a reading of Nietzsche by Paul Wiecke, actor from the court theater in Dresden, and an evening of recitations by Ludwig Wüllner. He also attends some premieres. He plans a trip to Florence to visit Heinrich.

At this time he also forms a friendship with Carl and Paul Ehrenberg, who are the sons of Carl Ehrenberg, the Dresden painter and professor at the Art Academy. The elder brother is a musician and composer at the Music Academy in Cologne. Paul is a painter and is studying at the Munich Art Academy. The three play trios, make bicycle trips, attend the Schwabing peasants' balls, and eat their evening meals together. "On New Year's Eve, your worthy brothers, the two Ehrenbergs, drank punch with us. Through his personality, Paul is the dearer fellow, but Carl has music on his side, the art which I pursue amorously because of the unrequited love in my heart." [Letter to Hilde Distel, *Briefe I*].

January 2, 1901

T.M. attends a performance of *Die Meistersinger*, with Emil Gerhäuser as Walter [von] Stolzing.

Before January 21, 1901

He gives a public reading of *The Way to the Churchyard, et al.* "It is true that Piepsam with almost every sentence caused lively excitement and was constantly applauded. I am especially pleased that I read well, and I am most proud of the appearance of Director Stollberg (from the Schauspielhaus), who seemed extraordinarily entertained, applauded me loudly, and received from me a special bow. Such a theater director is a very important power!" [Letter to Heinrich Mann, *Briefe I*]

February, 1901

T.M. studies background literature for his drama *Fiorenza: Savonarola and His Time* by Pasquale Villari, Jacob Burckhardt's *Kultur der Renaissance in Italien*, and Giorgio Vasari's biographies of artists.

During this winter, he has a deep friendship with the painter Paul Ehrenberg, who paints Mann's portrait. "When spring comes, I shall have behind me a winter that has moved me deeply and indescribably. The depressing feelings of a truly evil nature, which caused me to make serious plans for suicide, have been replaced by an unutterable, pure, and unexpected happiness." [Letter to Heinrich Mann, *Briefe I*]

"The younger, Paul, was also a painter; he was then at the Academy, a pupil of the famous animal painter Zügel, but he was a capital violinist as well. My feeling for him had originally something of my former feelings for my blond schoolmate; but, thanks to our having much more in common mentally and spiritually, the relationship was happier." [*A Sketch of My Life*]

Part Nine of *Buddenbrooks* is dedicated to "Paul Ehrenberg, the valiant painter, in memory of our musical-literary evenings in Munich."

From S. Fischer comes the news that *Buddenbrooks* will appear in October. A new collection of stories is prepared. T.M. works on the story *Tristan*: ". . . a burlesque that I am working on and that probably will be called 'Tristan' (That is true! A burlesque called 'Tristan'!)." He plans another "story with the unpleasant but intriguing title 'Litteratur.' (*Illae* lacrimae!)." [Letter to Heinrich Mann, *Briefe I*]

May, 1901

T.M. takes a trip to Florence and Venice. In Florence he makes friends with an English girl, Mary Smith. "*She is so very clever*, and I am so stupid always to love those who are clever, although I cannot constantly keep up with them." [Letter to Heinrich Mann, *Briefe I*]

". . . there followed a tender relationship and talk of marriage." [*A Sketch of My Life*]

The dedication of *Gladius Dei*, in English, reads, "To M.S. in remembrance of our days in Florence."

June, 1901

T.M. returns to Munich and continues work on *Tristan*.

July 10 to the end of August, 1901

He travels with Heinrich to Bozen, spends the night there, and continues alone to Mitterbad in South Tyrol. "I shall probably remain here until the end of next month." [Letter to Carl Ehrenberg, *Briefe III*]

October, 1901

Buddenbrooks appears in two volumes. Part Eight bears the dedication, "Dedicated to my brother Heinrich, the man and the writer."

BUDDENBROOKS (Berlin: S. Fischer, 1901. 1,000 copies)
BUDDENBROOKS (New York: Alfred A. Knopf, 1924. 2 vols.)

November 5 to December 20, 1901

In Riva on the Gardasee, T.M. visits a friend of the Mann brothers, Dr. von Hartungen at the Villa Cristoforo.

January, 1902

He takes a new apartment in Munich on Ungererstrasse 24.

Winter, 1901/1902

"I have not worked this winter. I have only lived, in quite a human way, and I have salved my conscience by writing a notebook full of observations." [Letter to Kurt Martens, *Briefe I*]

March, 1902

He attends several musical events: a violin concert by Willy Burmester (March 12), a concert of the Academy of Music directed by Hermann Zumpe in the Odeon (March 14), and a piano concert of Wagner by Franz von Fischer (March 15). "It is almost too much, but I don't want to let anything slip past me." [Letter to Hilde Distel, *Briefe I*]

May, 1902

"I have now decided to remain in Munich this summer, spend a short time in Starnberg, and in autumn go for a month and a half or two to Riva for a short time with Dr. von Hartungen . . ." [Unpublished letter to Kurt Martens]

June, 1902

T.M. works on *Tonio Kröger* and *Gladius Dei*. "I am also working again now. I am completing the collection of stories, which is to appear in early autumn." [Letter to Kurt Martens, June 2, 1902, *Briefe I*]

GLADIUS DEI (DIE ZEIT, Vienna, July 12 and 19, 1902)
GLADIUS DEI (STORIES OF THREE DECADES)

Summer, 1902

In Munich, he meets for the first time the publisher S. Fischer, who has good news about the financial success of *Buddenbrooks*. Fisher offers him an advance of a thousand marks.

July, 1902

From Starnberg, T.M. goes to Bad Kreuth for several days to visit Kurt Martens and his wife in their summer house.

About July 10, 1902

He returns to Munich.

September 1, 1902

"On September 1, I gave up my apartment, and until my departure I shall be staying at the Pension Gisela." [Letter to Kurt Martens, *Briefe I*]

September, 1902

T.M. makes the acquaintance of Richard von Schaukal, to whom the story *Little Lizzy* is dedicated. ". . . to my surprise I was particularly drawn to him. In any case, he is not a *Litterat* but rather a poet (even though sometimes a poor one, but that is less annoying). Moreover, he is courteous, well-dressed, discrete, and pleasantly bourgeois—that is, he is similar to you." [Letter to Kurt Martens, *Briefe I*]

October 2 to November 15, 1902

T.M. visits Dr. von Hartungen at Villa Cristoforo in Riva on the Gardasee. He reads some of the novels of Hermann Bang and Gustav Frenssen's *Jörn Uhl* and works on *Tonio Kröger*. "I am working just as usual, although very carefully and even more than usual line by line, because what I have in mind (a lengthy short story) is something so difficult that it will require considerable time. I am quite pressed, for I have already the proof sheets for the collection of stories, except for the one I am writing at the present, which is to be the final story of the collection. This story, however, is to appear before the collection in the *Rundschau*. I have a question and a request about it: this new story, which I have entitled *Tonio Kröger* and which I believe to be not of inferior quality, will suit you so well personally that I should like to dedicate it to you. *May I*? [Letter to Kurt Martens, *Briefe I*]

TONIO KRÖGER (NEUE DEUTSCHE RUNDSCHAU, February, 1903)
TONIO KRÖGER (in DEATH IN VENICE. London: Martin Secker, 1928)

November 15, 1902

T.M. takes a new apartment at Konradstrasse 11: "quite a pretty little apartment." [Letter to Kurt Martens, *Briefe I*]

November 27, 1902

He reads from *Tristan* before the Munich Academic Society. The study, *The Hungry*, may have been written about this time.

DIE HUNGERNDEN (DIE ZUKUNFT, Berlin, January 24, 1903)
THE HUNGRY (STORIES OF THREE DECADES)

ENGAGEMENT AND MARRIAGE

February, 1903

T.M. travels to Berlin and visits S. Fischer on Fasanenstrasse. "I was very cordially received . . . Yours, Tonio Kröger." [Letter to Paul and Carl Ehrenberg, February 8, 1903, *Briefe III*]

Spring, 1903

The collection of stories entitled *Tristan* appears. T.M. is introduced into the salon of Ernst Rosmer, pseudonym for the wife of the attorney Max Bernstein, and into the salon of Professor Alfred Pringsheim and his wife Hedwig, née Dohm, at Arcisstrasse 12, which is the parental home of Katja Pringsheim. "The atmosphere of the Pringsheim

TRISTAN, Novellen (Berlin: S. Fischer, 1903. 2000 copies)

home, that great family house that recalled my own early abode, enchanted me. I had known the traditional elegance that belonged to the great families; here I found it transformed and intellectualized in this stately society compact of art and literature." [*A Sketch of My Life*]

April 3, 1903

"For the first printing of *Tonio Kröger*, I have received 400 (four hundred) marks. Please tell everyone about it." [Letter to Carl Ehrenberg, *Briefe III*]

Summer, 1903

T.M. visits Kurt Martens and his wife in Bad Kreuth. Martens tells an anecdote from his time in the hussar regiment, which is made the theme of the short story *A Gleam*.

T.M. spends most of his time on the play *Fiorenza*.

July and August, 1903

He visits his mother, who is living in Polling near Weilheim at the house of a man named Schweighardt.

August, 1903

He hints of his possible marriage into the Pringsheim family to Otto Grautoff, to whom he dedicates Part Eleven of *Buddenbrooks*: "To my friend Otto Grautoff." Frau Hedwig Pringsheim is sympathetic to T.M.'s purpose: "The lady of the house came of a Berlin literary family, being the daughter of Ernst and Hedwig Dohm. My existence and my youthful performance were not lost upon her, nor did she oppose the passionate feeling that soon grew up in me for the only daughter of the house . . ." [*A Sketch of My Life*]

Beginning of October, 1903

T.M. makes a trip to Düsseldorf to visit his sister Carla and returns to Munich on October 6.

October, 1903

He reads from *Tonio Kröger* in Königsberg for the Literary Society and in Berlin for the Berlin Press Club.

On a visit to S. Fischer on Fasanenstrasse, T.M. meets Gerhart Hauptmann for the first time. "Meeting him was for me a great experience, and I only wished I could have given him a somewhat pleasanter impression of myself than he probably received." [Letter to S. Fischer, *Briefe I*]

November, 1903

He writes the short story *The Infant Prodigy* for the Christmas issue of the Vienna *Neue Freie Presse*. "I am no longer sitting in my little room alone, free and without obligations, creating art for art's sake. I feel as though I have fallen within range of an immense spotlight which has made me visible to the public eye and that I am now burdened with the responsibility of using my talents, which I have been foolish enough to reveal to others. The *Neue Freie Presse* has sent a telegram requesting a short story from my precious pen for their precious Christmas issue. Seriously, they have done just that, and after the second telegram I have promised them some sort of literary trifle. In the meanwhile, I have finished a study [*A Gleam*] for the first issue of the year of the *Neue Rundschau*, and I am supposed to do an essay [*Gabriele Reuter*] for *Der Tag*, and there is a mountain of important books I should like to read, and above all I must continue writing my Florentine dialogue . . ." [Letter to Walter Opitz, December 5, 1903, *Briefe I*]

DAS WUNDERKIND (NEUE FREIE PRESSE, Vienna, December 25, 1903)
THE INFANT PRODIGY (STORIES OF THREE DECADES)

EIN GLÜCK (NEUE RUNDSCHAU, January, 1904)
A GLEAM (STORIES OF THREE DECADES)
GABRIELE REUTER (DER TAG, Berlin, February 14 and 17, 1904)

He describes his plan for a new work: "I mean to say that one leads a symbolic, representative existence, similar to that of a prince. And behold! In this pathos lies the seed of a curious situation, about which I am thinking of writing—a novel of court life, a counterpart to *Tonio Kröger*, which will bear the title *Royal Highness* . . ." [Letter to Walter Opitz, *Briefe I*]

End of December, 1903

"Very serious and profound correspondence" is exchanged between Thomas and Heinrich Mann concerning Heinrich's novel *Die Göttinnen*. "Have you read it? What do you have to say about it? I am perplexed." [Letter to Kurt Martens, December 30, 1903, *Briefe I*]

1904

T.M. asks for the hand of Katja Pringsheim. "There was a ball in the gilded High Renaissance salons of the Pringsheim house, a brilliant and numerous gathering, where for the first time I was conscious of basking in the full sunshine of public favor and regard; it ripened in me the feelings upon which I hoped to base the happiness of my life." [*A Sketch of My Life*]

April 16 to May 6, 1904

T.M. visits at the Villa Cristoforo in Riva.

June, 1904

The story *At the Prophet's* is written as "harmless homage" to Frau Hedwig Pringsheim. T.M. writes the story after attending a reading from the "Manifesto" by Ludwig Derleth, a disciple of Stephan George.

BEIM PROPHETEN (in DAS WUNDERKIND. Berlin, 1914) *AT THE PROPHET'S* (STORIES OF THREE DECADES

July–September, 1904

Katja Pringsheim goes to visit her sick father in Bad Kissingen, and from there she goes with her mother to Switzerland. Finally she visits relatives in Northern Germany. During this time there is a lively exchange of letters between T.M. and her. "Unbelievable! The two or three days that I had to spend without you in M[unich] seemed to me like an unconquerable eternity, and now I have been able to spend almost three months without you and have remained in a tolerably good mood. Man is a staunch vertibrate." [Letter to Katja Pringsheim, *Briefe I*]

July 21, 1904

T.M. gives a reading in Göttingen before the Literary Society.

August–September 21, 1904

He is with his mother in Berchtesgaden.

October 3, 1904

He is engaged to Katja Pringsheim (born July 24, 1883 in Munich). ". . . along with expressing my regret that I could not be with you yesterday, I should like to announce that at that time I *became engaged to Katja Pringsheim* . . ." [Letter to Kurt Martens, October 4, 1904, *Briefe I*]

November 28, 1904

T.M. travels to Berlin with Frau Pringsheim and Katja for his first visit with his fiancee's grandmother, the writer Hedwig Dohm, "*Little Grandma.*"

November 29, 1904

T.M. reads from *Tonio Kröger, The Infant Prodigy*, and *A Gleam* before the Society for Art.

December 2, 1904

At the Lübeck Literary Society (*Lübecker Leseabend von 1890*) in the Alter Kasinosaal, he reads from *Fiorenza* and *The Infant Prodigy* before a "quite numerous audience." "The latter work was very appealing, but Herr Mann was not able to excite a great interest with the scenes from his play, although his reading of them may have been at fault." [From a Lübeck review]

T.M. returns to Berlin and visits Oskar Bie, editor of the *Neue Rundschau.*

January, 1905

He finishes *Fiorenza* just before his wedding. "The moods and feelings of this time have many of them been embodied in the undramatic dramatic dialogues of *Fiorenza.*" [*A Sketch of My Life*]

FIORENZA (DIE NEUE RUNDSCHAU July and August, 1905)

FIORENZA (STORIES OF THREE DECADES)

February 11, 1905

T.M. and Katja Pringsheim are married in Munich and take their wedding trip in Switzerland. "It was all a strange and confusing affair, and the whole day I was amazed, typically like a man at what a fix I had got myself into." [Letter to Heinrich Mann, from Zürich, February 18, 1905, *Heinrich und Thomas Mann: Die persönlichen, literarischen und weltanschaulichen Beziehungen der Brüder.* Alfred Kantorowicz. Berlin: Aufbau Verlag, 1956]

T.M. returns with his bride to Munich. They take an apartment at Franz-Joseph-Strasse 2, fourth floor.

SCHWERE STUNDE (SIMPLICISSIMUS, May 9, 1905)

A WEARY HOUR (STORIES OF THREE DECADES)

March, 1905

He writes a short story for an issue of *Simplicissimus* dealing with Schiller—*A Weary Hour.*

May, 1905

He mentions a plan for a "longer short story." [Letter to Philipp Witkop, May 14, 1905, *Briefe I*]

It is unclear whether this refers to *Royal Highness* or the plan for a novel about the life of Frederick the Great. ". . . my *shameless* plan of writing someday a novel about the life of Frederick the Great antedates *Royal Highness.*" [Letter to Ernst Bertram, January 28, 1910, *Briefe I*]

EIN NACHWORT (LÜBECKER GENERAL-ANZEIGER, November 7, 1905)

Summer, 1905

T.M. travels to Berlin for a visit with his wife's grandmother. He does not meet Maximilian Harden, a friend of the Dohm family, when Harden makes a visit. *The Blood of the Walsungs* is written at this time.

November, 1905

T.M. makes a protest against the Lübeck attorney Enrico von Brocken, who referred to *Buddenbrooks* as a *Bilse-Roman* [a term implying that the novel is an unethical exposé of real people].

November 9, 1905
T.M.'s first daughter, Erika Julia Hedwig Mann, is born.
December, 1905
He makes a lecture tour in Dresden and Breslau, reading from *Fiorenza* and various short stories.

WÄLSUNGENBLUT (written for DIE NEUE RUNDSCHAU and printed in January, 1906, but T.M. withdraws it, and the story does not appear until 1921, in a private edition with lithographs by Th. Th. Heine, published by the Phantasus-Verlag, Munich) *THE BLOOD OF THE WALSUNGS* (STORIES OF THREE DECADES)

1906–1913
FROM *ROYAL HIGHNESS* TO *DEATH IN VENICE*

End of January, 1906
T.M. reads in Basel from *Fiorenza* and various short stories.
February, 1906
He continues in the controversy concerning the right of an artist to portray people who are still alive by writing *Bilse und ich*.

BILSE UND ICH (MÜNCHENER NEUESTE NACHRICHTEN, February 15 and 16, 1906)

May, 1906
He reads in Dresden and ends his tour with a vacation at the sanatorium Weisser Hirsch. "I was on my way to Dresden, whither I had been invited by some men of letters: it was a literary and artistic pilgrimage, in short, such as, from time to time, I undertake not unwillingly. You make appearances, you attend functions, you show yourself to admiring crowds —not for nothing is one a subject of William II. And certainly Dresden is beautiful, especially the Zwinger; and afterwards I intended to go for ten days or a fortnight to the White Hart to rest, and if, thanks to the treatments, the spirit should come upon me, I might do a little work as well." [*Railway Accident*]
Frau Katja Mann is "not in the mood for travel." Probably about this time T.M. forms the conception of the *Confessions of Felix Krull, Confidence Man*, inspired by the memoirs of Manolescu.
Mid-June to mid-September, 1906
T.M. takes his summer holidays in Oberammergau at Villa Friedenshöhe and works on *Royal Highness*. ". . . in the middle of June, my wife and I are going with our daughter to Oberammergau for three months." [Letter to Kurt Martens, May 30, 1906, *Briefe III*]
November 18, 1906
T.M.'s first son, Klaus Heinrich Thomas Mann, is born.

February and March, 1907

T.M. contributes to a group of essays on "the cultural values of the theater." "I decided to interrupt work on my novel 'for a few days' . . . But instead of days, I spend weeks in in my struggle and was more than once sick to the point of despair with the whole thing . . . but I had agreed to write it, and so I obeyed my categorical imperative: 'Endure!' " [Report to the Literary Historical Society in Bonn].

VERSUCH ÜBER DAS THEATER (NORD UND SÜD, January and February, 1908)

May, 1907

T.M. makes a trip to Venice and to the Lido.

MITTEIL-UNG AN DIE LITERATUR-HISTOR-ISCHE GESELL-SCHAFT IN BONN (MITTEILUNGEN, Book 7, 1907)

May 11, 1907

Fiorenza receives its premiere at the Schauspielhaus in Frankfurt. T.M. and Katja attend the sixth performance on May 23. "The Frankfurt experiment succeeded beyond the general expectations. The dramatic effect of the work on the state—up until now not only questionable but not even discussed—has now been quite simply proven." [Letter to Hilde Distel, *Briefe I*]

IM SPIEGEL (LITERARISCHES ECHO, Berlin, December, 1907)

July to mid-September, 1907

T.M. takes his holidays in Seeshaupt at the Villa Hirt on Lake Würm. He makes some important comments to the Bonn Literary Historical Society on his method of writing. He writes an autobiographical sketch.

ÜBER FIORENZA (MÜNCHENER NEUESTE NACHRICHTEN, January, 1908)

December 17, 1907

Fiorenza is performed in the Munich Residenztheater. T.M. has a controversy with Hanns von Gumppenberg over the latter's criticism of the production.

January, 1908

He reads from *Royal Highness* at a benefit performance in Munich.

September 28, 1908

T.M. has a summer house (designed by Gabriel von Seidl) built in Bad Tölz, "During the summer we were in Tölz, where the air did us so much good that we bought some land and are having a little house built with a view of the town, the Isar, and the mountains. The rough brickwork is almost finished." [Letter to Philipp Witkop, November 1, 1908, *Briefe I*]

November, 1908

T.M. works on the final chapters of *Royal Highness*. "You ask about my novel. It is finished or as good as finished, but as is usual with my work, the novel is so bulky that it cannot be housed in the three October issues of the *Neue Rundschau* and has had to be postponed until January. Well, it will appear then after the first of the year, which is after all better than just before Christmas." [Letter to Philipp Witkop, *Briefe I*]

From the end of November to the beginning of December, 1908

T.M. is in Vienna.

November 26, 1908

He visits Arthur Schnitzler for the first time.

About November 27, 1908

Arthur Schnitzler, Jakob Wassermann, and T.M. go to the Semmering, where they are to meet Hugo von Hofmannsthal and his wife.

Beginning of December, 1908

T.M. visits Hugo von Hofmannsthal in Rodaun. He reads in Vienna from *Royal Highness*.

February 13, 1909

Royal Highness is finished.

KÖNIGLICHE HOHEIT (ROYAL HIGHNESS printed in serial in DIE NEUE RUNDSCHAU, January to September, 1909)

Spring, 1909

Thomas and Heinrich Mann travel to Italy (Livorno). T.M. begins work on a critical essay that is never completed.

March, 1909

He writes *Railway Accident* for the Easter issue of the *Neue Freie Presse*, Vienna.

DAS EISENBAHNUNGLÜCK (NEUE FREIE PRESSE, Vienna, Easter, 1909)
RAILWAY ACCIDENT (STORIES OF THREE DECADES)

March 27, 1909

T.M.'s third child and second son, Angelus Gottfried Thomas (Golo) Mann, is born.

May, 1909

T.M. is in the sanatorium of Dr. Bircher, Zürich.

Summer, 1909

He becomes acquainted with Max Reinhardt. "I have often been in Munich at the Reinhardt Theater, which was an important experience for me and caused me to do a great deal of thinking. My acquaintance with Reinhardt himself quite excited me, in the same childish way I am always excited whenever I come into contact with an inspired man." [Letter to Walter Opitz, August 26, 1909, *Briefe I*]

June, 1909

The basic conception of the Felix Krull novel is formed.

"My father's plans concerning *Krull* go back to June, 1909, at which time he had already explained to my mother the plot of the story." [Erika Mann, contributed by Hans Wysling, *Archivalisches Gewühle: Zur Entstehungsgeschichte des Hochstaplerroman. Blätter der Thomas Mann-Gesellschaft*, No. 5, 1965]

July, 1909

"Furthermore, I was in Bayreuth for *Parsifal*—too late actually, for even though I never really believed in Wagner, my passion for him has greatly diminished in the last years . . . But does it [*Parsifal*] still have a future? Isn't the mood, the tendency and taste expressed in it regarded already today as merely of historical interest?" [Letter to Walter Opitz, *Briefe I*]

July to September, 1909

At "Landhaus Thomas Mann" in Bad Tölz, T.M. works on an essay: "I have let myself in for a thing that has something to do with criticism, a treatise. In the morning I wear down my nerves so that in the afternoon I am nearer to nonsense than to letter-writing; indeed, Schiller is right when he says that it is more difficult to write a good letter than to create the best dramatic scene." [Letter to Walter Opitz, August 26, 1909, *Briefe I*]

DER LITERAT, DER KÜNSTLER UND DER LITERAT, Zwei Bruchstücke (MÄRZ, Munich, 1913)

September, 1909

He mentions further plans for his work: "I am working at the moment on an essay which will have the title *Geist und Kunst*. I am also busy with a smaller short story, *The Confidence Man*, which will be a kind of psychological supplement to my novel about court life. I am also making preliminary studies for a projected historical novel." [From an interview of September 2, 1909]

KÖNIGLICHE HOHEIT (Berlin: S. Fischer, 1909. 10,000 copies) *ROYAL HIGHNESS: A NOVEL OF GERMAN COURT LIFE* (Translated by A. Cecil Curtis. New York: Alfred A. Knopf, 1916. 362 pp.)

October, 1909

Royal Highness appears at the same time as Heinrich Mann's novel, *Die Kleine Stadt* (Leipzig: Insel Verlag).

January, 1910

T.M. begins work on *Felix Krull*. "I am gathering material, making notes, and studying for *The Confidence Man*, which will probably be my strangest work. Sometimes I am surprised at what I pull out of myself." [Letter to Heinrich Mann, January 10, 1910, *Heinrich und Thomas Mann: Die persönlichen, literarischen und weltanschaulichen Beziehungen der Brüder*. Alfred Kantorowicz. Berlin. Aufbau Verlag, 1956]

January 28, 1910

He begins a correspondence with the literary historian Ernst Bertram (1884–1957), who has lectured on *Royal Highness* to the Bonn Literary Historical Society.

February, 1910

"I am reading Kleist's prose in order to get my bearings properly." [Letter to Heinrich Mann, *Briefe I*]

March and April, 1910

T.M. writes a polemic against the philosopher and mathematician Theodor Lessing because of his disparaging article on the Weimar writer Samuel Lublinski. "That Thomas Buddenbrook's life . . . is the life of a modern hero is a fact which has been grasped up to now by only one critic—ugly little Lublinski. And I admit that only out of thanks to him for this have I broken a lance against that distorted imbecile of a Lessing." [Letter to Julius Bab, *Briefe I*]

DER DOKTOR LESSING BERICHTIGUNGEN (LITERARISCHES ECHO, March and April, 1910)

June 7, 1910

T.M.'s fourth child and second daughter, Monika Mann, is born. She is baptized in Bad Tölz on October 6.

Summer to Autumn, 1910

T.M. lives in his villa in Bad Tölz.

July 7, 1910

He reads the first chapter of *Felix Krull* to his family circle.

July 30, 1910

The actress Carla Mann, T.M.'s youngest sister, commits suicide at her mother's apartment in Polling. "A proud, disdainful nature, unconventional but refined, she loved literature, art, the manifestations of the mind; and the crude unkindly time drove her into an unhappy bohemian existence." [*A Sketch of My Life*]

In Bad Tölz, T.M. writes an essay on Theodor Fontane for Maximilian Harden's publication *Die Zukunft*. He again takes up his work on *Felix Krull*.

DËR ALTE FONTANE (DIE ZUKUNFT, October 1, 1910)
THE OLD FONTANE (ESSAYS OF THREE DECADES. New York: Alfred A. Knopf, 1947. 472 pp.)

August 28, 1910

He attends a performance of Friedrich Hebbel's *Gyges und sein Ring* in Munich.

September 2, 1910

Professor Pringsheim's sixtieth birthday is celebrated in Bad Tölz. "There was a mass of telegrams. On the eve of his birthday, the spa band gave a concert in our garden, I forced myself to make a speech at dinner, and on the evening of his birthday there was a torchlight procession and songs by the schoolchildren." [Letter to Paul Ehrenberg, *Briefe I*]

September 12, 1910

The premiere of Gustav Mahler's Eighth Symphony takes place in Munich. After the concert, T.M. is with Mahler and Max Reinhardt.

October 1, 1910

T.M. moves with his family into a new apartment in Herzogpark, Mauerkircherstrasse 13.

October 17, 1910

He attends the premiere of Frank Wedekind's *Liebestrank*.

November, 1910

On a lecture tour to Weimar, T.M. is the guest of his former school comrade, Count Vitzthum von Eckstädt ("touching hospitality"). He reads from *Felix Krull*.

December 11, 1910

He reads *The Fight Between Jappe and Do Escobar* to his family circle.

December, 1910

For the Christmas issue of the *Berliner Tageblatt*, T.M. writes a review of a new edition of Adelbert von Chamisso's *Peter Schlemihls wundersame Geschichte*, published by the Hans von Weber-Verlag, with illustrations by Emil Preetorius.

January, 1911

On a lecture tour in the Ruhr and Westphalia, T.M. reads from *Felix Krull* and various short stories: Coblenz, January 12; Düsseldorf, January 18; Bielefeld, January 19.

End of March, 1911

"I am so worn out in mind and body that I am on the point of retiring to a trustworthy naturopathic sanatorium for several weeks." [Unpublished letter to Korfiz Holm, March 20, 1911]

Middle of May, 1911

T.M. travels to Brioni, an island off the coast of Istria.

May 18, 1911

He learns of the death of Gustav Mahler.

From May 26 to June 2, 1911

He makes a sojourn on the Lido near Venice at the Hôtel des Bains. ". . . for Brioni was no place to remain for any length

WIE JAPPE UND DO ESCOBAR SICH PRÜGELTEN (SÜDDEUTSCHE MONATSHEFTE, February, 1911)

THE FIGHT BETWEEN JAPPE AND DO ESCOBAR (STORIES OF THREE DECADES)

PETER SCHLEMIHL (BERLINER TAGEBLATT, December 25, 1910)

of time." [Unpublished letter to Hans von Hülsen, contributed by Herbert Lehnert in *Thomas Mann's Interpretation of Der Tod in Venedig, Rice University Studies*, 1964]

At this time he forms the conception of *Death in Venice*. "My wife and I—not for the first time in our lives—spent a part of May on the Lido. There a series of curious circumstances and impressions combined with my subconscious search for something new to give birth to a productive idea, which then developed into the story *Death in Venice*. The tale as at first conceived was as modest as all the rest of my undertakings: I thought of it as a quick improvisation which should serve as interlude to my work on the Krull novel . . . But things . . . have a will of their own, and shape themselves accordingly . . ." [*A Sketch of My Life*]

End of May, 1911

At the request of the magazine *Der Merker* (Vienna) for its Bayreuth issue, T.M. writes once again his impressions from his trip to the Bayreuth Festival in 1909: "And I think that Wagner's star in the German cultural heavens is at the point of sinking." [*Auseinandersetzung mit Richard Wagner*]

"Only reluctantly and under pressure from an old promise to the editor of the *Merker*, have I decided to publish my opinion of Wagner . . . Only a barbaric and spiritually half blind nation, I thought in my bitterness, could build temples for these productions." [Letter to Ernst Bertram, on writing paper of the Hotel des Bains, *Bertram*]

AUSEINANDERSETZUNG MIT RICHARD WAGNER, (DER MERKER, Vienna, July, 1911)

June, 1911

T.M. reads from *Fiorenza* in a Munich winecellar to the students of Professor Arthur Kutscher's seminar.

June to October, 1911

He remains at his country house in Bad Tölz.

He writes the introduction to S. Fischer Verlag's Pantheon Edition of Adelbert von Chamisso's *Peter Schlemihls wundersame Gerschichte* and uses passages from his article on the work from the *Berliner Tageblatt* of 1910.

CHAMISSO (DIE NEUE RUNDSCHAU, October, 1911)
CHAMISSO (ESSAYS OF THREE DECADES)

He begins work on *Death in Venice*: "I am working now on a very strange thing that I brought back with me from Venice —a short story, serious and pure in tone, concerning the case of an aging artist's love for a young boy." [Letter to Philipp Witkop, July 18, 1911, *Briefe I*]

From September 2 to 19, 1911
Frau Katja Mann goes with her parents for the cure to Sils-Maria. "My wife returned yesterday. She has tolerably recovered, but she is constantly in need of care." [Letter to Josef Ruederer, September 20, 1911, *Briefe I*]

October, 1911
T.M. attends the premiere of Josef Ruederer's play *Der Schmied von Kochel* in Munich.

November, 1911
He gives a reading in Brussels.

November 20, 1911
He attends the premiere of Gustav Mahler's *Lied von der Erde*, conducted by Bruno Walter in Munich.

January, 1912
He goes on a lecture tour to Heidelberg, Bremen, and other cities.

February, 1912
He visits Hans von Weber to discuss printing *Death in Venice* in the latter's Hyperion Editions.

From March 10 to September 25, 1912
Katja Mann is in the forest sanatorium of Dr. Jessen in Davos. "In 1912 my wife had been attacked by a catarrh of the tip of the lung. Then, and again in the next year but one, she was obliged to stay for several months in the Swiss Alps. In May and June of 1912 I spent three weeks with her in Davos." [*A Sketch of My Life*]

April, 1912
Heinrich Mann finishes his play *Die grosse Liebe*. "Best wishes on the completion of your play! I should give much if I could report the same of my short story, but I cannot find an ending for it. Perhaps the change of air in mid-May will help me do it. My energies are now quite diminished." [Letter to Heinrich Mann, *Briefe I*]

April 27, 1912
T.M. tells his brother some experiences from his time as a recruit, which the latter employs in his novel *Der Untertan*.

From May 15 to June 12, 1912
T.M. visits his wife in the sanatorium at Davos. "Here I enjoy the company of my wife, who has improved but by no means completely recovered. I am only painfully becoming used to this altitude of five hundred feet. For a few days it

even made me feverish, and the Professor, smiling with an eye to profit, declared me obviously tubercular and in need of a lengthy cure." [Unpublished letter to Hans von Hülsen] He gathers impressions of his surroundings for a new short story. "I distinctly thought of it as another brief interlude to the *Confessions* . . . and as a satyr play to the tragic novella of decay just finished" [*Death in Venice*]. [*A Sketch of My Life*]

June 13, 1912

He returns to Munich and on the following day visits his parents-in-law on Arcisstrasse in order to report to them on the condition of their daughter. The doctors think her condition harmless but tedious. A six-month cure is necessary.

From June 15, 1912

T.M. retires to his country house at Bad Tölz with his mother and children. He finishes *Death in Venice*. "I was living at the time alone with the children at Tölz . . . and the sympathy and enthusiasm of the friends to whom I read the story aloud in the evenings in my little study might have prepared me for the almost stormy reception it was to have on its publication." [*A Sketch of My Life*]

He writes a review of Georg Hirschfeld's novel *Der Kampf der weissen und der roten Rose*.

Summer, 1912

Death in Venice appears.

September 25, 1912

Katja Mann returns from Davos.

Autumn, 1912

T.M. returns to his work on *Felix Krull*, Book Two (the exact time is uncertain).

November, 1912

After a lecture given by Maximilian Harden, he and T.M. are together "until around morning." They discuss the forthcoming production of *Fiorenza* at the Berlin Kammerspiele. "And if one takes "character" to mean not just moral but rather more aesthetic, in the sense of a figure, the actor of a picturesque role, then he is also a character." [Letter to Heinrich Mann, *Briefe I*]

November 16, 1912

T.M. attends the premiere of Gerhardt Hauptmann's *Gabriel Schillings Flucht* in Munich.

EIN WERK DES NATURALISMUS (MÜNCHENER NEUESTE NACHRICHTEN, July 22, 1912)

DER TOD IN VENEDIG (Munich: Hyperion Verlag Hans von Weber, 1912. 1,300 copies)

DEATH IN VENICE (London: Martin Secker, 1928. 272 pp.)

He becomes a member of the Munich censorship council and has differences with Frank Wedekind on account of a misunderstanding. ". . . I see it as my duty in being a member of the Censorship Council to inform the overseers of the public order when there is a violation in the area of literature." [Letter to Frank Wedekind, *Briefe I*]

November 27, 1912

T.M. inspects some possible building sites in Bogenhausen with the architect Ludwig.

End of December, 1912

He goes to Berlin to view a rehersal of *Fiorenza.* "I was recently at a rehearsal in Berlin. It will not go well. Though Winterstein, the director, is sympathetic and interested, he is not intellectually capable . . . Wegener is playing Lorenzo, and thus the production has at least a certain dramatic quality." [Letter to Maximilian Harden, *Briefe I*]

January 3, 1913

Fiorenza is performed at the Berlin Kammerspiele. Alfred Kerr writes a malicious review. "A poisonous howling, in which even the most imperceptive reader may detect a vindictive bloodthirstiness. What a character! Only a few realize how truly it is his own character that is speaking here . . ." [Letter to Hugo von Hofmannsthal, *Briefe I*]

January 16, 1913

Fiorenza is performed for the last time in Berlin.

End of January, 1913

T.M. goes on a lecture tour to Budapest.

From February, 1913

He remains at the country house in Bad Tölz with the exception of a few weeks until autumn.

Mid-February, 1913

He is visited by Ernst Bertram—their first private meeting.

February 25, 1913

A piece of property at Poschingerstrasse 1 is purchased. Katja Mann is made owner.

March 18, 1913

In the Concert Hall at Basel, T.M. reads *A Weary Hour*, from *Royal Highness*, from *Buddenbrooks*, and from *The Infant Prodigy*.

May 12, 1913

The poet Friedrich Huch dies.

May 15, 1913

T.M. gives a eulogy at the grave of Friedrich Huch. "Yesterday I was in Munich to say a few words over the coffin of the dear poet, and I was so moved I could hardly do it." [Letter to Ernst Bertram, *Bertram*]

FRIEDRICH HUCH GEDÄCHTNISREDE (SÜDDEUTSCHE MONATSHEFTE, June, 1913)

May 26, 1913

On account of unjustified attacks by Erich Mühsam, T.M. resigns from the Censorship Council and the Writers' Protective League, "as the radical ranters call themselves." "Thus may my social activity and the beautiful fiction of 'esprit de corps among writers' come to an end . . ." [Letter to Kurt Martens, *Briefe I*]

He receives a conciliatory letter from Frank Wedekind.

From June 19 to July 12, 1913

He spends his holidays in Viareggio.

1913–1915
THE MAGIC MOUNTAIN [FIRST PERIOD]

July, 1913

T.M. begins preliminary work on *The Magic Mountain.* "A three-weeks sojourn on the Mediterranean has again done me much good; nevertheless, I am still not working on my amazing novel but rather have turned to a short story, which appears to be developing into a kind of humorous counterpart to *Death in Venice.*" [Letter to Ernst Bertram, July 24, 1913, *Bertram*]

September, 1913

He writes a foreword to the novel *Nacht und Tag* by Erich von Mendelssohn.

VORWORT ZU EINEM ROMAN (SUDDEUTSCHE MONATSHEFTE, November, 1913)

He attends a performance of Paul Claudel's *The Tidings Brought to Mary* [*L'Annonce faite à Marie*] at the Hellerauer Festspielhaus. The translator is Jakob Hegner, who set the action in German medieval surroundings. Among those present are Rainer Maria Rilke, Max Reinhardt, and Martin Buber. "I declared at the time that I had received the strongest poetic impression, indeed the strongest artistic one which had been permitted me for a long time . . . Has it ever been observed to what degree Hegner's *Tidings* affects one as original poetry? How easily Anne Vercors of the French text becomes Andreas Gradherz of the German, Pierre de Craon becomes Peter von Ulm, the Mayor of Chevoche becomes the Mayor of Rothenstein! Love for this work comes above all from the joy in perceiving the brotherhood of those times, which is actually more than brotherhood: it is sense of unity." [*Betrachtungen eines Unpolitischen*]

September 9, 1913

T.M. begins to write *The Magic Mountain.*

October, 1913

Tonio Kröger is published as a single work with illustrations by Erich M. Simon.

TONIO KRÖGER, Novelle (Berlin: S. Fischer, 1913. 5,000 copies.)

TONIO KRÖGER (in DEATH IN VENICE. London: Martin Secker, New Adelphi Library, 1929)

October 16, 1913

T.M. attends a performance of *Aida* in Munich.

November 12 and 13, 1913

He goes on a lecture tour to Stuttgart.

From November 15 to December 21, 1913

Katja Mann goes to Merano for the cure.

December, 1913

T.M. writes a review of a volume of poetry, *Requiem*, by Bruno Frank, who had praised *Death in Venice* in detail in an article in the *Neue Rundschau*. This contact is the beginning of an enduring friendship that developed between them later on.

BRUNO FRANKS REQUIEM (DER ZWIEBELFISCH, June, 1914)

At this time the chapter *Of the Christening Basin, and of Grandfather in His Twofold Guise* in *The Magic Mountain* is probably written.

From January 4 to May 12, 1914

Katja Mann goes to Arosa for the cure.

About January 5, 1914

The Mann family moves into the new house at Poschingerstrasse 1. "I am very disturbed that my wife could not be here for the move. She has been in Arosa for two days. It was suggested that she spend several months in the Alps. It is hard." [Letter to Ernst Bertram, *Bertram*]

The Magic Mountain receives its title. Oskar Bie had announced the coming work in the *Neue Rundschau* as "The Sorceror's Apprentice" [*Der Zauberlehrling* instead of *Der Zauberberg*]. "I am behind in my story. Don't think that it is finished. By the way, the title is *The Magic Mountain* (Bie made the mistake), and the work can be something readable, if the nerves can stand it." [Letter to Ernst Bertram, January 6, 1914, *Bertram*]

January 19, 1914

T.M. reads in Zürich to the Hottingen Lesezirkel. "Here is the program: 1.) *A Weary Hour* (a study), 2.) A Selection from the Novel *Royal Highness*, intermission, 3.) A Selection from an Unpublished Novel [*Felix Krull*], 4.) *The Infant Prodigy* (a sketch)." [Letter to Hans Bodmer, *Briefe I*]

January 20 and 21, 1914

He reads in Lucerne to a group called the Freie Vereinigung Gleichgesinnter and in St. Gall to the Museum Society.

January 30, 1914

He reads from *The Magic Mountain* in Munich for the Galerie Caspari, sponsored by *Forum* (Wilhelm Herzog, director).

January 13, 1914

He attends a lecture by Karl Kraus.

February 18, 1914

A dinner is given in the new house. Among those invited are Ernst Bertram.

Spring, 1914

T.M. becomes a member of the Wedekind-Comité. He contributes to a gift and takes part in the presentation on the fiftieth birthday of Frank Wedekind.

May, 1914

He writes an article for the publication honoring Wedekind.

ÜBER FRANK WEDEKIND Later: *ÜBER EINE SZENE VON FRANK WEDEKIND* (DER NEUE MERKUR, Munich, July, 1914)

From July to mid-September, 1914

He remains at the country house in Bad Tölz.

July 2, 1914

He attends a performance of Shakespeare's *Tempest* at the Munich Künstlertheater, a guest-production by Luise Dumont and Gustav Lindemann, Düsseldorf.

July 15, 1914

He reads in Freiburg from *The Magic Mountain*.

August 1, 1914

World War I begins. "I am going as though in a dream—and yet one should now be ashamed of not thinking it possible, of not having foreseen that the catastrophe would have to come. What an affliction! How will Europe appear inwardly and outwardly when it is over?" [Letter to Heinrich Mann, *Briefe I*]

The wartime wedding of Viktor Mann, T.M.'s brother, and Magdalena (Nelly) Kilian from Munich takes place. Viktor and Heinz Pringsheim, Katja Mann's brother, say farewell on the battlefield.

Concerning *The Magic Mountain* at this time, T.M. writes, "At the outbreak of the war, no more than the first third of the first volume was written. Settembrini, as a comic adversary to the fascination of death, certainly belonged to my original intention." [Unpublished letter to Oskar A. H. Schmitz, Thomas Mann Archives, Zürich]

August 12, 1914

Heinrich Mann marries the actress Maria (Mimi) Kanova from Prague.

August and September, 1914

T.M. is at the country house in Bad Tölz.

He writes an article about the war. "I was heartily ashamed when I heard that you were in the service, and finally it was this shame that brought forth my small effort published in the *Rundschau*—the need to place at least my head in the service of the German cause." [Letter to Richard Dehmel, *Briefe I*]

GEDANKEN IM KRIEGE (DIE NEUE RUNDSCHAU, November, 1914)

Mid-September, 1914

He returns to Munich and writes the essay *Frederick and the Great Coalition*. "Since after writing the article in the *Rundschau*, I was not able to find my way back to my story, I have occupied the time in writing a lengthy historical sketch, 'Frederick and the Great Coalition of 1756' . . ." [Letter to Ernst Bertram, February 17, 1915, *Bertram*]

FRIEDRICH UND DIE GROSSE KOALITION (DER NEUE MERKUR, January/ February, 1915) *FREDERICK AND THE GREAT COALITION* (in THREE ESSAYS. New York: Alfred A. Knopf, 1929. 261 pp.)

October, 1914

The first edition of the collection of stories *Das Wunderkind* appears.

T.M. receives a visit from Geheimrat Professor Berthold Litzmann and his wife when they pass through Munich. They tell him of Ernst Bertram's lecture in Bonn, *Wie deuten wir uns?*

Mid-December, 1914

T.M. finishes his essay on Frederick the Great.

From the end of December, 1914 to February 3, 1915

He spends six weeks in Bad Tölz. ". . . it was a snowy experience. I had never seen so much snow in my whole life." [Letter to Ernst Bertram, *Bertram*] This experience was incorporated into *The Magic Mountain* in the chapter entitled "Snow."

DAS WUNDERKIND Novellen (Berlin: S. Fischer, 1914. 22,000 copies)

He is burdened with household cares. The children are ill, and Katja Mann overexerts herself in nursing them. T.M. is "swept up in the disturbances and worries of the time." He tries to return to his normal work, "after the first months of the war, I became involved in all sorts of political and historical trivia." [Letter to Frank Wedekind, January 11, 1915, *Briefe I*]

He reads Alfred Kubin's novel *Die andere Seite.*

Mid-February, 1915

There is a public reading of *Gedanken im Kriege* in Munich.

The alienation between Thomas and Heinrich increases. "I do not know how to treat my brother, who would welcome the Rhine as a border ('In those days we had a great literature') . . ." [Letter to Ernst Bertram, *Bertram*]

T.M. begins an extended correspondence with the Viennese philologist and art historian Paul Amann, an admirer of Romain Rolland. Their exchange of letters began after Amann wrote T.M. a critical letter concerning his *Gedanken im Kriege.*

From March, 1915

Ernst Bertram visits T.M. frequently. They discuss questions of art, philosophy, and politics. Bertram is working on his book about Nietzsche, which appears in 1918. T.M. continues to work on *The Magic Mountain.* "I have already been here in the country for a while and have been able to get back to my story. I shall not allow myself another interruption." [Letter to Julius Bab, March 5, 1915, "Letters by Thomas Mann to Julius Bab," ed. by John F. Frank. *The Germanic Review*, New York, vol. 36, no. 3, 1961]

May, 1915

T.M. writes a letter to the *Svenska Dagbladet* in answer to an inquiry.

Under the title *Friedrich und die grosse Koalition*, the three essays on the war appear, published by the S. Fischer Verlag.

THOMAS MANN OM TYSKLAND OCH VÄRLDKRIGET, (SVENSKA DAGBLADET, Stockholm, May 11, 1915)

FRIEDRICH UND DIE GROSSE KOALITION, (Berlin: S. Fischer, 1915 —Sammlung von Schriften zur Zeitgeschichte. 20,000 copies)

May 8, 1915
T.M. attends a performance of August Strindberg's *Ghost Sonata* at the Munich Kammerspiele.

June, 1915
Klaus, T.M.'s eldest son, becomes critically ill with appendicitis and peritonitis, resulting in an intestinal paralysis. Five serious operations are necessary, in which the life of the boy is at stake. Katja Mann also becomes ill and has to have an operation. "If the boy remains alive, it will be as though he had been given to us again." [Letter to Hedwig Fischer, *Briefe I*].

August 5 to October 1, 1915
The Mann family return to the country house in Bad Tölz, where the children and Katja gradually convalesce.

August 3, 1915
T.M. mentions for the first time his intention of interrupting work on *The Magic Mountain* in order to treat more thoroughly the political problems discussed in his former essays. "And all the while current developments give both head and heart so infinitely much to do, so much to cope with, and at this moment I do not know whether I can and should go on telling tales, or whether I must pull myself together for a thoroughgoing, sober discussion, a coming to terms on a personal and self-analytic basis with the burning problems of the day." [Letter to Paul Amann, August 3, 1915, *Amann*]

End of September, 1915
The collie, Motz, who was the original for Perceval in *Royal Highness* and who has been in the Mann family for years, is put to death because of old age. "For now Motz rests from all his noble-spirited madnesses in a respectable grave on the edge of the woods, behind our garden. The children, with whom he was close friends, have placed flowers on the grave, nor have we omitted to give him a stone, a field boundary stone that has served its day and now bears the simple inscription of his name." [Letter to Paul Amann, October 1, 1915, *Amann*]

1915–1918
BETRACHTUNGEN EINES UNPOLITISCHEN [Reflections of a Nonpolitical Man]

Beginning of November, 1915
T.M. begins work on the *Betrachtungen eines Unpolitischen.* "And then, by dint of repeated attacks, began my work on the *Reflections*—a thrashing through the pathless underbrush which was to go on for two years." [*A Sketch of My Life*]

November 7, 1915
"I have plunged into a critical—essayistic—work, a kind of essay—no, they are almost private scribblings, which attempt to create a fusion—a strange and rash experiment—between contemporary events and a revision of my personal point of view. The effort is a considerable psychological strain upon me." [Letter to Paul Amann, November 7, 1915, *Amann*]

November 20, 1915
After attending a lecture by Maximilian Harden, T.M., Harden, Wedekind, Bruckmann, Max Bernstein, and Richard Friedenthal meet together at the Hotel Continental.

December 3, 1915
T.M. attends the celebration of Alexander von Gleichen-Russwurm's fiftieth birthday at the Hotel Continental.

Beginning of January, 1916
From the attorney Maximilian Brantl, T.M. receives the November 1915 issue of *Weisse Blätter* containing Heinrich Mann's essay on Zola. T.M. is highly indignant about the invective only slightly concealed in the article. "Literature is *one* thing but I must confess that my indignation concerning the detestable intrigue is gradually increasing . . ." [Letter to S. Fischer, March 14, 1916, in the auction catalogue of the Stargardt firm in Marburg]
He replies with caustic polemics directed at his brother in the chapters *Der Zivilisationsliterat* and *Gegen Recht und Wahrheit* in the *Betrachtungen eines Unpolitischen.*

January, 1916
T.M. writes an article of protest against the suppression of Maximilian Harden's publication *Die Zukunft.* The article is

not published by the *Frankfurter Allgemeine* because of censorship.

PROTEST GEGEN DAS VERBOT DER ZUKUNFT (unpublished article, now lost)

February 18, 1916

T.M. is visited by Jakob Wassermann.

March, 1916

He becomes ill, at first with influenza and then erysipelas. "I don't understand it—I have never been ill before, and now I seem completely infected." [Letter to Ernst Bertram, *Bertram*]

He reads from *Felix Krull* at the Bonboniere in Munich for the series of "Intimate Afternoons."

From April 6 to mid-May, 1916

Again at the country house in Bad Tölz, T.M. resumes writing. "I am still somewhat shaky . . . , but I can live and put in at least two hours work daily [on the treatise], which for me is very important." [Letter to Paul Amann, April 15, 1916, *Amann*].

May, 1916

He returns to Munich. Accompanied by Monika, Katja goes to visit her mother, Hedwig Dohm, in Berlin. T.M. receives frequent visits from Ernst Bertram, and the *Betrachtungen* are read and discussed.

Mid-June to mid-September, 1916

After returning to Bad Tölz, T.M. purchases a dog named Bashan [German: Bauschan]. "In the neighborhood of Tölz there is a mountain inn, kept by a pleasingly buxom, black-eyed damsel, with the assistance of a growing daughter, equally buxom and black-eyed. This damsel it was who acted as go-between in our introduction to Bashan and our subsequent acquisition of him." [*A Man and His Dog*]

August, 1916

T.M. falls ill once again. "I . . . had a quite serious attack of nerves, which forced me to stop my work for a week." [Letter to Ernst Bertram, *Bertram*]

September, 1916

He finishes the chapter of *Betrachtungen* entitled *Einkehr* and works on the chapter entitled *Gegen Recht und Wahrheit*. "At the moment I am wrestling with Rolland—very reverently, as is only right . . ." [Letter to Paul Amann, September 5, 1916, *Amann*]

T.M.'s essay written for a new edition of Eichendorff's *Aus dem Leben eines Taugenichts* (later inserted in the chapter *Von der Tugend* of the *Betrachtungen*) appears in the *Neue Rundschau.*

DER TAUGENICHTS (DIE NEUE RUNDSCHAU, November, 1916)

October 5, 1916

T.M. reads from *Felix Krull* in Munich.

November 5–10, 1916

He reads to two groups in Berlin—"Secession" and the "German Society"—from *Felix Krull* with an introductory essay entitled *Der Entwicklungsroman.*

DER ENTWICKLUNGSROMAN (VOSSISCHE ZEITUNG, Berlin, November 4, 1916)

November 11, 1916

He is reexamined and declared unfit for military service because of weak stomach and nervousness.

November 25, 1916

He attends the premiere of Bruno Frank's *Die treue Magd* at the Munich Schauspielhaus.

December 10, 1916

He attends a Munich performance of Robert Schumann's oratorio *Das Paradies und die Peri.*

He writes a review of the German translation of Thomas Carlyle's *Frederick the Great.*

CARLYLE'S "FRIEDRICH" IN VOLLSTÄNDIGER DEUTSCHER AUSGABE (FRANKFURTER ZEITUNG, December 24, 1916)

He writes the article *Musik in München.* ". . . an undertaking for a friend [Bruno Walter] and absolutely the last diversion . . ." [Letter to Ernst Bertram, *Bertram*]

MUSIK IN MÜNCHEN (DER TAG, Berlin, January 20 and 21, 1917)

Beginning of January, 1917

"A few days" with the family on the Tegernsee. Kurt Hiller writes a harsh reply to the *Taugenichts* essay—*Taugenichts, tätiger Geist, Thomas Mann.* "To me Hiller is a distant, indeed, a repugnant spirit. Even in the face of the infamy of this polemic, he is a respectable but quite a foreign creature. His writing, as sharp as it may be, is not so bad . . ." [Letter to Carl Maria Weber, *Briefe I*]

March, 1917

T.M. works on the chapter of *Betrachtungen* entitled *Politik.* "When the present large chapter is finished, then there are only short, easily written things to do—and then freedom, that is art, which I think of as pleasure, music, celebration as I have never thought of them before." [Letter to Ernst Bertram, *Bertram*]

EINKEHR (DIE NEUE RUNDSCHAU, March, 1917)

April, 1917

He takes a week's vacation in Mittenwald and is very disappointed at having missed Paul Amann's visit in Munich.

June 1, 1917

He plans to sell his country house in Bad Tölz. "I am selling the house *with furniture* and a large garden of 4 acres for 80,000 marks. There is still a 12,000 mark mortgage on the house . . ." [Unpublished letter to Kurt Martens]

The release of sale is designated as a war loan.

June 12, 1917

Hans Pfitzner's *Palestrina* receives its premiere at the Munich Prinzregententheater under the direction of Bruno Walter. T.M. attends five performances. "I cannot describe how this *Palestrina* touches my heart . . . With its metaphysical mood, its ethos of 'cross, death and grave,' its uniting of music, pessimism, and humor (with which altogether I define the concept of humanity), it reaches my deepest, most personal needs. Indeed, its appearance just now means to me nothing less than a great happiness. It gives me a positive attitude and releases me from my polemics." [Letter to Bruno Walter, *Briefe I*]

June 15, 1917

T.M. receives a visit from Hans Pfitzner and his wife. "The Pfitzners spent an evening with us recently. I doubt that he was happy, although he drank at least five glasses of Mosel wine, ate a great number of cakes, and thus at least in this respect did what was required of him. He was not born to be happy—a difficult, wounded man of conflicting feelings . . ." [Letter to Bruno Walter, *Briefe I*]

He makes quick progress in his work on the *Betrachtungen*. His analysis of *Palestrina* is added to the chapter *Von der Tugend*.

PALESTRINA (DIE NEUE RUNDSCHAU, October, 1917)

Mid-June to mid-September, 1917

During his last sojourn at Bad Tölz, T.M. receives frequent visits from Ernst Bertram. The two have conversations and read to each other. It is the time of their closest friendship.

August, 1917

Dr. Willy Wiegand purchases the house at Bad Tölz, which for some time is used by the *Bremer Presse*.

Heinrich Mann's play *Madame Legros* is produced in Berlin with great success. "My brother's play (a Berlin humor sheet called it *Mme Engros* because of the length of the run) is unquestionably a powerful throw of the dice." [Letter to Paul Amann, August 27, 1917, *Amann*]

T.M. works on the chapter of the *Betrachtungen* entitled *Einiges über Menschlichkeit.*

October, 1917

He becomes ill with dysentery. While in the hospital, he reads Tolstoy's *War and Peace* and for the first time Adalbert Stifter, whose works in three volumes are a gift from Ernst Bertram with the inscription, "In memory of the last summer at Bad Tölz." T.M. works on the chapter of the *Betrachtungen* entitled *Vom Glauben.*

Beginning of November, 1917

He attends the premiere of the opera *Lanzelot und Eleine* by Walter Courvoisier, who is a neighbor on Mauerkircherstrasse. "The music originated in Mauerkircherstrasse over our heads, and we were quite touched to hear the familiar sounds again." [Letter to Peter Pringsheim, *Briefe I*]

November, 1917

The *Betrachtungen* are almost finished. The chapter *Aesthetizistische Politik* is completed. "We should think of cooling the champagne." [Letter of Ernst Bertram, *Bertram*]

December, 1917

T.M. reads from the chapter of the *Betrachtungen* entitled *Einiges über Menschlichkeit* to a group called *The Zwanglosen*. He is introduced by his brother-in-law, the bank director Löhr.

Christmas, 1917

He works on the last chapter of the *Betrachtungen* and rewrites the chapter entitled *Politik*. "I am now rewriting the section of the chapter *Politik* on my personal relationship to the state. Then only the foreword remains to be written . . ." [Letter to Ernst Bertram, December 25, 1917, *Bertram*]

There is a close friendship at this time between T.M. and Bruno Walter, who is General Music Director at the Munich Staatsoper from 1913 to 1922. "I have concerned myself much more again with music in the last years, probably because of my association with B. Walter, the good, fiery, childlike, enthusiastic General Music Director." [Letter to Peter Pringsheim, *Briefe I*]

December 30, 1917

Heinrich Mann begins an attempt at reconciliation with

T.M. Heinrich thinks of T.M.'s article *Weltfrieden?* "almost like a letter of which some parts were meant for me."

WELTFRIEDEN? (BERLINER TAGEBLATT, December 27, 1917)

January 3, 1918

T.M. gives up the attempt at reconciliation. "I ask myself . . . whether there is any point in pressing once again the painful thoughts of two years into a letter . . ." [Letter to Heinrich Mann, *Briefe I*, January 3, 1919]

January, 1918

T.M. goes westward on a lecture tour to Belgium and Northern Germany.

Beginning of January, 1918

In Strassburg, T.M. meets with Hans Pfitzner, who is the city music director.

In Essen, T.M. visits Krupp.

January 9, 1918

In Brussels, the three acts of *Fiorenza* are performed by the German dramatic troop at the Théâtre Royal du Parc. Because of T.M.'s late arrival, Saladin Schmitt, the director of the production, undertakes the reading of *The Infant Prodigy*. "I breakfasted with the commandant of the town, the Bavarian General Hurt, surrounded by his officers, all dapper and affable people, one and all, for what service I know not, decorated with the Iron Cross First Class. One of them—he had been a chamberlain at a Thuringian court—later addressed me in a letter as Herr Comrade-in-Arms; and really the vicissitudes of the war hit me as hard as they did these people." [*A Sketch of My Life*]

January 11, 1918

In Hamburg, T.M. reads *A Weary Hour*, from *Felix Krull*, from *Royal Highness*, and *The Infant Prodigy*.

In Rostock for a reading, he is the guest of the Grand Duke von Mecklenburg-Schwerin.

January 17, 1918

T.M. gives a reading at the Lübeck Stadttheater in a benefit performance for those injured in the war. He uses the same program.

February, 1918

Ernst Bertram finishes his book on Nietzsche. T.M. works on the foreword to the *Betrachtungen*.

March 16, 1918
The *Betrachtungen eines Unpolitischen* is finished. T.M. tries to secure paper for the printing.

March 17, 1918
T.M. visits Hans Pfitzner and attends a performance of the opera *Die Rose vom Liebesgarten*. "A true Schopenhauerian type—and the most unbelievable opposite to his humanity . . . I experienced again yesterday the voluptuous beauty of the music in the *Rose vom Liebesgarten*." [Letter to Ernst Bertram, *Bertram*]

March 18, 1918
He attends a concert conducted by Bruno Walter at the Academy—Beethoven's *Overture to Coriolanus* and *Pastoral Symphony*, also Karl Erb sings *An die ferne Geliebte*. He attends a performance of Wagner's *Flying Dutchman* with Erika and Klaus.

March, 1918
He begins work on *A Man and His Dog*. He and Ernst Bertram proofread the *Betrachtungen*.

April 24, 1918
Elisabeth Veronika Mann is born.
T.M. receives a visit from Dr. Günther Herzfeld, a lieutenant and a student, from whose correspondence during the war T.M. had quoted in the *Betrachtungen*. ". . . an unusually sympathetic person and an admirer of my work." [Letter to Ernst Bertram, August 6, 1918, *Bertram*]

June, 1918
"The chapter on the landscape in the Bashan idyll is giving me trouble with botany. I have to know how to call the ash and birch trees by name." [Letter to Ernst Bertram, June 29, 1918, *Bertram*]
T.M. receives help from the botanist Dr. Gruber, a neighbor. He reads Wieland's political writings. Monika becomes ill.

From mid-July to mid-September, 1918
In Abwinkel on the Tegernsee, Villa Defregger. "As I expected, the trip was hellish. But it's charming here. The children are happy about the rowboat." [Letter to Ernst Bertram, July 7, 1918, *Bertram*]
For the first time T.M. climbs a mountain of considerable

height, the Hirschberg, which is 5511 feet high. He spends some evenings playing ninepins with Bruno Frank. Because of the depreciation of the German currency, he has difficulties in supporting his family. "I nourish myself chiefly on honey, which is my favorite food anyhow, although I am not a bear in other respects, and my wife has hoarded an ample supply of it." [Letter to Paul Amann, *Amann*]

August, 1918

T.M. works on *A Man and His Dog*. He writes the description of the park streets. He reads Stifter—*Studien* and *Sommernacht*.

September 21, 1918

He writes an exhaustive letter to Ernst Bertram in appreciation of his book on Nietzsche, which T.M. has now read in its entirety.

October, 1918

The first edition of the *Betrachtungen eines Unpolitischen* appears. Kurt Martens writes the first review in the *Münchener Neueste Nachrichten*.

T.M. writes an article in memory of Eduard Count Keyserling.

October 15, 1918

"Have just . . . finished *A Man and His Dog*." [Letter to Hans von Hülsen, from the auction catalogue of the Stargardt firm, Marburg]

October 23, 1918

Elisabeth, the youngest daughter, is baptized by Pastor Kuno Fiedler. Godparents are Ernst Bertram and Günther Herzfeld. T.M. purchases a bust of Luther by Hans Schwegerle. He begins writing the *Gesang vom Kindchen*.

November 9, 1918

The November Revolution begins and with it the Armistice.

1919

T.M. first becomes acquainted with Josef Ponten through the latter's novel, *Der babylonische Turm*.

February–April, 1919

Revolution takes place in Munich. The President of the Cabinet Council Kurt Eisner is assassinated. A soviet is formed. Through the efforts of Ernst Toller, the Mann home is saved from being plundered.

BETRACHTUNGEN EINES UNPOLITISCHEN [Reflections of a Non-Political Man] (Berlin: S. Fischer, 1918. 6,000 copies)

ZUM TODE KEYSERLINGS (FRANKFURTER ZEITUNG, October 15, 1918)

PEINLICHE BEGEGNUNG (MÜNCHENER NEUESTE NACHRICHTEN, March 1, 1919)

GESANG VOM KINDCHEN (DER NEUE MERKUR, Munich, April–May, 1919)

March 21, 1919
"I hope it will be only a few days until I can read you the baptism poem . . . I have gone into this little undertaking with an appalling ignorance of meter." [Letter to Ernst Bertram, *Bertram*]

End of March, 1919
T.M. finishes the *Gesang vom Kindchen.*

April, 1919
The first edition of *A Man and His Dog* appears.

April 21 (Easter Monday), 1919
Michael Thomas Mann is born. "It was absurd, but we are safe. We came through the storms almost without a scratch, and when I count the heads of my little ones, I even find that they are increased by one more. On Easter Monday (the heavy artillery was firing) my wife gave birth to a little boy who is to be named Michael . . ." [Letter to Philipp Witkop, *Briefe I*]

HERR UND HUND (with a foreword not printed later. Munich, 1919. An edition of 120 copies for the benefit of needy writers) *BASHAN AND I* (Transl. Hermann George Scheffauer. London: W. Collins Sons & Co., Ltd. 1923. 247 pp.) *A MAN AND HIS DOG* (STORIES OF THREE DECADES)

1919–1924
THE MAGIC MOUNTAIN [SECOND PERIOD]

End of April, 1919
T.M. resumes writing *The Magic Mountain.*

March, 1919
He takes a short vacation at Feldafing on Lake Würm.
He reads Oswald Spengler's *Decline of the West* (see T.M.'s later essay *On the Theory of Spengler*).

June, 1919
He reads Hermann Hesse's novel, *Demian,* which was published under the pseudonym "Emil Sinclair." "I was very moved and inquired pressingly about the author, his age, etc." [Letter to Josef Ponten, *Briefe I*]

June 4, 1919
Ernst Bertram makes his *Habilitation* at Bonn. Hedwig Dohm, Katja Mann's grandmother, dies at 86 in Berlin.

June 16, 1919
Hans Pfitzner's fiftieth birthday is celebrated at the restaurant Palais Preising in Munich, where T.M. gives the talk, *Tischrede auf Pfitzner*. He attends a production of Pfitzner's *Der arme Heinrich*.

TISCHREDE AUF PFITZNER (SÜDDEUTSCHE MONATSHEFTE, October, 1919)

July, 1919
Hans Schwegerle finishes a bronze bust of T.M.

Mid-July to the beginning of August, 1919
T.M. is the guest of S. Fischer at the beach hotel in Glücksburg on the Flensburg Fjord. "Here I am refreshing my memories of youth, and I am pleased with the really *primitive* fare—this region is untouched in every way." [Letter to Kurt Martens, *Briefe I*]

August 3, 1919
T.M. receives an honorary doctorate through the philosophical faculty of the Rheinische Friedrich Wilhelm-Universität at Bonn.

August 21, 1919
With Erika and Klaus, T.M. attends a performance of Heinrich Marschner's *Hans Heiling* at the Staatsoper. Katja Mann spends the holidays with the four younger children at Stock on the Chiemsee.

September, 1919
T.M. meets Josef Ponten. "I am happy about our meeting and relationship. I arranged for this because my reading of the *Turm* made me certain that you were a man and a soul whose conversation and friendship would be honorable and profitable . . ." [Letter to Josef Ponten, *Briefe I*]

October, 1919
T.M. returns for a while to Feldafing on Lake Würm.

December 4–10, 1919
He travels to Vienna with Bruno Walter, who is to give some concerts there. On the way, T.M. gives a reading of *Gesang vom Kindchen* in Nuremberg. In Vienna he attends a performance of *Fiorenza*. "I may recall here one happy theatrical experience, which fell to my lot in Vienna soon after the war: a performance of *Fiorenza*, forever memorable because it was given under such favorable circumstances that for the first time I felt none of the pangs of conscience that usually assail the author on such occasions. Dr. Wilhelm Rosenthal, then Director of the Volkstheater, was a lover of this work of mine. He had entrusted its performance to a dramatic company selected from the Burg and the Volkstheater so that even the smallest rôles were interpreted by artists who were arresting personalities and masters of diction. It was given in the Akademietheater, with its ample stage and inti-

AUFRUF ZUR GRÜNDUNG DES HANS PFITZNER-VEREIN FÜR DEUTSCHE TONKUNST
(In REDE UND ANTWORT, Berlin, 1922)

BRIEF AN DEN DEKAN DER PHILOSOPHISCHEN FAKULTÄT IN BONN
(In REDE UND ANTWORT, Berlin, 1922)

mate auditorium, the latter filled with a warmly disposed and international audience. I sat in a box near the stage, and my own lively interest astonished me." [*A Sketch of My Life*] He reads from *Gesang vom Kindchen* in the great hall of the Chancery with a introductory speech by Vice-Chancelor Dr. Jodok Fink. He attends a concert by Arnold Rosé (violin) and Bruno Walter (piano); the Beethoven *Spring Sonata* is among the works performed.

December 25, 1919

T.M. writes an article on the 100th birthday of Theodor Fontane.

ZUM 100. GEBURTSTAG THEODOR FONTANE (BERLINER TAGEBLATT, December 25, 1919)

January, 1920

The dog Bashan is put to death because of a purulent lung infection.

T.M. writes an open letter to Hermann, Count Keyserling on the occasion of the founding of the "School of Wisdom" in Darmstadt. The letter concerns the *Betrachtungen eines Unpolitischen*.

KLÄRUNGEN (DAS TAGEBUCH, Berlin, March 31, 1920)

January 28, 1920

He sends the manuscript of *The Hungry* to Stefan Zweig for the latter's collection.

February, 1920

In Feldafing on Lake Würm. T.M. works on *The Magic Mountain*. "I have slipped once again into my natural habitat, the mousehole. My wife was also here a few days but unfortunately before the good weather came." [Letter to Ernst Bertram, *Bertram*]

March, 1920

Katja Mann is very ill with influenza.

T.M. works on the chapter of *The Magic Mountain* entitled *Sudden Enlightenment*. "The Magic Mountain is growing slowly but evenly, may I say. Recently some decidedly curious scenes have formed, such as the one I am writing now which takes place in the X-ray laboratory—an institution that is to my mind quite unpermissible." [Letter to Ernst Bertram, March 16, 1920, *Bertram*]

April 22, 1920

T.M. reads in Augsburg from *The Magic Mountain*. The critic Bert Brecht writes of the reading: "Mann read from his novel *The Magic Mountain*, which, if the excerpts are typical, describes a kind of refined or naïve guerrilla war against death. The careful description is never lacking in metaphysical implications. The general fate of the many who are awaiting death has created a peculiar culture—a certain *savoir mourir*, perhaps—which in its playful charm hides the painful difficulties which have been inwardly overcome. For those who are safe from death, it is in relation to life a kind of laziness, but this observation is made relatively and not without a certain respect. The story of the dying woman who does not want to die, who kicks her legs in opposition when the priest comes to her, is incomparable in its mixture of profound horror and charming grandeur. So also is the story of the dying boy who makes a frivolous little play for the ladies out of his terrible lonely and intense battle with death in its mixture of restraint and love." [From the newspaper *Der Volkswille*, Augsburg]

May 9–14, 1920

The first chapter of *The Magic Mountain* is printed in a newspaper.

CHAPTER I: ARRIVAL, NUMBER 34, IN THE RESTAURANT from THE MAGIC MOUNTAIN (NEUE ZÜRCHER ZEITUNG, May 9–14, 1920)

May, 1920

Along with Hugo von Hofmannsthal, Jakob Wassermann, Ricarda Huch, and Count Hermann Keyserling, T.M. plans the publication of a periodical *Figura*, which is never published.

Ernst Bertram gives a lecture in Bonn on the *Betrachtungen eines Unpolitischen*.

May–June, 1920

Katja Mann is in Oberammergau at Pension Waldhaus for recuperation.

June 3, 1920

T.M. attends a performance of Wagner's *Die Walküre* "with my two eldest, who are an ever greater delight to my eyes and are more and more in my heart." [Letter to Ernst Bertram, *Bertram*]

Mid-July, 1920

He spends several days in Feldafing.

Mid-August, 1920

In Garmisch-Partenkirchen at the Fürstenhof, T.M. writes an evaluation of Verlaine's *Femmes* and *Hombres* in Kurt Moreck's translation for the publisher Paul Steegemann.

BRIEF AN EINEN VERLEGER (In REDE UND ANTWORT, Berlin, 1922)

September, 1920

Again in Munich, T.M. reads Georg Brandes' *Die roman-*

tische Schule in Deutschland, which is important for later chapters of *The Magic Mountain* and leads to T.M.'s acquaintance with Novalis' writings.

November 2–22, 1920

T.M. goes on a three-week lecture tour of the occupied Rhineland and the Ruhr. He reads from *The Magic Mountain* and the short stories.

November 2, 1920

He leaves on the night train from Munich to Frankfurt to Cologne.

November 3, 1920

In Mülheim-Speldorf, he is the guest of the Wilhelm Buller family (Frau Hedwig Buller is the daughter of Dr. Max Hoefer, the Mann family doctor at Bad Tölz.)

November 4, 1920

He reads in Mülheim.

November 5, 1920

He reads in Duisburg.

November 7, 1920

He reads in the afternoon in Dortmund, in the evening in Bochum.

November 11, 1920

While reading in Elberfeld, he is the guest of Ernst Bertram's mother.

November 18, 1920

In Cologne, He gives a reading as well as a talk to the students at the University. ". . . to the young people who live under the impression of a permanent and inconceivable insult . . ." [Unpublished letter to Rudolf Pannwitz]

November 20, 1920

He is in Bonn for a reading at the University.

November 7, 1920

He reads in Wiesbaden.

January–February, 1921

He makes a lecture tour in Switzerland. "When peace had been made after a fashion and Germany was suffering so greatly at the hands of the world, I took a few breaths outside the prison. Your land was the first foreign country I chose to visit after the war . . . Traveling to see you is no adventure. Lindau can be reached in comfort. One simply

sails across Lake Constance and sets foot on your honest soil . . ." [*Brief über die Schweiz*]
He reads *The Thermometer* from *The Magic Mountain*, from *Felix Krull*, and *The Infant Prodigy*.

January 17, 1921

In Winterthur: "Three stars by the name of this city! It was charming there, and I lived with the dearest people."

January 18, 1921

He reads in Zürich for the Hottingen Lesezirkel.

January 19, 1921

He reads in Aarau and Solothurn, "whose cathedral and town hall are among my strongest architectural impressions."

January 26, 1921

He reads before the student body of the University of Bern.

January 28, 1921

He reads in Saint Gall.

January 29, 1921

In Lucerne, he reads before a group called the Gesellschaft der Gleichgesinnten. "The trip from Lucerne was unforgettable. I had spent some time in the circle of like-minded people ["*Gleichgesinnten*"] and had found them liking [*wohlgesinnt*] me very much. On the surface of the Wallensee I saw the peaks of the Seven Kurfürsten clearly reflected. Then upward on worn paths into the holy, phantasmagoric world of snow covered mountains opening up before me, toward the strangely distant spot with whose name for such a long time my tears and thoughts have been so closely bound . . ." [*Brief über die Schweiz*]

January 30, 1921

T.M. spends four days in Davos at the sanatorium. "In the place itself, dear Bertram! You can imagine that I am all eyes. It is more than curious—the reality—after I have had it so long in my mind, to be able to see it actually again before me." [Letter to Ernst Bertram, *Bertram*]

February, 1921

He writes an introduction to the special issue of the *Süddeutsche Monatshefte* that deals with masterpieces of Russian literature. He goes on a lecture trip to North Germany and Thuringia, using the same works for reading.

ZUM GELEIT SÜDDEUTSCHE MONATSHEFTE, February, 1921)

February 19, 1921

In Berlin, he reads in the auditorium of the Werner Siemens Gymnasium. "an almost stormy success with my description of Hofrat Behrens [chief doctor at the sanitorium—*trans.*] and *The Thermometer*." [Letter to Robert Faesi, *Briefe I*]
The tour ends with readings in Jena, Coburg, and Weimar. "There were three high points: Standing a quarter hour before one of Hodler's murals at the University of Jena, a goiter operation, which I attended disguised as a visiting doctor at the Coburg Hospital; and a visit with the old Lama [Elisabeth Föster-Nietzsche] at the Weimar Archives." [Letter to Robert Faesi, *Briefe I*]

March 18, 1921

Writing on Wolfgang Born's illustrations for *Death in Venice*, T.M. states, "What I find most favorable about your pictures is that they move the story away from a naturalistic perspective, cleanse it of the pathological, sensational elements, and leave only the poetic." [*Vorwort zu einer Bildermappe*]

BILDER ZUM "TOD IN VENEDIG" (VOSSISCHE ZEITUNG, September 8, 1921)

April, 1921

T.M. selects articles for the volume of essays *Rede und Antwort* (the first title was *Improvisationen*). "Now I am as busy as it is possible for me to be in preparing for publication a collection of essays, *Improvisationen*, and every morning pushing the novel a bit further along." [Letter to Robert Faesi, *Briefe I*]

FOREWORD TO REDE UND ANTWORT, (Berlin: S. Fischer, 1922. 10,000 copies)

May, 1921

He spends a week in Feldafing and finishes the chapter *Walpurgis-Night* (the end of volume one in the German edition).

May 29, 1921

He writes a review of Hermann Ungar's collection of short stories entitled *Knaben und Mörder*.

KNABEN UND MÖRDER (VOSSISCHE ZEITUNG, May 29, 1921)

June 6, 1921

On his birthday he attends a performance of Bizet's *Carmen* with Erika, Klaus, and Golo (Monika is ill).

June 8, 1921

He attends an evening of recitations by the Indian poet Rabindranath Tagore at the home of the publisher Kurt Wolff.

June 10, 1921
He begins work on his lecture *Goethe and Tolstoy* for the "Nordic Week" in Lübeck.

GOETHE UND TOLSTOI (DEUTSCHE RUNDSCHAU, Berlin, March, 1922)
GOETHE AND TOLSTOY (in THREE ESSAYS. London: Martin Secker, 1932. 261 pp.)

July, 1921
"Concerning my essay, I am already involved in it and indeed quite articulate. Without any preparation, I have simply begun to write with the delusion that I could say everything. Recently I have read to my wife for two hours without ever reaching a stopping point." [Letter to Ernst Bertram, *Bertram*]

August 8–23, 1921
T.M. spends the holidays with Ernst Bertram on the beach in Timmendorf at the Villa Oda.

August 24 to September 2, 1921
He concludes his holidays with a week in Wenningstedt on Sylt at Haus Erika. He finishes his essay *Goethe and Tolstoy.*

September 2–8, 1921
In Lübeck for the "Nordic Week," he is the guest of the writer Ida Boy-Ed at her apartment on the Burgtor.

September 4, 1921
He gives his lecture *Goethe and Tolstoy* in the auditorium of the Johanneum. "The hour and a half lecture had a turbulent and enthusiastic reception. The house on Mengstrasse has been purchased by the city and restored. On the first floor there is to be a 'Buddenbrook Book Shop.'" [Letter to Ernst Bertram, *Bertram*]
He attends a performance of the *Dance of Death* at the Ägidienkirche.

September 10, 1921
In Berlin, T.M. repeats the *Goethe and Tolstoy* lecture at the Beethoven Hall.

September 12, 1921
In Munich, he resumes work on *The Magic Mountain*, beginning the chapter *Changes*.

October, 1921
He defends Oskar A. H. Schmitz's book *Das rätselhafte Deutschland* against unjustified critical attacks.

EIN BRIEF VON THOMAS MANN (GEORG MÜLLERS NEUESTE NACHRICHTEN, issues 12–14, 1921)

October 31, 1921
He gives the *Goethe and Tolstoy* lecture in Munich at the Vier Jahreszeiten. "The large hall was overcrowded, and the audience gave its deepest attention." [Letter to Ernst Bertram, *Bertram*]

November 6–12, 1921
In Zürich, T.M. reads *The Thermometer* from *The Magic Mountain* to the Hottingen Lesezirkel. In the auditorium of the University he gives the *Goethe and Tolstoy* lecture. Every day he visits the outpatient department of the hospital, gathering material for *The Magic Mountain.*
He writes a review of Kurt Martens' *Schonungslose Lebenschronik.*

EIN SCHRIFTSTELLERLEBEN (NEUE ZÜRCHER ZEITUNG, November 30, 1921)

November, 1921
The collection of essays *Rede und Antwort* appears.

Mid-December, 1921
T.M. works on an essay on the problem of German–French relations, which is an answer to André Gide's essay *Les rapports intellectuels entre la France et l'Allemagne* in the *Nouvelle Revue Française*, November, 1921.

DAS PROBLEM DER DEUTSCH-FRANZÖSISCHEN BEZIEHUNGEN (DER NEUE MERKUR, January, 1922)

January, 1922
With Katja Mann, T.M. makes a lecture trip to Prague, Brünn, Vienna, and Budapest. He reads *Goethe and Tolstoy.* While staying at the Hotel Imperial in Vienna, T.M. is robbed in a "criminal adventure."
He has his first meeting with the Marxist literary historian and writer, Georg Lukács, at whose father's house in Budapest T.M. is frequently a guest. "Dr. Georg Lukács is a man whose intellectual nature and attitude toward the world and society are in no way mine but whose strong, pure and proud spirit I honor and admire from an ethical point of view . . . Once in Vienna he explained his theories to me for an hour. For as long as he spoke he was right. And even if after his talk there remained with me an impression of almost uncanny abstractness, I also felt his clarity and intellectual generosity." [*Brief an Dr. Seipel*]
In the chapter of *The Magic Mountain* which soon followed this meeting, *A New-Comer*, T.M. made his description of the Jesuit Naphta to resemble Lukács.
Ernst Bertram is called to a professorship at Cologne University. Heinrich Mann becomes seriously ill with appendicitis and peritonitis. T.M. and his brother become reconciled at this time. "Those were difficult days that lie behind us, but now that we are over the mountain, things will go better for us together, if you are sincere as I am." [Letter to Heinrich Mann, January 31, 1922, *Briefe I*]

January 29, 1922

T.M. writes a review of Knut Hamsun's *The Women at the Pump.*

DIE WEIBER AM BRUNNEN (PRAGER PRESSE, January 29, 1922)

February 27 to March 31, 1922

T.M. is in Frankfurt for the Goethe Week, sponsored by the Friends of the Frankfurt Goethe Museum. He gives a lecture at the University. Among those present are Reichspräsident Friedrich Ebert and Gerhart Hauptmann. The title of the lecture is *The Idea of Organic Unity Through Confession and Education* (*Goethe and Tolstoy*, pp. 159–160 in *Essays of Three Decades*).

March 1, 1922

T.M. gives a talk before the festival production of Mozart's *Zauberflöte* at the Frankfurt Opernhaus.

March 4, 1922

The Buddenbrook Book Shop is opened in Lübeck with T.M. present.

March 19–20, 1922

In Berlin at the Theater am Kurfürstendamm and at the Sezession, T.M. reads the chapter from *The Magic Mountain* entitled *Analysis*.

April, 1922

He spends a short time in Feldafing.

He writes a review of Hans Reisiger's translation of the works of Walt Whitman. "The day came (an important day for me personally) when in an open letter about Walt Whitman—who had made a very great impression on me, in Reisiger's noble translation—I proclaimed the unity of humanity and democracy; I asserted that the first was only a classistic, old-fashioned name for the second, and felt no scruple in coupling the godlike Weimarian name and that of the Manhattan thunderer . . ." [*The German Republic*]

HANS REISIGERS WHITMAN WERK (FRANKFURTER ZEITUNG, April 16, 1922)

Klaus and Erika are in the state boarding school, Bergschule Hochwaldhausen on the Vogelsberg. Being declared nuisances at school, they leave in August at the end of their first term. Erika prepares herself for her final examinations at home. Klaus goes to the Odenwaldschule under the supervision of Paul Geheeb.

June, 1922

Katja Mann takes the children to the island of Reichenau in Lake Constance. She visits Kurt Hahn, an old acquaintance, who is the director of the state boarding school, Schloss Salem.

Beginning of July, 1922

T.M. repeats his lecture *Goethe and Tolstoy* in Heidelberg at the Kollegienhaus. "Heidelberg was charming. It was the first time I have been there, and I was enchanted by the romantic landscape and the youthful spirit of the academic world." [Letter to Ernst Bertram, *Bertram*]

He is guest of the law historian Professor Fehr. He meets the professors Hoops, Oncken, and Alfred Weber and visits a colleague of Professor Fehr.

Progress on *The Magic Mountain* has reached the chapter *Choler. And Worse.*

HIPPE and *ANALYSIS* from THE MAGIC MOUNTAIN (WISSEN UND LEBEN, Zürich, October, 1922)

July, 1922

T.M. begins writing the speech *The German Republic*. "I am thinking of writing a birthday article about Gerhart Hauptmann in the form of a manifesto, in which I shall speak to the consciences of the youth who will listen to me." [Letter to Ernst Bertram, *Bertram*]

VON DEUTSCHER REPUBLIK (DIE NEUE RUNDSCHAU, November, 1922)

THE GERMAN REPUBLIC (in ORDER OF THE DAY: POLITICAL ESSAYS AND SPEECHES OF TWO DECADES. New York: Alfred A. Knopf, 1942. 280 pp.)

August, 1922

He takes his holidays in Ahlbeck, "where I wrote the largest portion of my republican manifesto." [Letter to S. Fischer, Auction Catalogue of the Stargardt Firm, Marburg]

September, 1922

Financial problems increase because of the inflation. "Without foreign money I should not be able to manage these days with a family like mine. Like everyone else, I am considering how to earn something extra . . . Thus I am becoming in middle age a bustling businessman . . . Now I am returning to *The Magic Mountain*, but . . . immediately I have these American letters to write, which of course sustain us." [Letter to S. Fischer, Auction Catalogue of the Stargardt Firm, Marburg]

GERMAN LETTER I (THE DIAL, New York, December, 1922)

October 6, 1922

He reads *The German Republic* to his friends in Munich—Kurt Martens, Heinrich Mann, Emil Preetorius, Bjørn Bjørnson.

October 10–November 3, 1922

T.M. makes a lecture tour through Germany and Holland.

October 10, 1922

While visiting S. Fischer in Berlin, T.M. meets Oskar Loerke.

October 15, 1922
He reads from *The German Republic* in the Beethoven Hall in Berlin. "I attempted to explain my idea of humanity in *The German Republic*, for which I have been accused of being un-German and of contradicting the *Betrachtungen*, when in reality this speech is a direct continuation of them." [Letter to Félix Bertaux, *Briefe I*]
He gives readings in Hanover, Münster, Düsseldorf, and Cleve. Using Amsterdam as headquarters, he gives readings in Nijmwegen, Utrecht, Amsterdam, and other Dutch cities.
October 31, 1922
Before 2,500 people in the Saalbau in Frankfurt, T.M. reads *Hippe* from *The Magic Mountain* and the medical examination scene from *Felix Krull*. He is the guest of Emil Liefmann, M.D.
November 3, 1922
T.M. returns to Munich. "The whole trip was quite successful. Satiated with the world, cheerful, and tired, I return to my harbor." [Unpublished letter to the Wilhelm Buller family, his hosts in Duisburg.]
November, 1922
He makes new plans for lecture tours because of the growing inflation. "I . . . shall be stationary now until the middle of January. Then I go once again to Switzerland. At the beginning of March, it will be Sweden's turn, and in mid-April, Spain's. It is a mad life and a difficult feat to collect a tremendous composition and form it into a work of art which is crying to be finished." [Letter to Kurt Martens, *Briefe I*]
December 20, 1922
He takes part in a séance at the home of Baron von Schrenck-Notzing (later also on January 6 and 24, 1924). Out of his notes on the sitting comes the essay *An Experience in the Occult*.
January, 1923
The Ruhr is occupied. "It is as though everyone else sees Germany not at all as a republic like any other, but rather as a leaderless land, an unfeeling torso with which one may do as he pleases." [Letter to Ernst Bertram, *Bertram*]
Mid-January, 1923
T.M. goes on a lecture trip to Chur, Zürich, and other Swiss cities.

RUSSISCHE DICHTER-GALERIE Introduction to Alexander Eliasberg's BILDERGALERIE ZUR RUSSISCHEN LITERATUR (PRAGER PRESSE, December 3, 1922)

OKKULTE ERLEBNISSE (DIE NEUE RUNDSCHAU, March, 1924)

AN EXPERIENCE IN THE OCCULT (THREE ESSAYS. New York: Alfred A. Knopf, 1929. 261 pp.)

January 31, 1923
At Tübingen in the Schiller Hall of the Museum, T.M. gives a lecture from *Goethe and Tolstoy* at the invitation of the General Student Committee.

Mid-February, 1923
In Dresden as guest of Professor Arthur Nikisch, the son of the conductor, T.M. reads from *The Magic Mountain*.

He goes to Berlin to discuss the filming of *Buddenbrooks*. "A stupid and sentimental film-drama . . . , about which my soul knows nothing, but in Scandinavia, Holland, and America, there seems to be considerable interest in it . . ." [Letter to Ernst Bertram, *Bertram*]

February 27, 1923
He reads *An Experience in the Occult* in Augsburg, "where the audience sat on the stage."

March 11, 1923
T.M.'s mother dies in Wessling at the age of 73. "I do not believe that I have ever been so sad in all my life." [Letter to Ernst Bertram, *Bertram*]

March, 1923
Félix Bertaux makes plans to translate *Death in Venice*.

March 25–April 8, 1923
T.M. goes eastward on a lecture tour to Austria, Hungary, and Czechoslavakia, reading *An Experience in the Occult*.

March 25–30, 1923
At the Hotel Imperial in Vienna, T.M. encounters Arthur Schnitzler and Raoul Auernheimer.

March 31, 1923
He makes an excursion to Semmering.

April 1, 1923
He visits Hugo von Hofmannsthal in Rodaun.

April 2, 1923
He is in Budapest.

April 5, 1923
In Prague, T.M. visits Mimi Mann.

There are problems with Erika and Klaus during the inflation. Klaus is sent to an occultist and follower of Rudolf Steiner, Alexander von Bernus, at the Neuburg Foundation on the Neckar.

April 19–May 22, 1923
T.M. travels to Spain. "In the spring of 1923 came a voyage

to Spain undertaken by water in the still necessary avoidance of France: from Genoa to Barcelona, Madrid, Seville, and Granada, then back across the peninsula to Santander in the north, through the Bay of Biscay and via Plymouth to Hamburg [with the Hapag steamer, Toledo]. I shall not soon forget Ascension Day in Seville, the mass in the cathedral, the glorious organ music, the gala *corrida* in the afternoon. But, on the whole, Andalusia and the south appealed to me less than the classic Spanish domain, Castile, Toledo, Aranjuez, Philip's granite fortress, and the drive past the Escorial to Segovia beyond the snow-topped Guadarrama." [*A Sketch of My Life*]

He gives lectures from *Goethe and Tolstoy, An Experience in the Occult, et al.* at the German School in Diego de León and at the German School in Madrid. Present at the Madrid lecture is Professor Adolfo Bonilla, Dean of the Philosophical Faculty of the University. T.M. is received by the Infanta Isabella and is a guest at the Ullmann house.

He writes *German Letter II.*

Beginning of June, 1923

The chapter of *The Magic Mountain* entitled *Snow* is finished.

June 6, 1923

At T.M.'s birthday party, those present are Viktor Mann, Dr. Hallgarten, Emil Preetorius, Berthold Litzmann, and their wives.

June, 1923

T.M. gives a speech at the Rathenau memorial service for the Republican students in Munich: *Geist und Wesen der deutschen Republik.*

September, 1923

He writes *German Letter III.*

October, 1923

He spends his holidays in Bozen at the Hotel Austria.

From his meeting with Gerhart Hauptmann, T.M. forms the conception of the character of Mynheer Peeperkorn for *The Magic Mountain*. "I have sinned against you. I was in sore need, was led into temptation, and gave in to it. My need was artistic. I was searching for a figure whom for a long time I had foreseen as necessary to my composition but whom I could not visualize or hear or possess. Restless, care-worn, and perplexed in the search, I came to Bozen, and

GERMAN LETTER II (THE DIAL, New York, June, 1923)

SNOW from THE MAGIC MOUNTAIN (DIE NEUE RUNDSCHAU, December 1923)

GEIST UND WESEN DER DEUTSCHEN REPUBLIK (FRANKFURTER ZEITUNG, June 28, 1923)

GERMAN LETTER III (THE DIAL, New York, October, 1923)

there, while I was drinking wine, there offered itself to me unwittingly that which personally I should never have been able to take but which, in a moment of human weak judgment, I did take and believed myself permitted to take . . ." [*Brief an Gerhart Hauptmann*]
With his brother, Viktor, T.M. writes a filmscript of *Tristan and Isolde*. The film is never made.

November 15, 1923

The inflation comes to an end when the mark is stablized by basing it on land values.

Winter, 1923

T.M. writes several short articles for the newspapers, among them a review of some writings of Ernst Tröltsch.
He is visited by the painter Hermann Ebers, who shows him a series of illustrations of the Joseph story from the Old Testament. "At about this time . . . , a Munich artist, an old friend of my wife, showed me a portfolio of illustrations of his, depicting quite prettily the story of Joseph the son of Jacob. The artist wanted me to give him a word or so of introduction to his work, and it was partly in the mind to do him this friendly service that I looked up in my old family Bible . . . the graceful fable . . ." [*A Sketch of My Life*]
His first intention is to write a novella about Joseph in the form of a triptych of historical tales.

December 12–14, 1923

He gives a lecture from *An Experience in the Occult* in Berlin at the Singing Academy and at Lübeck in the aula of the Johanneum.

December 25, 1923

"*The Magic Mountain* is printed as far as the manuscript is finished; that is, it is still not completed. Fischer's Loerke finds the work 'magnificent.'" [Letter to Ernst Bertram, *Bertram*]

February–March, 1924

While Katja Mann spends six weeks resting at Clavadel near Davos, T.M. is alone with the children.
He writes an essay about Spengler's *Decline of the West*.
Erika passes her final examinations and becomes an actress.

Beginning of April, 1924

T.M. is ill with influenza. Katja Mann returns from Clavadel.

TRISTAN UND ISOLDE (published 1949 by Viktor Mann in his book, WIR WAREN FÜNF)
NATURRECHT UND HUMANITÄT (FRANKFURTER ZEITUNG, December 25, 1923)
EUROPÄISCHE SCHICKSALSGEMEINSCHAFT (BERLINER TAGEBLATT, December 25, 1923)
GERMAN LETTER IV (THE DIAL, New York, January, 1924)
ÜBER DIE LEHRE OSWALD SPENGLERS (ALLGEMEINE ZEITUNG, Munich, March 9, 1924)
ON THE THEORY OF SPENGLER (PAST MASTERS AND OTHER PAPERS. New York: Alfred A. Knopf, 1933. 275 pp.)

April 10, 1924

Hermann Ebers' illustrations are printed. "I am extraordinarily pleased, and the plan for giving the charming story a fresh retelling pleases me also. Nothing could make me more excited than these pictures, which reflect so much of the delightfulness of the story." [Letter to Hermann Ebers, in Herbert Lehnert, *Thomas Manns Vorstudien zur Josephtetralogie. Jahrbuch der Deutschen Schillergesellschaft,* 1963]

End of April, 1924

T.M. prepares for a trip to England. "I have only just now organized and begun the conclusion of *The Magic Mountain*. During July I hope to be finished." [Letter to Ernst Bertram, *Bertram*]

May, 1924

T.M. travels to Holland and England.

May 2–4, 1924

In Amsterdam, he is the guest of the *Letterkundige Kring*. His dinner speech is entitled *Demokratie und Leben.*

DEMOKRATIE UND LEBEN (VOSSISCHE ZEITUNG, Berlin, May 23, 1924)

May 5, 1924

He travels from Vlissingen to London.

May 6, 1924

He does some sightseeing in London and is guest of honor at the PEN Club. John Galsworthy, president of the club, gives a speech welcoming him, and he is the guest of Galsworthy in Hendon. "The dinner in London was a *Demonstration*—pretty, delightful, and touching." [Letter to Ernst Bertram, *Bertram*]

May 12, 1924

He visits Oxford. "Youth and the centuries are becoming to each other." [Letter to Ernst Bertram, *Bertram*]

He returns via Southampton to Hamburg, then continues on to Berlin, where Erika is finishing her dramatic studies.

June, 1924

He writes a greeting to Ricarda Huch on her sixtieth birthday.

ZUM 60. GEBURTSTAGE RICARDA HUCHS (FRANKFURTER ZEITUNG, July 18, 1924)

July 1, 1924

He writes an article in memory of Wolfgang von Weber.

From the middle to the end of July, 1924

With Gerhart Hauptmann, T.M. spends some holidays at the cloister on [the island of] Hiddensee, at the hotel Haus am Meer. "It was on Hiddensee . . . , I was also there once and stayed at the house that received the famous guest every year—the Haus am Meer. We spent many an evening there under the lamp, and on one of these Hauptmann honored and pleased us by reading in person from his manuscript of *Eulenspiegel*, which was still a secret. It was the first song, which we heard with great feeling. On the following evening, he asked to hear something of *The Magic Mountain*, which he knew I was working on at that time. I was embarrassed, for I did not wish to take my candle from under the bushel after the impressions of the previous evening, and I said as much with a polite refusal. Hauptman was searching for a response. It was one of those typical and tense moments when his expressions and hands were preparing something which, when it occurred, would surprise with its simplicity . . . I realized in a few seconds that my hesitation had been false and fearful. He said, 'You are wrong. In my father's house are many mansions.' " [*Herzlicher Glückwunsch*]

BRIEF AN WOLFGANG VON WEBER (DER ZWIEBELFISCH, Munich, September, 1924)

August, 1924

To conclude his holidays, T.M. goes to Bansin and stays at Haus Seeblick until August 16, and then to Ahlbeck, where he stops at Haus Heimdahl, from the 18th to the 25th. "The children are truly sad about leaving the lake, both the big ones and the little ones, just as I used to be . . . After my morning swim, which is delightful, I have been constantly working hard . . . *The Magic Mountain* has made great progress toward its completion. I believe I shall finish by the end of October." [Letter to Ernst Bertram, *Bertram*]

August 18, 1924

At Stralsund, T.M. gives a speech in memory of those who fell in World War I.

AUS DER REDE AM 18. AUGUST 1924 IN STRALSUND (In JOACHIM VON WINTERFELDT ZUM 60. GEBURTSTAGE AM 15. 5. 1925. Berlin, 1925)

September 1, 1924

Erika Mann is hired by the Reinhardt-Bühnen in Berlin.

Klaus becomes the second drama critic on the *12-Uhr-Mittags-Blatt* and begins his literary career with some essays for the *Weltbühne* and the collection of short stories, *Vor dem Leben*.

Michael and Elisabeth have appendectomies.

A NEWCOMER from THE MAGIC MOUNTAIN (DIE NEUE RUNDSCHAU, September, 1924)

September 28, 1924

T.M. celebrates finishing *The Magic Mountain* with Ernst Bertram.

October, 1924

With Ernst Bertram, he spends a ten-day vacation in Sestri Levante. "Here I'm resting up." he writes another *German Letter.*

GERMAN LETTER V (THE DIAL, New York, November, 1924)

November 4, 1924

He gives a speech at the Odeon in Munich on the occasion of the eightieth birthday of Friedrich Nietzsche.

REDE ZUR FEIER DES 80. GEBURTSTAGES FRIEDRICH NIETZSCHES (In ARIADNE, Yearbook of the Nietzsche Society, Munich, 1925)

NIETZSCHE AND MUSIC (PAST MASTERS AND OTHER PAPERS)

November 8, 1924

For the first time, he reads the Peeperkorn chapters from *The Magic Mountain* publicly, at the Galerie Caspari.

November 12–26, 1924

T.M. makes a lecture tour of Stuttgart, Freiburg, and Dresden, during which time he is the guest of Professor Nikisch. Going on to Hanover and finally Berlin, he meets Katja and Erika. At the home of the publisher, Georg Bondi, he meets Stefan George. "At Bondi's, on the threshold, I had a weird meeting with HIM." [Letter to Ernst Bertram, *Bertram*]

He puts together the collection of essays entitled *Bemühungen.*

November 28, 1924

The Magic Mountain appears in two volumes. The first printings are quickly bought up. "It was in 1924, after endless intermissions and difficulties, that there finally appeared the book which, all in all, had had me in its power not seven but twelve years. Its reception would have needed to be much more unfavorable than it was, to surpass my expectations . . . . Certain it is that ten years earlier the book would not have found readers—nor could it have been written. It needed the experiences which the author had shared with his countrymen; these he had to ripen within him in his own good time, and then, at the favorable moment, as once before, to come forward with his bold production." [*A Sketch of My Life*]

DER ZAUBERBERG (Berlin: S. Fischer, 1924. 2 volumes.)

THE MAGIC MOUNTAIN (New York: Alfred A. Knopf, 1927)

He writes a review of the works of Selma Lagerlöf and Robert Louis Stevenson.

December 14–23, 1924

He makes a lecture tour of Denmark. He reads in Aarhus, and in Copenhagen he is the guest of the German ambassador, Gerhart von Mutius.

GROSSE UNTERHALTUNG (BERLINER TAGEBLATT, December 12, 1924)

December 18, 1924

He gives a lecture to the Student Union from *Goethe and Tolstoy*.

December 20, 1924
At the celebration for the establishment of the society called Friends of German Literature at the Odd Fellows Hall, he reads from his works. Then he returns to Berlin. "It was a delightful trip, both in a personal and a national sense." [Letter to Ernst Bertram, *Bertram*]

December 31, 1924
With his children Elisabeth and Michael, T.M. attends a performance of Humperdinck's *Hänsel und Gretel.*

1925
HIS FIFTIETH BIRTHDAY

January 1, 1925
T.M. goes to a "solemn breakfast" at the home of the privy counselor, Berthold Litzmann.

January, 1925
He again takes to work on the *Goethe and Tolstoy* essay. "I am working again on *Goethe and Tolstoy* for the collection of essays. It had become cold, but it is warming up again now." [Letter to Ernst Bertram, *Bertram*]
Hermann Hesse visits T.M.

January 11, 1925
In Dresden, he visits Professor Nikisch and attends a performance in the evening of Mozart's *Don Giovanni* conducted by Fritz Busch.

January 12–13, 1925
In Breslau, he gives two lectures. The one at the University is from *Goethe and Tolstoy.*

End of January, 1925
Enmity developes between T.M. and Josef Ponten, who in an open letter attacked T.M.'s concept of *Dichter* and *Schriftsteller* in the essay on Ricarda Huch.

February, 1925
Besides expanding the essay *Goethe and Tolstoy*, T.M. writes a foreword to the Epikon edition of Goethe's *Wahlverwandtschaften,* a short story for the Thomas Mann Birthday Issue of the *Neue Rundschau*, and a political article for *L'Europe Nouvelle*. He buys his first car. "I must tell you *entre nous* that I have earned some seventy thousand marks by selling tickets to my mystical-comical aquarium; thus I have purchased an automobile, a pretty six passenger Fiat. Our

GOETHE AND TOLSTOY (In BEMÜHUNGEN, Berlin, 1925)
ZU GOETHES WAHLVERWANDTSCHAFTEN (DIE NEUE RUNDSCHAU, April, 1925)
L'ESPRIT DE L'ALLEMAGNE ET SON AVENIR ENTRE LA MYSTIQUE SLAVE ET LA LATINITÉ OCCIDENTALE (L'EUROPE NOUVELLE, March 14, 1925)

windbag, Ludwig, thinks of himself as an accomplished chauffeur, and so I shall travel into the city now with 33 horses and wave affably in all directions." [Letter to Ernst Bertram, *Bertram*]

March 1, 1925

T.M. writes an article to the memory of the President of the Republic, Friedrich Ebert.

ZU FRIEDRICH EBERTS TOD (FRANKFURTER ZEITUNG, March 6, 1925)

March 5–25, 1925

He takes a cruise on the Mediteranean at the invitation of the Stinnes Lines aboard the M.S. *General San Martin*. "I am living in no luxury suite and am quite satisfied. I have been given an officer's cabin on the main deck that was formerly the doctor's—a tightly, practically furnished little space with a table for writing and many spacious drawers under the bed and in the chest. It is nice but not too nice, which means it is as it should be for me. My lounge chair for reading is just outside the door." [*Unterwegs*]

He visits Venice, Cattaro, Port Said, Cairo, Luxor, and Karnak."We were in *Luxor*, in *Karnak*, in the tombs of the Pharoahs at Thebes. We traveled back and forth at night in a pullman." [*Unterwegs*]

UNTERWEGS (VOSSISCHE ZEITUNG, Berlin, April 12, 1925)

He mentions for the first time his plans for a novel about Joseph. "I shall be traveling in this manner about four weeks, . . . during which time, without wanting to concern myself too much with the humanistic elements, I am primarily interested in Egypt. I shall take a look at the desert, the pyramids, and the sphinx, for these can be useful in some of my definite, though perhaps ulterior plans which I have laid in secret." [Letter to Ernst Bertram, February 4, 1925, *Bertram*]

The trip continues to Constantinople, where he is officially received by the Turkish Harbor Control, then on to Athens and Naples, from whence he returns to Germany.

April, 1925

He writes the short story *Disorder and Early Sorrow*.

UNORDNUNG UND FRÜHES LEID (DIE NEUE RUNDSCHAU, June, 1925)

April 30, 1925

"My short story is almost finished. The first half has already gone to print." [Letter to Ernst Bertram, *Bertram*]

May, 1925

With Gerhart Hauptmann and his son, Benvenuto, T.M. attends a full rehearsal of Hauptmann's *Festaktus*, written for the formal opening of the Deutsches Museum in Munich. "We shook a lot of hands, and everything is again in order. He is such a fine figure; I am very fond of him. And the play is also a charming bit of prattle." [Letter to Erika Mann, *Briefe I*]

EARLY SORROW (Transl. Hermann George Scheffauer. London: Martin Secker, 1929. 100 pp.) *DISORDER AND EARLY SORROW* (STORIES OF THREE DECADES)

May, 1925

Klaus Mann's first book, the collection of short stories *Vor dem Leben*, appears.

May 9–25, 1925

T.M. goes on a journey to Italy.

May 9–16, 1925

He attends the International Cultural Week in Florence as the representative of Germany along with Professor Ulrich von Wilamowitz-Moellendorf. He gives a lecture from *Goethe and Tolstoy* and is a guest at the country house of Dr. Richter.

May 17–25, 1925

He is in Venice and on the Lido.

June 6, 1925

On T.M.'s fiftieth birthday, numerous greetings and articles appear in the European press. He also receives personal greetings from Stefan Zweig, Max Rychner, Alfred Kubin, Hans Pfitzner, Gerhart Hauptmann, Jakob Wassermann, Hugo von Hofmannsthal, and others.

At the official celebration in the Old Counsel Hall in Munich, Franz Munckner makes the main address. There is a speech by Mayor Scharnagl of Munich, and Karl Vossler gives his lecture on the character and rôle of Settembrini. Heinrich Mann's speech was a "short, moving remembrance of childhood birthdays and brought not only me to tears." [Letter to Ernst Bertram, *Bertram*]

In reply to these speeches, T.M. states, "If . . . my studies and writings have the effect of developing, guiding, helping in the outside world, then it is an accidental effect, which surprises me to the same degree that it makes me happy . . . What my work ought to accomplish—something musical, something moral, something of both—God alone, who gave me the ability, knows . . . In any case, it is a wonderful, gratifying thing to belong to a great cultural people like the

REDE ZUM 50. GEBURTSTAG: Rekonstruktion (In ALMANACH 1926 DES S. FISCHER VERLAGS, Berlin, 1925)

Germans, to use their language, to be permitted to follow and continue to develop their great heritage." [*Tischrede bei der Feier des fünfzigsten Geburtstages*]

June 7, 1925

There is a program in his honor at the Munich Residenztheater: Mozart's chamber music, a lecture by Professor Fritz Strich, a reading from *Felix Krull* by T.M., who, after a roundelay by some young ladies, is crowned with a laurel wreath.

He expresses his thanks. ". . . I had to speak once again, which I did cordially without restraint." [Letter to Ernst Bertram, *Bertram*]

June 8–11, 1925

At the PEN Club in Vienna, he gives the speech, *Natur und Nation*. Raoul Auernheimer gives a speech at the PEN Club banquet, and T.M. replies to it with the speech, *Zum Problem des Österreichertums.*

ZUM PROBLEM DES ÖSTERREICHERTUMS (NEUE FREIE PRESSE, Vienna, June 11, 1925)

DANKSAGUNG (FRANKFURTER ZEITUNG, June 11, 1925)

1925–1928
THE *DEMANDS OF THE DAY* AND THE JOSEPH NOVEL

Mid-June, 1925

T.M.'s new literary undertakings are a contribution to Hermann Keyserling's *Ehe-Buch*, another *German Letter*, an article on cosmopolitanism for the *Literarische Welt*, and a dispute with some medical doctors about problems in *The Magic Mountain*. The bookdealer, Ida Herz, systematizes T.M.'s library. "I am just now having my library put in order, which to be sure has a rather jumbled character . . ." [Unpublished letter to Korfiz Holm]

Ida Herz makes a private collection of T.M.'s publications in newspapers and magazines. As a result, a lifelong friendship and correspondence develops between the two of them.

T.M. plans to write a novella triptych. "What I had in mind, of course, was a novella which should serve as one wing to a historical triptych, the other two dealing with Spanish and German subjects, the religious-historical theme running through the whole." [*A Sketch of My Life*]

"VOM GEIST DER MEDIZIN" (DEUTSCHE MEDIZINISCHE WOCHENSCHRIFT, Leipzig, July 17, 1925)

July, 1925

He takes an automobile trip to the state boarding school,

GERMAN LETTER VI (THE DIAL, New York, October, 1925)

Schloss Salem on Lake Constance, which Golo and Monika Mann are attending. He gives a reading to the students. A schoolmate of Golo and Monika "of Spanish blood" is to become, "because of his exotic beauty, a model for my father's young Joseph." [Monika Mann, *Vergangenes und Gegenwärtiges*]

July 15, 1925

He attends a performance of Wagner's *Parsifal* at the Munich Residenztheater. Erika Mann becomes an actress in the Bremen Schauspielhaus.

August, 1925

"I have finished the marriage article for Keyserling and did it in quite a respectable manner, it seems to me. It became a rather comprehensive document, highly moral, and includes a basic argument against homoeroticism . . ." [Letter to Erika Mann, *Briefe I*]

DIE EHE IM ÜBERGANG (In DAS EHE-BUCH, ed. Count Hermann Keyserling. Celle, 1925)

August 20–30, 1925

T.M. attends the Salzburg Festival. At Alt-Aussee he visits Jakob Wassermann, who "has a magnificent piece of property." He meets there his publisher, S. Fischer.

In Salzburg, T.M. attends *Mirakel* by Karl Gustav Vollmöller, *Das grosse Welttheater* by Hugo von Hofmannsthal, *Das Apostelspiel* by Max Mell, and Donizetti's *Don Pasquale* directed by Bruno Walter.

WAS VERDANKEN SIE DER KOSMOPOLITISCHEN IDEE? (LITERARISCHE WELT, Berlin, October 9, 16, and 23, 1925)
COSMOPOLITANISM (PAST MASTERS AND OTHER PAPERS)

Beginning of September, 1925

He proofreads his volume of essays, *Bemühungen*. "But I am often worried about when I shall again do something new." [Letter to Ernst Bertram, *Briefe I*]

September, 1925

He has a holiday with Michael and Elisabeth at the Hotel Pithecusa in Casamicciola on the island of Ischia.

October, 1925

The first edition of the volume of essays, *Bemühungen*, appears.

BEMÜHUNGEN: Neue Folge der Gesammelten Abhandlungen und kleinen Aufsätze (Berlin: S. Fischer, 1925. 12,000 copies)

October 9–10, 1925

At the delayed celebration of T.M.'s birthday in Lübeck, there is a production of *Fiorenza* at the Stadttheater. Before the performance for the Volksbühne, T.M. makes a speech.

In Berlin he sits for a portrait by Max Liebermann. S. Fischer has asked for an etching to be included in the collected works, which are to appear in ten volumes. T.M.

visits Professor Hönn, editor of the periodical, *Deutsche Politik*.

November, 1925

Klaus Mann's first play, *Anja und Esther*, receives its premiere at the Hamburg Kammerspiele, with Klaus and Erika. Gustaf Gründgens and Pamela Wedekind play the main rôles. T.M. sees the production in Munich.

November 8, 1925

T.M. gives a speech at the beginning of the "Book Week" in Munich.

DAS DEUTSCHE BUCH (PRAGER TAGEBLATT, December 6, 1925)

He makes preparations for his Joseph novella. "I am happy now for at least a few weeks of free time to carry out my plans." [Unpublished letter to Ida Herz]

December, 1925

He writes an article for the *Frankfurter Zeitung* about the new Christmas publications and prepares his lecture to be given at Carnegie Institute in Paris. "But I have decided from now on to occupy myself with something entirely different, and I am looking forward to talking to you about Abraham and Hammurabi, Joseph and Amenhotep IV." [Letter to Ernst Bertram, December 25, 1925, *Bertram*]

KATALOG (FRANKFURTER ZEITUNG, December 13, 1925)

January 12–29, 1926

He travels to Paris at the invitation of the Carnegie Foundation.

LES TENDENCES SPIRITUELLES DE L'ALLEMAGNE D'AUJOURD'HUI (L'ESPRIT INTERNATIONAL, Paris, January, 1927)

January 12–18, 1926

He gives readings in Heidelberg, Cologne, Marburg, and Mainz, where he meets his wife Katja.

January 19, 1926

He takes a guided walking tour through Mainz and in the evening departs for Paris.

January 20, 1926

He arrives in Paris and registers at the hotel Palais d'Orsay. He takes a walk through Paris in the morning and gives a lecture in the afternoon at the Dotation Carnegie pour la Paix Internationale. He is introduced by Professor Henri Lichtenberger of the Sorbonne. The subject of T.M.'s lecture is intellectual trends in modern-day Germany. A reception given for T.M. by the German ambassador is attended by, among others, the following: Minister of Education Édouard Daladier, Minister of Labor Anatole de Monzie, Minister of War Paul Painlevé, State Secretary for Foreign Affairs

Philippe Berthelot, the Austrian Ambassador Dr. Grünberger, the African scholar Leo Frobenius, Benjamin Crémieux, Dagny Bjørnson-Langen (now Mme Sautreau), the critic Alfred Kerr, Félix Bertaux, and Alfred Fabre-Luce.

January 21, 1926

T.M. attends a meeting of the Union pour la Vérité. "One gets the impression that he is attending a conventicle, an assemblage of gentle conspirators for the good." [*Pariser Rechenschaft*]

He is greeted formally by the chairman Paul Desjardins and makes an impromptu reply. Afterwards he attends a meeting of the Union Intellectuelle Française, where there are speeches in his honor by Félix Bertaux, Maurice Boucher, and Charles du Bos. T.M. says a short word of thanks. Later at a dinner in the Cercle Volney, among those present are Deputy Émile Borel, the mathematician and physicist Paul Langevin, the writer Pierre Viénot, and the writer of comedies Paul Zifferer.

January 22, 1926

At his hotel, T.M. is interviewed by the *Chicago Tribune* correspondent Marcus Aurelius Goodrich. He visits the German–Italian Guido Isenburg. He has breakfast with Joseph Chapiro at the Café Palais d'Orsay. He has tea at the apartment of Charles du Bos with Edmond Jaloux. "Simple, serious, thoughtful, almost without gestures, more cheerful than sparkling, he [Jaloux] seems to me on repeated meetings to be the epitome of the French intellectual . . ." [*Pariser Rechenschaft*]

He attends *Les Nouveaux Messieurs* by de Flers and de Croisset at the Athéneé with Count Coudenhove-Kalergi and his wife, Ida Roland. He dines later with Weber. "Coudenhove, with the little *cocarde* of pan-Europeanism in the lapel of his dinner jacket, is one of the most interesting and, by the way, handsomest men I have ever met. Half Japanese and the other half a mixture of European noble blood, he represents a type of Eurasian aristocrat who is quite captivating and makes the average German feel rather provincial." [*Pariser Rechenschaft*]

January 23, 1926

T.M. visits Notre Dame. He has dinner at the home of Dr. Zifferer with the Austrian ambassador Dr. Grünberger,

Alfred Fabre-Luce, and Pierre Viénot. He has a discussion with Dr. Grünberger about Spain. "In the evening at the Comédie: *Robert et Marianne*—marriage misunderstandings by Géraldi. Very elegant production." [*Pariser Rechenschaft*]

January 24, 1926

T.M. has breakfast with Félix Bertaux in Sèvres. They discuss Egypt at the time of the pharaohs. He has tea with the Russian poet Leo Schestow. "Indeed, there was suddenly a Russian atmosphere in the little, very human space for living room and study. There was a mood of openness, of childishness, and of great good humor, not without a touch of wildness in the strong tea and cigarettes." [*Pariser Rechenschaft*] He has dinner at the home of M. and Mme Sautreau. Among the guests are Minister of War Painlevé, Victor Basch, Mme Paul Clemenceau (sister-in-law of the "Tiger"), Dr. Zuckerkandl, and the wife of the Austrian ambassador.

January 25, 1926

He has breakfast with the Count and Countess de Ponge in the Faubourg Saint Germain. Among the guests are Henri Lichtenberger, Maurice Muret, and Alfred Fabre-Luce. He has tea at the Institut International de Coopération Intellectuelle, of which Julien Luchaire and Robert Eisler are cochairmen. Afterwards he has dinner at the home of Salomon Reinach at Boulogne-sur-Seine. "This man is probably the greatest polyhistor of the present day. He is above all . . . a mythologist, a religious historian, a scholar on human prehistory." [*Pariser Rechenschaft*]

January 26, 1926

"I made a formal visit to the Louvre. The circumstances prevented any kind of serious musing." He has breakfast at the German Embassy with Ambassador von Hoesch. He gives a lecture from *Goethe and Tolstoy* at the École Normale Supérieure. He has dinner at the Paris PEN Club with the Cercle Littéraire International; among those present are Edmond Jaloux, Jules Romains, François Mauriac, Benjamin Crémieux, Walter Hasenclever, Charles du Bos, Félix Bertaux, Ivan and Claire Goll, and Leo Schestow. A speech is given by Benjamin Crémieux with a brief reply by T.M. "They spoke French, and I spoke German, and we understood each other perfectly. Let us be symbolic and understand this communicating as a symbol for Europe, in which we hope and believe." [*Pariser Rechenschaft*]

January 27, 1926

T.M. is guided through Paris by Dr. Zifferer and Pierre Viénot. He visits the Russian poet Ivan Shmelyov, author of *Sonne der Toten*, and receives a disturbing impression of the existence of an emigrant: ". . . utter poverty, in an apartment for the poor." In the evening he attends a work by Alfred Savoir in the Théâtre Michel.

January 28, 1926

He has a discussion at the Kra Publishing Co. about a French edition of his collected works. Dmitri Merezhkovski and Ludwig Lewisohn visit T.M. at his hotel. T.M. departs for Munich in the evening.

Beginning of February, 1926

He spends several days in Ettal at the Klosterhotel with his two youngest children.

February 10, 1926

In Munich again with Katja. T.M. is ill with influenza, which is complicated by a lung infection. During his illness he writes *Pariser Rechenschaft* and the essay on the death penalty. "I am reading much and have even written a little article on the death penalty." [Unpublished letter to Ida Herz, February 14, 1926]

March, 1926

Golo Mann passes his final examinations. At Heidelberg, he studies History and German under Karl Jaspers, among others.

April, 1926

The short story *Disorder and Early Sorrow* appears

He prepares his speech for the Lübeck seven hundredth anniversary.

May 5–28, 1926

While relaxing at the Waldsanatorium in Arosa, he writes an article about Lübeck.

He visits Professor Philipp Witkop in Freiburg, among others, in an effort to gain an honorary doctorate for S. Fischer on his publishing firm's fortieth anniversary.

He gives a speech to the PEN Club Congress in Berlin.

May 30 to June 2, 1926

He spends a short time in Munich.

PARISER RECHENSCHAFT (DIE NEUE RUNDSCHAU, May–July, 1926)

DIE TODESSTRAFE (VOSSICHE ZEITUNG, Berlin, March 10, 1926)

UNORDNUNG UND FRÜHES LEID (Berlin: S. Fischer, 1926. 20,000 copies)

EARLY SORROW (Transl. Herman George Scheffauer. London: Martin Secker, 1929. 100 pp.)

DISORDER AND EARLY SORROW (STORIES OF THREE DECADES)

LÜBECK ALS GEISTIGE LEBENSFORM (Lübeck: Otto Quitzow, 1926)

DEM KONGRESS (LITERARISCHE WELT, Berlin, May 21, 1926)

June 3–9, 1926
The 700-Year Jubilee of the Hanseatic City of Lübeck takes place.

June 4, 1926
There is a production of *Fiorenza*.

June 5, 1926
T.M. gives a speech in the Stadttheater. ". . . when choosing for my lecture the title *Lübeck as a Spiritual Form of Life,* what I mean is the form of life and the course of life of a Lübecker, the Lübecker who speaks before you today, who has become an artist, a writer, *Dichter*, if you will, and who has remained as an artist and writer a Lübecker." [*Lübeck als geistige Lebensform*]
He is awarded the title "Professor" by the Senate.

June 6, 1926
He visits his old school, the Katharineum.

June 8, 1926
He gives a reading in Hamburg.

June 28, 1926
Katja Mann returns from Arosa.

Mid-July, 1926
Erika Mann is married to Gustaf Gründgens, the main director at the Hamburg Kammerspiele.
T.M. writes the introduction to Frans Masereel's *Mein Stundenbuch*.
He makes a brief visit to Lake Constance and to Schloss Salem, where Golo and Monika Mann are in school.

EINLEITUNG (to Frans Masereel's MEIN STUNDENBUCH. Munich: Kurt Wolff, 1926)

August 1, 1926
He makes preparations for writing the Joseph novel. "I am sitting deep in preparation for a short, difficult, but thoroughly charming novel, *Joseph in Egypt*. It is the biblical story itself that I wish to retell in a realistic and humorous manner." [Unpublished letter to Félix Bertaux, Thomas Mann-Archives, Zürich]

August 31 to September 13, 1926
He spends a vacation at Forte dei Marmi, where he writes an introduction to Joseph Conrad's *The Secret Agent* and, at the request of the *Berliner Tageblatt*, the article, *Die Unbekannten*.
He sees a magician, whom he later gives a literary form in the short story *Mario and the Magician*.

EINLEITUNG ZUM ROMAN DER GEHEIMAGENT VON JOSEPH CONRAD (In DAS 40. JAHR 1886–1926. Berlin: S. Fischer, 1926)

September, 1926
He becomes a member of the Committee on Pan-European Union, whose president is Count Coudenhove-Kalergi.

End of September, 1926
He goes for a week with Katja Mann and Ernst Bertram to Lausanne, where Monika Mann is now studying piano. "We stayed in Ouchy, visited Montreux, Geneva, Caux, etc., spent some time in Swiss cities, . . . and stood for a long time by the waterfalls at Schaffhausen." [Unpublished letter to Ida Herz]
He returns to Schloss Salem.

JOSEPH CONRAD'S THE SECRET AGENT (PAST MASTERS AND OTHER PAPERS)
DIE UNBEKANNTEN (BERLINER TAGEBLATT, October 10, 1926)

October, 1926
Klaus Mann's *Kindernovelle* appears. "I read Eissi's *Kindernovelle* last evening straight through and was able to laugh quite a bit. But doubts crept upon me here and there." [Letter to Erika Mann, *Briefe I*]

October 16, 1926
T.M. takes part in the funeral of Professor Berthold Litzmann and writes a eulogy.

ABSCHIED VON BERTHOLD LITZMANN (MÜNCHENER NEUESTE NACHRICHTEN, October 21, 1926)

October 18–28, 1926
He travels to Berlin and Hamburg.

October 19, 1926
He gives a lecture on Joseph Conrad, and Monika reads from *The Magic Mountain* on a Berlin radio program.

October 21–24, 1926
In Hamburg, he stays at the Hotel Atlantic, visits Klaus Mann, and gives a reading from *The Magic Mountain.*

October 27, 1926
In Berlin, the Prussian Minister of Education Dr. Becker calls a meeting for the preliminary election of members to the Literary Section of the Prussian Academy of Arts. The electors are Ludwig Fulda, Gerhart Hauptmann (not present), Arno Holz, T.M., and Hermann Stehr. Among the 21 members to be voted upon are Hermann Hesse, Ricarda Huch, Oskar Loerke, Heinrich Mann, Josef Ponten, Arthur Schnitzler, Jakob Wassermann, and Franz Werfel. Ricarda Huch writes about her election, "I was elected to the Academy and refused quietly, but they tormented me so (through Thomas Mann) that, for good or evil, I had to accept." (November 10, 1926).

November 2, 1926
T.M. gives a speech at the founding of the Münchener Gesellschaft 1926 in Steinecke Hall.

REDE ZUR ERÖFFNUNG DER MÜNCHENER GESELLSCHAFT 1926 (DER ZWIEBELFISCH, Munich, Book 1, 1926/27)

November 18, 1926
A formal meeting of the Prussian Academy of Arts takes place under its president Max Liebermann, with Minister of Education Dr. Becker present. The literary section is founded. T.M. replies to speeches by Max Liebermann and Dr. Becker. ". . . I did not let slip the opportunity to refer to that antagonism to academic thought which exists in the German intellectual sphere, and to indicate the possibility of obviating it. . . . It was not chance that I had been asked to speak; as perhaps no other, I had suffered in my own person, with whatever violent struggles, the compulsion of the times, which forced us out of the metaphysical and individual stage into the social . . ." [*A Sketch of My Life*]

November 23 or 24, 1926
Formal meeting of the German Academy at the Hotel Vier Jahreszeiten in Munich. There is a speech by T.M., who has just been elected a senator of the Academy.

November 25, 1926
Dorothea Angermann by Gerhart Hauptmann receives its premiere in the Munich Kammerspiele. At the formal celebration in the Munich City Hall, T.M. gives the main address.

AN GERHART HAUPTMANN (in DIE FORDERUNG DES TAGES. Berlin, 1930)

November 30, 1926
At the formal declaration of "Munich as a Center of Culture" in the Tonhalle, there are speeches by T.M., Heinrich Mann, Leo Weismantel, Willi Geiger, Walter Courvoisier, Paul Renner. "Last evening in the Tonhalle before a giant audience, we made a 'politico-cultural announcement'—six speeches against the Munich Reaktion amidst frantic applause. It was an explosion." [Letter to Rudolf Goldschmit-Jentner, *Briefe I*]

BLEIBT MÜNCHEN KULTURZENTRUM? (VOSSISCHE ZEITUNG, Berlin, December 7, 1926)

December 12 and 13, 1926
T.M. goes on a lecture tour to Heidelberg and Cologne. He has a meeting with Ernst Bertram.

December 23, 1926
He attends a performance of Wolfgang Goetz's *Gneisenau.* "A ridiculous demand, which, however, we are to carry out." [Letter to Erika Mann, *Briefe I*]

Christmas, 1926
On Christmas Eve, the Mann family has numerous guests, among whom are Professor Alfred Pringsheim and his son, Professor Peter Pringsheim, Bruno Frank, and their wives. Wilhelm Speyer is also present. All of T.M.'s children are at home except Erika and Klaus.

December, 1926
T.M. writes the introduction to the Joseph novel, *Descent into Hell*. "I am quite happy to be writing again. One actually feels and knows something about himself only when he does something . . . Joseph is growing page by page, even if at present it is only a kind of essayistic or humorous pseudo-scientific method whereby I can amuse myself. For this thing gives me more pleasure than anything else. It is at the same time something new and something spiritually worthwhile. To these people, meaning and being, myth and reality are constantly intertwined; Joseph is a kind of mythical confidence man." [Letter to Erika Mann, December 23, 1926, *Briefe I*]

January, 1927
Ernst Bertram is offered a position at the University of Munich; to T.M.'s great disappointment, he refuses it in order to keep his chair at Cologne.

T.M. writes *Worte an die Jugend*.

WORTE AN DIE JUGEND (LITERARISCHE WELT, Berlin, January 7, 1927)

End of January to mid–February, 1927
During a short stay in Ettal near Oberammergau, T.M. writes a cordial letter to Karl Arnold about his book *Schlaraffenland*. T.M. and Hermann G. Scheffauer act as editors for a series of novels entitled *Romane der Welt*. T.M. writes the foreword to the first volume, which is Sir Hugh Walpole's *Portrait of a Man With Red Hair*.

AN KARL ARNOLD (BERLINER TAGEBLATT, February 11, 1927)

ROMANE DER WELT (PRAGER PRESSE, March 23, 1927)

About March 6, 1927
In Berlin at a meeting of the literary section of the Prussian Academy of Arts, T.M. reads Heinrich Mann's protest against the censorship law that is pending in the Reichstag.

March 8–15, 1927
T.M. travels to Warsaw at the invitation of the Polish PEN Club. "The year 1927 brought a visit to Warsaw, where society welcomed the German writer with an unforgettable guesture of high-hearted hospitality and readiness to be friendly. I say *society* advisedly; for not only the closed circle

of the PEN Club—which for the space of a week exhausted itself in attentions—but also nobility and officialdom united to give me the impression that there prevailed a sincere respect and gratitude for German culture . . ." [*A Sketch of My Life*]

There is an official reception at the train station by the members of the PEN Club. At the PEN Club dinner, with members of the literary, social, and diplomatic circles present, there are speeches in German, Polish, and French by Stanislaw Przybyszewski, Horcyca, Juliusz Kaden-Bandrowski. T.M. replies with his *Rede in Warschau*. He has breakfast with Prince Janusz Radziwill, the leader of the Conservative Party. At a visit to Kaden-Bandrowski, Adjutant Marshal Jozef Pilsudski is present and discusses his position in the country with T.M. "I received the impression of a moderate personality, who is highly honored and, although of the military, not a militarist." [From an interview]

REDE, GEHALTEN BEIM FESTESSEN DES PEN-CLUBS IN WARSCHAU (in DIE FORDERUNG DES TAGES. Berlin, 1930)

Count Branicki gives a reception at his palace in Wilanow; the writer F. A. Ossendowski is present. In the evening, the German trade representative Dr. Eberhard von Pannwitz gives a reception. T.M. visits the library in Cracow.

He attends a performance at the Teatr Polski and later meets the actors. In the evening at the crowded hall of the Hotel Europejski, T.M. gives the lecture *Freiheit und Vornehmheit*. He visits the German Department of the University of Warsaw, accompanied by Rector Boleslav Hrymiewiecki and Professor Lempicki. In the evening he takes part in the PEN Club's meeting in honor of E. T. A. Hoffmann in the historic wine cellar, Fugger, where there is a lecture by Horcyca on Hoffmann. T.M. says goodbye to Kaden-Bandrowski and Professor Lempicki. He is given an official farewell at the train station by the State Secretary of Foreign Affairs Grabowski.

FRAGMENT (article in Jacques Mortane's book DAS NEUE DEUTSCHLAND Zürich: Orell Füssli, 1927)

March 16, 1927

He gives a reading for the Art Society in Danzig.

March, 1927

He writes an article for Jacques Mortane's book *Das Neue Deutschland*, about German–French relations.

DIE ROMANE DER WELT Answer to an open letter from Stefan Grossmann (DAS TAGEBUCH, Berlin, May 28, 1927)

March 4–7, 1927

He goes on a reading tour to Essen and Heidelberg and reads from *Disorder and Early Sorrow*.

May 6, 1927
While resting in Königswinter, he takes a trip to Grafenwerth, an island in the Rhine.

May, 1927
He has a dispute with the editor of the *Tagebuch*, Stefan Grossmann, about the editorship of the *Romane der Welt*.

Mid-July, 1927
He spends a short time in Bad Kreuth. "I was alone for a week and a half in Kreuth (the old 'Wildbad,' favorite excursion spot of my parents) and have finished the first section of *Joseph*. [Letter to Ernst Bertram, *Bertram*]

He writes a greeting to Max Liebermann on his eightieth birthday.

MAX LIEBERMANN ZUM 80. GEBURTSTAG (KUNST UND KÜNSTLER, Berlin, July, 1927)

August 10 to September 11, 1927
He takes a vacation at Kampen on the island of Sylt, staying at Haus Kliffende with his wife and the three youngest children. "The sea is lovely there. I still have the soft thunder of the breakers in my ears, and besides this at Haus Kliffende we were treated excellently. I am ashamed of not having done anything. Except for undemanding trivia, nothing was finished. And *Joseph* is still resting untouched." [Letter to Ernst Bertram, *Bertram*]

August 14, 1927
T.M. writes a greeting to John Galsworthy on his sixtieth birthday.

JOHN GALSWORTHY ZUM 60. GEBURTSTAG (NEUE FREIE PRESSE, Vienna, August 14, 1927)

September–October, 1927
He writes an essay on Heinrich von Kleist's *Amphitryon*. "The weeks of loving preoccupation with Kleist's comedy and the wonder of his metaphysical brilliance . . ." [*A Sketch of My Life*]

DIE GROSSE SZENE IN KLEISTS AMPHITRYON (VOSSISCHE ZEITUNG, October 16, 1926)

October 10, 1927
Before the festival production of *Amphitryon* in the Munich Schauspielhaus, T.M. gives the lecture *Kleist's Amphitryon*.

KLEIST'S AMPHITRYON (ESSAYS OF THREE DECADES)

October, 1927
Klaus and Erika take a trip around the world, through the United States to Japan, Korea, and Russia. "Your cable yesterday had a cheering and comforting effect, for we were rather worried not only about the reports of storms on the Atlantic (about this not very serious concern, though it awakened some small anxiety) but also with regard to your landing and first impressions." [Letter to Klaus and Erika Mann, *Briefe I*]

October 20–28, 1927
T.M. travels to Berlin and gives readings in Stettin and Frankfurt on the Oder from *Disorder and Early Sorrow* and *Kleist's Amphitryon.*

November 8, 1927
At the Auditorium Maximum in Munich, he reads from the Joseph novel.

November 30 to December 10, 1927
He goes on a long reading tour to the following cities: Karlsruhe, Wiesbaden (*Freiheit und Vornehmheit*), Aachen, Mönchen-Gladbach, Krefeld, Düsseldorf (*Natur und Nation*). During this time he is guest of the Wilhelm Buller family in Duisburg, where he meets again Professor Werner Heuser, with whom he had become acquainted in Kampen. Heuser later becomes director of the Düsseldorf Academy of Art. T.M. ends his tour with Trier and Frankfurt on the Main.

January 10, 1928
There is a meeting of the Literary Section of the Prussian Academy in Berlin. The new members elected are Theodor Däubler, Leonhard Frank, Alfred Döblin, Alfred Mombert, and Fritz von Unruh.

January 12, 1928
T.M. gives a reading from the Joseph novel in Berlin.

Beginning of February, 1928
He travels to Vienna, where there is a reception given at the city hall. He reads to the Kulturbund from the Joseph novel.

February, 1928
He writes an article in the *Literarische Welt* concerning his dispute with the nationalistic and National Socialist press—the *Berliner Nachtausgabe*, the *Tag*, the *Völkischer Beobachter, et al.*—about his relations with France.

March, 1928
He defends himself against an accusation by Arthur Hübscher, who had stated that by shortening the *Betrachtungen eines Unpolitischen* for the collected edition of his works, T.M. had changed the meaning of the book. In an article defending himself, T.M. returns to his early sympathetic attitude toward the idea of a socialistic society. "What would be needed, what would after all be typically German, would be an alliance, a compact between the conservative culture-

DESCENT INTO HELL First chapter of THE TALES OF JACOB (DIE NEUE RUNDSCHAU, December, 1927)

THOMAS MANN GEGEN DIE BERLINER NACHTAUSGABE (LITERARISCHE WELT, February 24, 1928)

KULTUR UND SOZIALISMUS (PREUSSISCHE JAHRBÜCHER, April, 1928)

idea and revolutionary social thought: to put it pointedly, as I have elsewhere done once before, an understanding between Greece and Moscow." [*Culture and Socialism*]

March 12, 1928

New Members are initiated at the Prussian Academy of Arts in Berlin.

April, 1928

T.M. takes a spring automobile tour to Zürich, Geneva, Neuchâtel, Aix-les-Bains, Grenoble, Cannes, St. Raphaël, and Marseille.

May 21–24, 1928

He reads at the University of Frankfurt, attends the International Press Exhibition (Pressa) in Cologne with Ernst Bertram, and gives a reading in Düsseldorf.

June–August, 1928

The dispute with Arthur Hübscher grows sharper. In an open letter in the *Süddeutsche Monatschefte* Hübscher repeats the charge that in shortening the book of the *Betrachtungen eines Unpolitischen* T.M. consciously changed its meaning. After the unauthorized publication of five private letters, the attacks take on the appearance of an act of revenge for T.M.'s refusal to allow *Das Tagebuch* to print any more of his articles.

End of June, 1928

T.M. continues work on the Joseph novel. "The novel demands my attention in spite of all hindrances. Rachel has just been introduced, the mother of the lamb, and I think she will please you better than grayish little Dinah." [Letter to Ernst Bertram, *Bertram*]

July, 1928

He attends the memorial exhibition in Nuremberg on the four hundredth anniversary of Albrecht Dürer's death.

August 1–30, 1928

He takes a vacation in Kampen at Haus Kliffende and is visited by Ernst Bertram.

September, 1928

He writes a speech for the Reclam publishing firm's jubilee—*Hundert Jahre Reclam*. He writes introductions to Ludwig Lewisohn's *Der Fall Herbert Crump*, Edmond Jaloux's *Die Tiefen des Meeres*, and the Reclam edition of the selected works of Theodor Fontane.

CULTURE AND SOCIALISM (PAST MASTERS AND OTHER PAPERS)

EINE ERKLÄRUNG (MÜNCHENER NEUESTE NACHRICHTEN, June 19, 1928)
UM THOMAS MANNS BETRACHTUNGEN (SÜDDEUTSCHE MONATSHEFTE, July, 1928)
KONFLIKT IN MÜNCHEN (DAS TAGEBUCH, August 11, 1928)
DIE FLIEGER, COSSMANN UND ICH (BERLINER TAGEBLATT, August 13, 1928)

DÜRER: ZUM 400. TODESTAG (HAMBURGER NACHRICHTEN June 28, 1928)
DÜRER (PAST MASTERS AND OTHER PAPERS)

October 1, 1928

The centennial celebration of the founding of the Reclam firm takes place in the Altes Theater in Leipzig. T.M. gives the main address. Among the guests are Gerhart Hauptmann, Kurt Martens, Börries Baron von Münchhausen, Josef Ponten, and Jakob Schaffner.

October 31 to November 9, 1928

T.M. goes on a reading tour to Austria and Switzerland. He reads from the Joseph novel and gives a talk as introduction.

November 5, 1928

He reads in Vienna to the Kulturbund, an artistic society.

November 7, 1928

He reads in Basel at the Stadtcasino.

November 9, 1928

He reads in Lucerne.

November 25 to December 12, 1928

He makes a reading tour through Germany: ". . . on a very rigorous reading tour with a tight schedule . . ." [Letter to Ivan Shmelyov, *Briefe I*]

He reads from the Joseph novel.

November 25, 1928

In Duisburg, he is the guest of the Wilhelm Buller family.

November 26 and 27, 1928

In Cologne, he discusses a matter concerning the Nietzsche Society with Ernst Bertram.

December 1, 1928

In Hamburg, he gives a reading in the great auditorium of the University.

December 2–4, 1928

He attends an organ concert at the Marienkirche in Lübeck. "Now I am in the city of my fathers where I was born and grew up. I heard a beautiful concert yesterday evening of the music of Buxtehude in the church where I was confirmed." [Letter to Hildegard und Gabrielle Buller, *Briefe I*]

He gives a reading in the new aula of the Oberrealschule at the cathedral.

He attends a performance of Richard Strauss' *Ägyptische Helena* at the Stadttheater.

He gives readings in Magdeburg, Liegnitz, and Berlin.

December, 1928

He writes several book reviews at Christmas time for the newspapers.

HUNDERT JAHRE RECLAM (Leipzig: Philipp Reclam jun., 1928)

EIN WORT ZUVOR: MEIN JOSEPH UND SEINE BRÜDER (NEUE FREIE PRESSE, Vienna, October 31, 1928)

BÜCHERLISTE (DAS TAGEBUCH, December 1, 1928)

JAKOB WASSERMANN, LEBENSDIENST (RECLAMS UNIVERSUM, Leipzig December 13, 1928)

DIE WELT IST SCHÖN (BERLINER ILLUSTRIERTE ZEITUNG, December 23, 1928)

THE STORY OF DINAH from THE TALES OF JACOB (DIE NEUE RUNDSCHAU, January, 1929)

THE NOBEL PRIZE

January, 1929
In Ettal, near Oberammergau, T.M. works out his speech on Lessing.

January 21, 1929
He gives his speech at the celebration of the two hundredth birthday of Gotthold Ephraim Lessing by the Prussian Academy of Arts in Berlin. There are also speeches by Max Liebermann and Professor Julius Petersen.

January 22, 1929
A filmed recording of parts of the Lessing speech are made.

LESSING (PAST MASTERS AND OTHER PAPERS)
ZU LESSINGS GEDÄCHTNIS (BERLINER TAGEBLATT, January 20, 1929)
REDE ÜBER LESSING (NEUE SCHWEIZER RUNDSCHAU, February, 1929)

About April 10, 1929
In Munich, Jakob Wassermann gives a speech sponsored by the Goethe Society: *Unterhaltung mit dem Leser*. At the banquet following, T.M. gives a speech about Wassermann: "Early he realized his most difficult and adverse opponent, the actual immorality which suppresses life, and gave it the name, 'the idleness of the heart.' This phrase is so well chosen because it may be understood both artistically and morally. For the artist, idleness comes primarily from the heart. 'The idleness of the heart' is the natural opponent to all art. It is this that causes art to go wrong and the heart to mutiny." [*Tischrede auf Jakob Wassermann*]

TISCHREDE AUF JAKOB WASSERMANN (BERLINER TAGEBLATT, April 10, 1929)

April–May, 1929
T.M. interrupts his work on the Joseph novel to write an essay on Freud. "I have just left my essay, *Freud's Position in the History of Modern Thought*, in which I unload all my feelings about the problem of revolution. It is full of pedagogical intentions which in this case are to recognize the psychoanalytical movement as the only manifestation of a modern antirationalism, which in no way offers a pretext for reactionary misuse." [Letter to Charles du Bos, May 3, 1929, *Briefe I*]

May 16, 1929
T.M. gives *Freud's Position in the History of Modern Thought* as a lecture in the Auditorium Maximum in Munich at the invitation of the Democratic Students' Club. "On the 16th I gave my lecture on Freud here to a massive throng of students. It was an encouraging evening." [Letter to Ernst Bertram, *Bertram*]

DIE STELLUNG FREUDS IN DER MODERNEN GEISTESGESCHICHTE (PSYCHOANALYTISCHE BEWEGUNG, Vienna, May/June, 1929)
FREUD'S POSITION IN THE HISTORY OF MODERN THOUGHT (PAST MASTERS AND OTHER PAPERS)

May 25 to June, 1929

He goes for a rest to Bad Gastein. "The curious bathers here almost suffocate me on the promenade. The whole thing is too confining. But the water is decidedly having its effect . . . We have had beautiful summer days, but now we are covered with thick cold clouds. I have not been able to work at all. The correspondence takes up the morning hours which I had planned to use for writing." [Letter to Erika Mann, *Briefe I*]

June, 1929

He is visited by students about to be graduated from the Lübeck Katharineum (Gymnasium) with their director, Dr. Georg Rosenthal, on their class trip. "They were on their way south and visited me in Munich as a group. It was—at least for me—a delightful hour. We drank a glass of beer and chatted." [*Ansprache an die Jugend*]

He prepares for publication the collection of essays entitled *Die Forderung des Tages*.

July 8, 1929

He writes the *Rede über das Theater*.

July 15, 1929

Hugo von Hofmannsthal dies. T.M. writes a eulogy. ". . . recently for the last time . . . we sat with our wives and chatted. We spoke of Germany, of her great men, of the relation of the people to politics, of the inner strife and animosity which this new element has caused in the soul of the people. We spoke of the severity of the demands which for the last fifteen years—the time in which we both became forty—the times have placed on the German people's ability and willingness to learn. [*In memoriam Hugo von Hofmannsthal*]

IN MEMORIAM HUGO VON HOFFMANSTHAL (NEUE FREIE PRESSE, Vienna, July 21, 1929)

July 20, 1929

The Heidelberg Festival is opened with T.M.'s giving his *Rede über das Theater*. There are productions of Shakespeare's *Midsummer Night's Dream* and Gerhart Hauptmann's *Florian Geyer*. The city gives a festival banquet in honor of Hauptmann and T.M.

REDE ÜBER DAS THEATER (DIE NEUE RUNDSCHAU, September, 1929)

July 29 to August 23, 1929

T.M. takes his vacation with the youngest children at the spa at Rauschen, Samland.

August 4, 1929

He writes Knut Hamsun greetings on his seventieth birthday. He works on a new novella, *Mario and the Magician.* "It was not feasible to take the swollen manuscript of *Joseph* upon this extended though easy trip. But I have no talent for unoccupied recreation, it is always sure to do me more harm than good; so I resolved to spend my mornings on the easy task of writing out an incident of a previous holiday in Forte dei Marmi, near Viareggio, and the impressions of our stay there; in other words with a piece of work which needed no apparatus but could be written 'straight out of my head' in the easiest possible way." [*A Sketch of My Life*]

GLÜCKWUNSCH ZU KNUT HAMSUNS 70. GEBURTSTAG (Vossische Zeitung, August 4, 1929)

TRAGISCHES REISE ERLEBNIS later title: *MARIO UND DER ZAUBERER* (Velhagen und Klasings Monatshefte: Bielefeld and Leipzig, April, 1930)

MARIO AND THE MAGICIAN (London: Martin Secker, 1930. 138 pp.)

He purchases some property at Nidden in Memelland. "Our holidays had a practical result over and above the literary result. We visited the Kurische Nehrung, whose landscape had often been recommended to us—it can boast that no less a person than Wilhelm von Humboldt has sung its praises—and spent a few days in the fishing village of Nidden in Lithuanian Memelland. We were so thrilled by the indescribable and unique beauty of nature in this place—the fantastic world of sandy dunes mile on mile, the birch and pine groves full of elk between The Haff and the Baltic, the wild splendor of the beach—that we decided to acquire a dwelling-place in this remote spot . . ." [*A Sketch of My Life*]

T.M. engages an architect to build a summer house there.

August 29, 1929

In Königsberg, T.M. gives a reading from the Joseph novel to the "Goethe-Bund." Walter von Molo gives a speech to greet him.

September, 1929

He writes a review of Arthur Eloesser's German literary history.

DIE DEUTSCHE LITERATUR (Die Neue Rundschau, December, 1929)

October 1, 1929

The Buddenbrook Book Shop in Lübeck is forced to liquidate. "Only a few years ago, Thomas Mann in his inimitable way—both careless and tense—stood on the stairway with his hand on his watch chain and opened the Buddenbrook Book Shop." [*Das Ende der Buddenbrook-Buchhandlung* by Fritz Endres]

November 12, 1929

T.M. is offered the 1929 Nobel Prize for literature by the Nobel Prize Committee of the Swedish Academy. He receives the telegram at noon on November 12. The *Berliner Zeitung am Mittag* publishes the news on the same day. "The year was not to close without agitating events. The famous award of the Swedish Academy, which once more, after a space of seventeen years, fell to Germany's lot, had, I knew, hovered over me more than once before and found me not unprepared. It lay, I suppose, upon my path in life—I say this without presumption, with calm if not uninterested insight into the character of my destiny, of my 'rôle' on this earth which has now been gilded with the equivocal brilliance of success; and which I regard entirely in a human spirit, without any great mental excitement. And just so, in such a spirit of reflective and receptive calm, I have accepted as my lot in life the resounding episode, with all its festal and friendly accompaniments, and gone through it with the best grace I could muster—even inwardly, which is a harder matter." [*A Sketch of My Life*]

November 14, 1929

Articles of homage and congratulations appear in the press throughout the world. T.M. receives congratulations from the Chancellor of the Reich, Hermann Müller, from the Senate of Lübeck, the city of Munich, and the Bavarian government.

November 16, 1929

The Union of German Writers holds a Nobel Prize celebration, at which T.M. reads from *Mario and the Magician*.

November 18, 1929

T.M. gives a lecture to the Society for Medical Psychology in Munich: *Freud's Position in the History of Modern Thought*.

November 19, 1929

The Munich Rotary Club gives a celebration in honor of T.M., at which Emil Preetorius gives a speech in his praise and T.M. gives a speech entitled *Bürgerlichkeit*.

BÜRGERLICHKEIT (JUGEND, Munich, January, 1930)

T.M. writes a review of André Gide's autobiography, *Si le grain ne meurt*. . . . "I should have liked to have been more thorough about the story of your life; however, I followed the command of the publisher at a time of great turmoil. I am not satisfied with the article." [Letter to André Gide, *Briefe I*]

SI LE GRAIN NE MEURT (DIE LITERATUR, Stuttgart, December, 1929)

November 26–30, 1929
He takes a trip into the Rhineland, stopping at Bochum, Duisburg, Cologne, and Bonn. "The Stockholm event lent festal emphasis to a long-arranged-for lecture tour on the Rhine. The ceremonies in the Aula of the University of Bonn—whose Philosophical Faculty had conferred on me the degree of *doctor honoris causa* shortly after the war—will remain ever memorable to me by reason of a press of students who subjected the ancient flooring to a serious test—so I was told by some worried professors." [*A Sketch of My Life*]
There is a formal celebration in the Auditorium Maximum with speeches by the Dean and Oskar Walzel.
In the Beethoven Hall, after an introductory speech by the blind poet Adolf von Hatzfeld, T.M. reads from the Joseph novel.

December 7–23, 1929
With Katja, T.M. travels to Stockholm to receive the Nobel Prize.

December 7, 1929
In Berlin, T.M. is interviewed in the morning by correspondents of the international press. In the afternoon, there is a reception given by the International Student Association at Humboldt-Haus, where speeches are given by Willy Haas and Rudolf Kayser, and T.M. reads from *Felix Krull*. In the evening, he gives a reading from *Mario and the Magician*, in the Great Concert Hall of the Hochschule für Musik, sponsored by the Union of German Writers. Arnold Zweig gives an introductory speech. Afterward T.M. is with Heinrich Mann and some friends, including Wilhelm Herzog, at Restaurant Frolicz on Fasanenstrasse.

December 9, 1929
T.M. arrives in Stockholm and is received by representatives of the Swedish Academy, the German Society, and the German–Swedish Society. He stays at the Grand Hotel. Representatives of the Scandinavian press interview him. The German ambassador, Dr. von Rosenberg gives a reception. T.M. gives a reading from *Buddenbrooks* and the Joseph novel sponsored by the German–Swedish Society.

December 10, 1929
T.M. is formally awarded the Nobel Prize for literature by King Gustaf V, in the presence of the Crown Prince and

Princess, members of the Swedish Academy, and other scholarly groups in the Great Hall of the Konserthuset. Other recipients were Professor Louis Victor de Broglie and Sir Owen Williams Richardson (physics), Professor Arthur Harden and Professor Hans von Euler-Chelpin (chemistry), and Sir Frederic Hopkins (medicine). Former President of the Cabinet Council Hammerskjöld, chairman of the arrangements, gives the formal greetings. There are speeches by some Swedish professors to the prizewinners, and the King awards the certificates. Professor Frederick Böök gives an address in praise of T.M. in German. T.M.'s certificate reads, "Thomas Mann, receiver of the Nobel Prize for Literature 1929, especially for his great novel, *Buddenbrooks*, which in the course of the years has found greater and greater recognition as a classic work of the present day."

In the evening there is a banquet at the Grand Hotel, at which the prizewinners give short addresses. T.M.'s speech closes with four cheers for the Nobel Institute. "I am proud to lay this international prize, which more or less accidentally bears my name, at the feet of my country and people—a country and people with whom those of my ilk feel more closely bound today than in the period of Germany's most jarring display of power. The Stockholm world prize this year again after many years is dedicated to the German soul, in particular to German prose; and it would be difficult for you to imagine the sensitive awareness, which this wounded and greatly misunderstood people feels, of these signs of world sympathy." [*Rede in Stockholm*]

REDE IN STOCKHOLM (BERLINER TAGEBLATT, December 15, 1929)

December 11, 1929

At the Stockholm Rotary Club breakfast, the Club's President, Director Belfrage, Head of the Stockholm Stock Exchange, gives a formal greeting. In the evening, at a dinner in the Royal Palace, among those present are earlier Nobel Prizewinners Selma Lagerlöf and Archbishop Nathan Söderblom, as well as the publisher Albert Bonnier.

December 12, 1929

At the German–Swedish Society, T.M. gives a reading before about five hundred members of the German colony from *Felix Krull*, *Tonio Kröger*, and *The Infant Prodigy*.

December 14, 1929

T.M. departs for Copenhagen.

December 15, 1929
Ulrich von Hassell gives a reception at the German Embassy in Copenhagen, where Professor Roos from the University of Copenhagen gives a lecture in which he praises T.M. Among the guests are President of the Cabinet Council Stauning, Foreign Minister Dr. Munch, and Bjørn Bjørnson. T.M. is later guest at the celebration of the twenty-fifth anniversary of the Danish Journalist's Union at the Hotel d'Angleterre.

December 16, 1929
T.M. gives a reading from *Buddenbrooks* and the Joseph novel at the Student Union.

December 19, 1929
In Berlin, at a banquet of the German PEN Club in the Zoological Garden, T.M. is greeted in a speech by Chairman Fedor von Zobeltitz. Arthur Eloesser gives the main address. There are speeches by the Prussian Minister of Education Dr. Becker, by René Lauret as representative of the French PEN Club, and by Oskar Loerke representing the Literary Section of the Prussian Academy. T.M. gives his thanks with the assurance that it was the recognition of his homeland which made him happiest.

T.M. writes greetings to Samuel Fischer on his seventieth birthday.

ZU S. FISCHERS 70. GEBURTSTAG (LITERARISCHE WELT, Berlin, December 19, 1929)

December 20, 1929
T.M. speaks on the radio and gives an extemporaneous description of the Stockholm festivities. In the evening, he gives a reading from the *Tales of Jacob* at the home of Hugo Simon for the benefit of the Jewish Care for the Aged.

December 23, 1929
The city of Munich gives a banquet in the City Hall, where the mayor of Munich, Dr. Scharnagl gives T.M. formal greetings, and T.M. replies.

Christmas, 1929
"We had quite a pleasant celebration and felt ourselves safe in the harbor after a stormy voyage . . ." [Letter to Ernst Bertram, *Bertram*]

January, 1930
While in Ettal near Oberammergau for two weeks, T.M. begins writing *A Sketch of My Life* and finishes it in February.

LEBENSABRISS (DIE NEUE RUNDSCHAU, June, 1930)
A SKETCH OF MY LIFE (Paris: Harrison, 1930. 69 pp. New York: Alfred A. Knopf, 1960. 90 pp.)

February 11, 1930
On his silver wedding anniversary, T.M. writes: "Here again I do not know how to thank enough the wife who now for five and twenty years has shared my life—this difficult, so easily tired and distracted life, which asks, above all, for so much patience; I do not know how, without the wise, courageous, delicate yet energetic assistance of my incomparable companion and friend, I should sustain it even as well as I do." [*A Sketch of My Life*]

THE JOSEPH NOVEL [CONTINUATION]

Mid-February to mid-April, 1930
T.M. travels to Egypt and Palestine, has a stormy crossing from Genoa to Alexandria.
February 21, 1930
He goes on the Nile steamer "Aswan-Vadi Halfa" to Nubia, where he spends several days.
Beginning of March
He returns to Alexandria by way of Aswan and Luxor.
March 2, 1930
He sends Arthur Eloesser greetings on his sixtieth birthday from Aswan. He returns to Cairo. Katja Mann falls ill with dysentery.

ZU ARTHUR ELOESSERS 60. GEBURTSTAG (VOSSISCHE ZEITUNG, Berlin, March 20, 1930)

March 18, 1930
A reception is held for T.M. at the (literary) Club Al Diafa in Cairo.
March 19, 1930
He receives an invitation to visit the Arabian newspaper *Al Mocattam.*
March 26 to April 1, 1930
In Jerusalem, T.M. also becomes ill with dysentery and is cared for at the German Diaconate Hospital. ". . . in Cairo my wife had to have dysentery, and now I have fallen ill with the same here in Palestine, so that we both find ourselves in a quite lamentable situation in the local hospital." [Letter to Ernst Bertram, *Bertram*]
April 8, 1930
T.M. and Katja return home via Italy. "It was a meaningful trip, far up the Nile into Nubian country, then to Aswan,

Luxor, Cairo, through the Canal into the Near East. I took care!" [Letter to Maximilian Brantl, *Briefe I*]

May 18, 1930

In Berlin, T.M. gives a speech to the Pan-European Congress at the Singing Academy—*Die Bäume im Garten*.

DIE BÄUME IM GARTEN (VOSSISCHE ZEITUNG, May 20, 1930)

June, 1930

He takes part in the International PEN Club Congress at The Hague in the Knights' Hall of the Inner Court.

July 7, 1930

He gives a reading from the Joseph novel at the University of Munich. He works on the introduction to Theodor Storm's collected works. "I have had great demands put upon me by a project which had to be put together very quickly—the introduction to the Knaur Verlag edition of Theodor Storm's works." [Unpublished letter to Ida Herz, June 23, 1930]

DER LYRIKER THEODOR STORM—THEODOR STORM, DER MENSCH (DAHEIM, Berlin, November, 1930) *THEODOR STORM* (ESSAYS OF THREE DECADES)

July 16 to the beginning of September, 1930

T.M. spends holidays at the new house on the dunes at Nidden on the Kurische Nehrung. "At that time we had a house in the Kurisch area up on the Baltic. My father was born on the Baltic, and he was constantly attracted there or to some other sea . . . The house lay in the Kiefern Forest, a quarter hour from the beach. It had brown wooden walls, blue shutters, a straw roof, and a view of the Inner Sea, the so-called Haff." [From *Vergangenes und Gegenwärtiges* by Monika Mann]

T.M. writes the foreword to *Colberts Reise und andere Erzählungen*, a posthumous collection of novellas by Hermann Ungar.

HERMANN UNGAR (BERLINER TAGEBLATT, October 10, 1930)

September 2, 1930

Professor Alfred Pringsheim celebrates his eightieth birthday at Nidden. "Then 'Ofei' is eighty. That is quite fantastic. One must realize that he has the wittiest eyes in the world, a mouth which never gives one peace but streams with jokes and merry puns . . . that he never drives a car and rarely rides the tram, . . . that he plays the piano like a young man, that he still studies mathematics in his little mysterious study with its gallery and astronomical equipment, that he can prepare cold duck, carve a roast, spice a salad . . ." [From *Glückwunsch* by Erika Mann]

September 13, 1930

T.M. gives a speech in The Hague at the Rotary Club Regional Conference on Europe and Africa. He discusses the intellectual situation of writers of the time.

September 14, 1930

At the election in the Reichstag, there is a great increase in the number of National Socialists.

T.M. gives a reading from the Joseph novel in Geneva at the Athenée. He is invited to visit the German Foreign Minister Dr. Curtius. He attends the full assembly of the League of Nations.

Mid-September, 1930

He writes an essay on Platen for a conference of the Platen Society.

End of September, 1930

He visits Ernst Bertram in Munich. There is a developing opposition in the political views of the two. "Monday I ventured out against T.M., among the three of us . . . he was in a terrible rage about Hitler." [Letter by Ernst Bertram to a friend]

October 4, 1930

T.M. gives the main speech at the conference of the Platen Society in Ansbach. He is awarded the Platen Plaque by the President of the Society, Hans von Hülsen.

October, 1930

The collection of essays, *Die Forderung des Tages*, appears.

October 15–19, 1930

T.M. is in Berlin.

October 15, 1930

He gives a reading from *The Magic Mountain* and the Joseph novel at the Teachers' Union.

October 17, 1930

In a speech—*An Appeal to Reason*—at the Beethoven Hall in Berlin, T.M. warns of the growing danger of National Socialism. The political position of the citizen, he says, should be on the side of social democracy. Those on the radical right and the National Socialists attempt to interrupt the speech, but in spite of unrest and fighting in the hall, T.M. finishes his speech.

October 19, 1930

He gives a reading from the Joseph novel at the Singing

DIE GEISTIGE SITUATION DES SCHRIFTSTELLERS IN UNSERER ZEIT (NEUE FREIE PRESSE, Vienna, September 14 and 16, 1930)

PLATEN-TRISTAN-DON QUICHOTTE (DIE NEUE RUNDSCHAU, January, 1931)

PLATEN (ESSAYS OF THREE DECADES)

DIE FORDERUNG DES TAGES: REDEN UND AUFSÄTZE AUS DEN JAHREN 1925–1929 (Berlin: S. Fischer, 1930. 8,000 copies)

DEUTSCHE ANSPRACHE: EIN APPELL AN DIE VERNUNFT (Berlin: S. Fischer, 1930. 6,000 copies)

AN APPEAL TO REASON (ORDER OF THE DAY

Academy as guest of the Union of German Writers. He is introduced by Jakob Schaffner.

End of October, 1930

T.M. probably finishes the first volume of the Joseph novel, *The Tales of Jacob*.

December, 1930

T.M.'s plan to write a book about Goethe, to be published in 1932, is strongly supported by the publishing firms Knaur and S. Fischer, but he finally gives up the plan. "You can imagine that the Joseph book is my main reason for giving up the Goethe plan. Besides this, it is not like me to accept an order for a work however important it may be to my career and to my reputation and for which I shall receive a high fee paid in advance; I have never done this. My books came about freely, from necessity and amusement, and their success has been an unexpected and comforting by-product . . ." [Letter to Ernst Bertram, *Bertram*]

He writes *Das Bild der Mutter* at the request of an illustrated periodical.

He writes a review of Heinrich Mann's new novel *Die grosse Sache*.

DAS BILD DER MUTTER: ERINNERUNGEN (ILLUSTRIERTE LEIPZIGER ZEITUNG December 11, 1930)

ANMERKUNGEN ZUR GROSSEN SACHE (LITERARISCHE WELT, Berlin, December 12, 1930)

End of December, 1930

Ernst Bertram visits T.M. in Munich. "The little ones played nicely at T.M.'s house. They gave a concert for me. I had a long walk with Tom . . ." [Letter by Ernst Bertram to a friend]

January, 1931

"I am still spinning away my bibical-mythological tale, which is a highly capricious undertaking for me and perhaps too much an experiment for me to have invested so much time and energy in it." [Letter to Ivan Shmelyov, *Briefe I*]

Mid-January to February 12, 1931

At the Chantarella, St. Moritz, T.M. is with Jakob Wassermann, who reads from his novel, *Der Fall Maurizius*. "Jakob read several times from his new novel. It is very grand and rather humorous as always." [Letter to Erika Mann, *Briefe I*]

During this time T.M. works on the political essay, *Die Wiedergeburt der Anständigkeit*.

DIE WIEDERGEBURT DER ANSTÄNDIGKEIT DER STAAT SEID IHR, (Berlin, March 2–23, 1931)

March, 1931

The historian and philosopher, Erich von Kahler, invites

T.M. to Wolfratshausen near Munich, so that he could read to T.M. from his new work, *Der deutsche Charakter in der Geschichte Europas.* T.M. refuses because of being overburdened, but from this correspondence there develops a lifelong friendship between the two.

March 27, 1931

There is a celebration of Heinrich Mann's sixtieth birthday at the Prussian Academy of Arts in Berlin, with speeches by Minister of Education Adolf Grimme, Gottfried Benn, Lion Feuchtwanger, T.M., and a word of thanks by Heinrich Mann. T.M.'s speech states, "Lübeck gothic and a dash of the Latin—it would be a mistake for one to search in our works for either the one or the other—Old Germany in me, for writing *Buddenbrooks*; the Latin in you for writing the *Herzogin*, the *Kleine Stadt*, and so many novellas . . . There is so much of our native gothic spectre in *Professor Unrat* that one can see that apparition completely in this novel, but it is merely necessary to look more carefully in your works to find it in other places as well." [*Vom Beruf des deutschen Schriftstellers in unserer Zeit*]

VOM BERUF DES DEUTSCHEN SCHRIFT-STELLERS IN UNSERER ZEIT (DIE NEUE RUNDSCHAU, Berlin, May, 1931)

THE COAT OF MANY COLOURS from YOUNG JOSEPH (DER MORGEN, Darmstadt, April, 1931)

May, 1931

T.M. travels to Paris at the invitation of the publisher Fayard for the appearance of the French edition of *The Magic Mountain.*

May 5, 1931

In Strassburg, at the Conservatory, he gives a lecture, *Die geistige Situation des Schriftstellers in unserer Zeit*, and reads from the Joseph novel.

May 6, 1931

He arrives in Paris.

May 7, 1931

At noon he has a breakfast at the German Embassy, and in the evening he lectures at the Institut International de Coopération Intellectuelle on *Vornehmheit und Freiheit*, with an introduction by Stephan Valot and Jules Romains.

May 11, 1931

At the Germanistic Institute of the Sorbonne, he gives the lecture, *Freud's Position in the History of Modern Thought.* He visits Félix Bertaux, and he has his first personal meeting with André Gide and Jean Schlumberger.

June 11, 1931
In Erlangen at the invitation of the Republican Student Union, T.M. gives the lecture, *Europa als Kulturgemeinschaft*.

EUROPA ALS KULTURGEMEINSCHAFT (See DIE BÄUME IM GARTEN, May, 1930)

June 12, 1931
He gives the same lecture in Munich.

July, 1931
He is visited by André Gide for several days in Munich.

July 5, 1931
At the University of Munich, he gives a reading from the Joseph novel, with André Gide present. "To my great pleasure, André Gide was in Munich a few days, and I had opportunity to experience his charming and deeply remarkable personality more intensively than was possible in Paris. We made a nice little trip *en famille* to Lake Würm, and he was even so courteous as to attend a reading from my bibical novel, which I gave at the University in the evening. He said to me some astonishingly impressive things about it, which I took as proof of his intuition." [Letter to Jean Schlumberger, *Briefe I*]

July 6–8, 1931
He takes part in a meeting of the Comité Permanent des Lettres et des Artes at Geneva. Director of the conference is President Jules Destrée of Belgium. Others attending are Paul Valéry, Gonzague de Reynold, Gilbert Murray, Henri Focillon, Josef Strzygovsky, Wilhelm Waetzoldt, Ugo Ojetti, John Masefield, Ragnar Ostberg, Nini Roll Anker, Hélène Vacaresco (Elena Vacarescu), George Oprescu, Adolfo Costa du Rels, Béla Bartók, Karel Čapek, Roberto Paribeni, Julien Luchaire, and Salvador de Madariaga. "This is the group. We found ourselves on July 6, 1931 in the breezy, comfortably furnished . . . Hall of the Palace of the League of Nations in Geneva—for the most part, strangers to each other at first, but each of us well acquainted with the works of the other, each emerging from his productive loneliness, but each with the good intention of releasing the strain of his loneliness in sociable discussion." [*Der Geist in Gesellschaft*] The theme of the conference is the advancement of intellectual relations through technical means of communication. The high point is a statement by Paul Valéry, to which T.M.

refers in his final speech: "The new image must be found—the synthetic man of the new humanism, the new European . . ." [From the minutes of the conference]

From mid-July to the beginning of September, 1931

T.M. takes a vacation in his summer house at Nidden.

August 21, 1931

In a letter to the editor of *Nouvelles Littéraires*, Maurice Martin du Gard, T.M. protests against a subjective, disparaging review of the French edition of *The Blood of the Walsungs*.

September 3, 1931

In Königsberg, T.M. gives a lecture from *Goethe and Tolstoy*.

September 4, 1931

In Elbing, he gives a reading from *Buddenbrooks, The Magic Mountain*, and the Joseph novel.

September 7, 1931

The four hundredth anniversary celebration of the Katharineum in Lübeck takes place. After many speeches and talks comes T.M.'s speech, *Ansprache an die Jugend*, in the Katharinenkirche. "It is no more than a suitable return visit which I am paying at this time to the city of my fathers and to its old school—a return visit to the young people. There occurs to me now a summer evening about two years back when I saw on our garden terrace in Munich some very charming guests. They were young people, Lübeck young people, the youth of the Katharineum." [*Ansprache an die Jugend*] [In a fine review of the first German edition of the present work, Herbert Lehnert remarks on the fact that T.M.'s September 7 speech also contained "warnings directed against antiliberal radicalism. According to one observer, these met with loud protests from the students." (*Modern Language Notes* [1967, p. 515]—*trans. note*]

In the evening there is a performance of Plautus' *Menaechmi* by the upper sixth form.

September ?, 1931

T.M. writes an article for Harald Braun's book, *Dichterglaube*.

December, 1931

He is ill with "a catarrh and the usual stomach and intestinal infection." "On Christmas Eve, a quarter hour before we

SANG RÉSERVÉ (French translation of THE BLOOD OF THE WALSUNGS, LES NOUVELLES LITTÉRAIRES, Paris, August 29, 1931)

ANSPRACHE AN DIE JUGEND (VOSSISCHE ZEITUNG, Berlin, September 8, 1931)

FRAGMENT ÜBER DAS RELIGIÖSE (In DICHTERGLAUBE, a collection of writers' descriptions of their religious experiences, ed. Harald Braun. Berlin-Steglitz: Eckart-Verlag, 1931)

THE WEDDING (from THE TALES OF JACOB. (CORONA, Munich, Zürich, November, 1931)

were to open our presents, when the children sing, I stood up a bit and was truly pleased with my main present, which we bought in order to stimulate the economy—a combination radio and phonograph, which plays the records through the loudspeaker, a treat for the ears." [Letter to Ernst Bertram, *Bertram*]

1932
THE GOETHE-YEAR

January, 1932
The German economic and financial crisis worsens. Six million people are unemployed.
T.M. works on his lecture, *Goethe as Representative of the Bourgeois Age*. "This year is truly a year of honor for the German and for German culture. The emergence of self-consciousness, which is connected with this honor, is needed by a people who have suffered like the Germans." [*Ansprache bei der Einweihung des erweiterten Goethe-Museums in Frankfurt am Main*]
February 5–24, 1932
He travels to St. Moritz. "We have had a week of full sunshine, and today for the first time there is a light snow with a magical veil of mist around the mountains. It is difficult to say which is more beautiful." [Letter to Robert Faesi, *Thomas Mann/Robert Faesi, Briefwechsel*. Zürich: Atlantis Verlag, 1962]
He works on his lecture, *Goethe's Career as a Man of Letters*, and writes a review of Alfred Jeremias' *Handbuch der altorientalischen Geisteskultur*, which was a main source for the Joseph novel.
February 25, 1932
In Bern, T.M. gives the lecture *Goethe as Representative of the Bourgeois Age*.
February 26, 1932
He gives the same lecture in Lucerne.
March 13–22, 1932
"The second Goethe-trip."
March 14, 1932
In Prague, he lectures at the Goethe Memorial Celebration in the New Theater. He is guest of the Prague PEN Club.

DEMÜTIGUNG UND ERHEBUNG (DIE GRÜNE POST, Berlin, December 27, 1931)
GOETHE ALS REPRÄSENTANT DES BÜRGERLICHEN ZEITALTERS (DIE NEUE RUNDSCHAU, April, 1923)
GOETHE AS REPRESENTATIVE OF THE BOURGEOIS AGE (ESSAYS OF THREE DECADES)
GOETHES LAUFBAHN ALS SCHRIFTSTELLER (CORONA, Munich, Berlin, Zürich, February, 1933)
GOETHE'S CAREER AS A MAN OF LETTERS (FREUD, GOETHE, WAGNER. Transl. Rita Matthias-Reil. New York: Alfred A. Knopf, 1937. 211 pp. ESSAYS OF THREE DECADES)

March 15, 1932
In Vienna, at the Hotel Imperial after a lecture, he speaks in an interview about Hitler's injurious effect upon Germany.

March 18, 1932
In Berlin, T.M. gives the main address at the Prussian Academy's celebration of the one hundredth anniversary of Goethe's death—*Goethe as Representative of the Bourgeois Age*. "Let me invoke the feelings that overcame me when, years ago, I went for the first time through Goethe's family house, in the Hirschgraben in Frankfurt.

"These stairs, these rooms, were familiar to me of yore: their style, their atmosphere. Here were the origins, the 'sources,' just as they are in the books—and in the book of my own life. And at the same time they were the first beginnings of the prodigy. I was 'at home,' and at the same time I was a timid and tardy guest on this native heath of genius." [*Goethe as Representative of the Bourgeois Age*]

T.M. is awarded the Goethe Medal "for valuable work at the Goethe Centennial" along with a certificate signed by Hindenburg.

DIE EINHEIT DES MENSCHENGEISTES (VOSSISCHE ZEITUNG, Berlin, February 17, 1932)

March 21, 1932
In Weimar, T.M. gives the main address at the Goethe Memorial Week—*Goethe's Career as a Man of Letters. Torquato Tasso* is performed by a visiting troop from the Burgtheater in Vienna.

April, 1932
He spends some time at Villa Castagnola in Lugano.

May 10/11, 1932
In Nuremberg, he gives a lecture for the Volkshochschule in the Hall of the Transportation Museum—*Goethe's Career as a Man of Letters.*

May 12–14, 1932
There is a conference of the Comité Permanent des Lettres et des Arts in the Roman Assembly Hall in Frankfurt on Main: "Entretiens sur Goethe." There is a formal opening of the conference at the opera house. Rudolf G. Binding gives the welcoming speech, and there are addresses by Jules Destrée and other members of the Comité.

The theme of the first meeting is "Goethe Européen," at which T.M. gives the paper *Goethe et la Vocation d'Écrivain*, and Hélène Vacaresco (Elena Vacarescu), Salvador de

Madariaga, and Paul Valéry also give papers. In the evening, *The Magic Flute* is performed at the opera house. Theme of the third meeting is "Les Voyages," at which George Oprescu, Roberto Paribeni, and Wilhelm Waetzoldt give papers, and T.M. gives the closing speech—*Goethe et l'Allemagne*.

GOETHE ET L'ALLEMAGNE (In ENTRETIENS SUR GOETHE, Paris, 1932)

May 14, 1932

T.M. gives a speech at the dedication of the enlarged Goethe Museum in Frankfurt. "I am deeply gripped by the honor which this hour gives me, of accepting this deeply felt labor of love, this hoard of reliques—the Frankfurt Goethe Museum—and I accept it in faith as a representative of the nation . . . Indeed, I have loved him from childhood—why should I not say it here and now—with a love that was of the greatest feeling of kinship and was an affirmation of my own self through his radiance, ideality, and perfection." [*Ansprache bei der Einweihung des erweiterten Goethe-Museums in Frankfurt am Main*]

ANSPRACHE BEI DER EINWEIHUNG DES ERWEITERTEN GOETHE-MUSEUMS IN FRANKFURT AM MAIN (In FESTGABE ZUM GOETHEJAHR 1932, Halle, 1932)

He is awarded the Master Medal of the Free German Foundation of Frankfurt on Main, with green ribbon, which makes him canon of the Foundation with perpetual membership. He returns to Munich via Heidelberg and Stuttgart.

He is visited by Leopold Schwarzschild, editor of the *Tagebuch*, who makes plans to publish his periodical in Munich, but he later gives up this plan.

June 8, 1932

T.M. gives the lecture *Goethe's Career as a Man of Letters* in Munich. "Yesterday, before fifteen or sixteen thousand people in the Auditorium Maximum, I gave the lecture that seemed so washed out in Weimar. The people—many of them young—proved to be quite strongly moved. One may say of Germany what one will: my sort will never be alone." [Letter to Ernst Bertram, *Bertram*]

The expression "washed out" (*ins Wasser gefallen*) is to be understood literally: on the day of the lecture in Weimar there was heavy rain.

End of June, 1932

Probably around this time the second volume of the Joseph novel, *Young Joseph*, is finished.

July 2 to September 4, 1932

T.M. spends a vacation at the summer house in Nidden. For

the first two weeks, Hans Reisiger, "a pleasant companion," visits him. On July 15, Katja arrives with the children. T.M. continues to work on the Joseph novel. "I am writing on the third volume of *Joseph*. Fischer wanted to publish the two already finished, but I refused. I should like to present the whole thing at one time." [Letter to Ernst Bertram, July 23, 1932, *Bertram*]

THE JOURNEY TO THE BROTHERS from YOUNG JOSEPH (DIE NEUE RUNDSCHAU, August and September, 1932)

July 31, 1932

At the Reichstag election, the National Socialists win a great number of votes: 230 of 608.

August, 1932

T.M. gives a strong opinion of the riots of the National Socialists in Königsberg: "Will the bloody atrocities of Königsberg open the eyes of the admirers of this sentimental 'Movement,' which calls itself National Socialism, to the true nature of this sickness of the people, this mishmash of hysteria and outmoded Romanticism, whose exaggerated Teutonism is the caricature and vulgarization of everything German? Even the pastors, professors, teachers, and men of letters follow chattering along after it." [*Was wir verlangen müssen*]

WAS WIR VERLANGEN MÜSSEN (BERLINER TAGEBLATT, August 8, 1932)

Political developments hinder his progress on the Joseph novel. "I have come a good piece further with the third volume of *Joseph*, and, were it not for politics, it would be still longer and better." [Letter to Ida Herz, *Briefe I*]

October, 1932

In Munich, he writes his recollections of the conference of the Comité Permanent des Lettres et des Arts at Geneva and Frankfurt. He writes a speech for the Viennese workers—"a convincing declaration of sympathy for their cause."

DER GEIST IN GESELLSCHAFT (NEUE ZÜRCHER ZEITUNG, October 9 and 10, 1932)

October 22, 1932

He gives a speech to workers in Vienna-Ottakring. "It happens that I, a writer born of the middle class, am speaking for the first time before a socialistic audience of workers, and not only is this situation symptomatic of the times, which have brought it about, but also it is, I feel, decisive for my personal life and intellectual development." [*Rede vor Arbeitern in Wien*]

REDE VOR ARBEITERN IN WIEN (in GESAMMELTE WERKE IN ZWÖLF BÄNDEN, Volume XI)

October 23, 1932

He reads from the Joseph novel on the Vienna Radio.

Beginning of November, 1932
While visiting Ernst Bertram in Cologne-Marienburg, he talks with Hans Carossa.

December, 1932
He writes a review of Arthur Eloesser's German literary history, second volume. He interrupts his work of the Joseph novel to write an essay to commemorate the fiftieth anniversary of the death of Richard Wagner (on February 13, 1933).

ELOESSERS ZWEITER BAND (DIE NEUE RUNDSCHAU, January, 1933)

December 11, 1932
He gives a speech at the Munich National Theater for the celebration of Gerhart Hauptmann's seventieth birthday. "This childish rhyme, '*Kunst bringt Gunst*,' defines and explains his character, his dignity, and his popularity quite completely and more happily than any other current expression." [*An Gerhart Hauptmann*]

AN GERHART HAUPTMANN (VOSSISCHE ZEITUNG, Berlin, December 15, 1932)

1933–1938
THE YEARS IN SWITZERLAND AND THE JOSEPH NOVEL [CONTINUATION]

LEIDEN UND GRÖSSE RICHARD WAGNERS (DIE NEUE RUNDSCHAU, April, 1933) *SUFFERINGS AND GREATNESS OF RICHARD WAGNER* (In FREUD, GOETHE, WAGNER and ESSAYS OF THREE DECADES)

January 1, 1933
Erika Mann, with her friend Therese Giehse and other young actors, opens the literary cabaret, Die Pfeffermühle, in the Bonboniere at Munich, but it soon has to close because of the political situation.

January 2, 1933
T.M. works on the Wagner essay. "My health is not of the best: my nerves and head tire very quickly. I have a bit too much to bear. There are times when I do not work on Joseph at all. I am preparing a lecture on Wagner for the fiftieth anniversary of his death to be given in Amsterdam, Brussels, and Paris—a ticklish, exciting task with great difficulties of composition caused by the rush of my thoughts." [Letter to Adele Gerhard, *Briefe I*]

January 20, 1933
T.M. declines to take part in the assembly of the Social Cultural Union at the Berlin Volksbühne. His speech is to be read by someone else. The assembly planned for February

BEKENNTNIS ZUM SOZIALISMUS (SOZIALISTISCHE BILDUNG, Berlin, February, 1933)

19 does not take place because it is forbidden after the National Socialists seize power.

January 30, 1933
Adolf Hitler becomes the Chancellor of the Reich.

January 30 to February 9, 1933
T.M. is in Garmisch-Partenkirchen at Pension Nirvana. Heinrich Mann leaves Germany after he receives warnings from friends.

February 10, 1933
T.M. gives his lecture *Sufferings and Greatness of Richard Wagner* at the invitation of the Goethe Society in Munich, at the Auditorium Maximum, for the fiftieth anniversary of Richard Wagner's death.

February 11, 1933
T.M. departs for Holland, without realizing that this trip is the beginning of his exile.

February 13, 1933
He gives the main address at the Wagner Memorial Celebration of the Amsterdam Wagner Society, in the Concertgebouw in Amsterdam.

February 14, 1933
In Brussels, he repeats the Wagner lecture in French for the meeting of the PEN Club in the Palais des Beaux Arts. Afterwards there is a reception at the German Embassy.

February 18, 1933
In Paris, he gives the Wagner lecture at the Théâtre des Ambassadeurs and again at the Foyer de l'Europe.

February 26 to mid-March, 1933
He takes a rest at the Neues Waldhotel in the Swiss town of Arosa. "There was much social life connected with giving the lectures, and since previously I had worked so hard, we thought it a good idea to come here from Paris to rest for a few weeks. Medi has joined us for skiing." [Letter to Lavinia Mazzucchetti, *Briefe I*]

February 27, 1933
The Reichstag burns. T.M. receives warnings from Germany that his safety cannot be guaranteed. ". . . I am on the list of those guilty of 'intellectual high treason' for 'pacifistic excesses.' Moreover, it is questionable whether there will ever be room for my sort in Germany, whether I will be able to breathe the air there again. I am too good a German, too closely involved with the cultural traditions and language of

my country for the prospect of a year-long or perhaps lifelong exile not to have a hard, ominous meaning for me." [Letter to Lavinia Manzzucchetti, *Briefe I*]

March 12, 1933

Erika and Klaus Mann return to Germany. They telephone their parents from Munich, warning them of the "bad weather" in Germany. Erika leaves again immediately; Klaus departs for Paris March 13.

Mid-March to the end of March, 1933

T.M. and Katja make an "improvised sojourn" in Lenzerheide at Chalet Canols. T.M. visits Hermann Hesse at Montagnola.

March 22, 1933

"This morning for the first time, I have been able to work on *Joseph*. I wanted at least to concentrate on the gigantic task that still remains to be finished. Concentration and composure are my primary goals. I have left the Academy, resigned from the post of Chairman of the Union [of German Writers], and want to be rid of all the showy frippery of officialdom, in order to live, wherever it may be, in retirement, tending to my own affairs . . ." [Unpublished letter to Ida Herz]

March, 24, 1933

The Act of Authorization, which opens the way for Hitler's dictatorship, is accepted by all parties of the Reichstag except the Social Democrats (the Communists have already been excluded). "My ears are ringing with the stories of murder and horror in Munich that are accompanying the regular and continuous atrocities of a political nature: the crude mistreatment of the Jews . . . There is no pause in the violence." [*Leiden an Deutschland*]

End of March to the beginning of April, 1933

T.M. is in Lugano at Villa Castagnola.

April 17, 1933

"I am beginning slowly to work a bit after some difficult weeks. The Bruno Franks are here, also the Ludwig Fuldas, Emil Ludwig, Remarque, and, above all, Hermann Hesse, whom I love and honor very much." [Letter to Stefan Zweig, *Briefe I*]

April 16/17, 1933

He recieves a protest against his Wagner lecture from the "Richard Wagner City of Munich." It is signed by Bavarian

Minister of Education Hans Schemm, President of the Academy of Fine Arts German Bestelmeyer, General Director of the Bavarian State Art Collection Friedrich Dörnhöffer, General Director of the Bavarian State Theater Clemens von Franckenstein, Chairman of the Musical Academy Eduard Niedermeyer, President of the Chamber of Industry and Commerce Josef Pschorr, and also by Hans Knappertsbusch, Hans Pfitzner, Richard Strauss, Olaf Gulbransson, Angelo Jank, and Bernhard Bleeker. T.M. thanks the critic Willi Schuh for his defense against the protest in his article *Thomas Mann, Richard Wagner, und die Münchener Gralshüter*. "Your article is to me primarily a sign and assurance that the dishonor will go to the originators of this sad folly and to their more or less compelled followers." [Letter to Willi Schuh, *Brief I*]

April 25, 1933

T.M. directs Golo Mann, who has remained in Munich to complete his studies, to send him the materials for the Joseph novel that had been left behind in Munich. Ida Herz packs the most important sections of T.M.'s library and sends them under another name and address to Switzerland.

May 10 to June 17, 1933

At the suggestion of René Schickele, T.M. moves with his family temporarily to the Grand Hotel in Bandol (department of Var), on the French Riviera. His plan to find lodgings in Basel has failed. From Bandol, he searches for a less expensive suitable place for a longer stay. "I have my wife and children with me and the most necessary books. The climate is highly pleasing, and there is no lack of signs of sympathy and good will. But the exhaustion of my nerves manifests itself in a disinclination and sluggishness of spirit, which on every bright morning after a few lines triumphs over my good intentions of pressing forward." [Letter to Alfred Neumann, *Briefe I*]

May, 1933

In Munich, Erika Mann saves T.M.'s manuscripts, among which is the Joseph novel. "After the overthrow of the government by the National Socialists, my eldest daughter ventured back to Munich into our house, which had already been confiscated, and brought the manuscript to me in South France; there, after the initial confusion of new, uprooted circumstances, I began slowly to write again on the work which had been continued in our Swiss refuge on the Lake of Zürich, which we had enjoyed for five years." [From *Joseph und seine Brüder*, a lecture]

June 18 to September 20, 1933

T.M. moves with his family to Sanary-sur-Mer, to a little house called La Tranquille. "For ten days we have lived in this nicely situated and charmingly furnished little house, in which we have with us our four youngest children. Our future plans are very uncertain." [Letter to Robert Faesi, *Thomas Mann/Robert Faesi, Briefwechsel.* Zürich: Atlantis Verlag, 1962]

July, 1933

"Here the summer heat is at its peak, but it is never really so terrible since there is almost always a breeze, and the evenings are refreshing. I often sit until late on the little porch outside my study, smoke my cigar, look at the stars, and think of the strangeness of my life." [Letter to A.M. Frey, *Briefe I*]

August, 1933

T.M. prepares for publication the first volume of the Joseph novel, *The Tales of Jacob*. "I have just finished revising the page proof and was touched again by the death of Rachel as when I wrote it. There is something of the unusual and of beauty in the volume, for example, the betrayal of the blessing and Jacob's wedding. This latter chapter I read aloud recently with about twenty people sitting in the garden, and I used our little terrace as a podium. Those listening seemed quite touched." [Letter to Gottfried Bermann Fischer, *Briefe I*]

Sanary-sur-Mer becomes a meeting place for German emigrants: Arnold Zweig, Lion Feuchtwanger, Ernst Toller, Bert Brecht, Erwin Piscator, Antonina Valentin, Fritzi Massary, Hermann Kesten, Fritz Wolf, Franz Werfel, Wilhelm Herzog, Rudolf Leonhard, Balder Olden, Ludwig Marcuse, and others. Heinrich Mann, who is beginning work on his novel, *Henri Quatre*, lives, as does René Schickele, in Nizza; Julius Meier-Grafe, in St. Cyr. On August 23, Heinrich Mann is deprived of his German citizenship.

September 21, 1933

The trial concerning the burning of the Reichstag begins.

T.M. follows its progress attentively. (See the notebook, *Leiden an Deutschland: Tageblätter aus den Jahren 1933 und 1934*.)

Early autumn, 1933

T.M. moves with his family to a permanent dwelling in Küsnacht near Zürich, Schiedhaldenstrasse 33. The apartment is arranged for by the wife of Robert Faesi.

In Amsterdam, Klaus Mann edits a periodical for German emigrants, *Die Sammlung*, under the patronage of André Gide, Aldous Huxley, and Heinrich Mann. [Herbert Lehnert, in his review in *Modern Language Notes* (1967, p. 515), states that T.M. had to withdraw his name from the list of contributors in order to ensure the publication of *Joseph and his Brothers* in Germany.—*trans. note*] In Munich, Golo Mann interrupts his studies shortly before his final examination and accepts a position as Reader of German at an education institute in St. Cloud. Monika, still in Sanary, plans to go to some friends in Florence. Michael is accepted as violinist in the master class at the Zürich Conservatory. Elisabeth, "who in the summer continued her studies diligently on her own," attends the lower sixth form of a Gymnasium in Zürich.

October 10, 1933

The first volume of the Joseph tetralogy, *The Tales of Jacob (Joseph and His Brothers)*, appears. T.M.'s friendship with Ernst Bertram ends. "Too much stands between us, which, to discuss in letters, is painful, leads nowhere, and is not without danger . . . but I know that your spiritual vigor was never sufficient. It is sufficient now for you to support and glorify that which to me is loathsome and, at the same time, invite me cordially to carry on the common civilities with you. I can take your admonitions only as an expression of a rather thoughtless good humor." [Letter to Ernst Bertram, *Bertram*]

DIE GESCHICHTEN JAAKOBS (Berlin: S. Fischer, 1933. 10,000 copies)
JOSEPH AND HIS BROTHERS later title: *THE TALES OF JACOB* (New York: Alfred A. Knopf, 1934. 428 pp.)

November, 1933

T.M. supports Carl J. Burckhardt's intervention with the Rockefeller Foundation for the Jewish philosopher Heinrich Hellmund, who has emigrated to Switzerland and is destitute.

November 8, 1933

He gives a reading from the Joseph novel at the University of Zürich.

December, 1933
He refuses an offer of membership in the Literary Chamber of the Reich, whose chairman is Hans Friedrich Blunck. "I shall in no case sign the application for membership of that compulsory organization in Berlin." [Letter to A. M. Frey, *Briefe I*]

December 4, 1933
Stefan George dies in Minusio near Locarno.
T.M. uses his influence to help Julius Meier-Graefe attain a position as a regular contributor to the *Neue Zürcher Zeitung*. The German Political Police demand payment from T.M. of the "Refugee Tax." "The fact that my property—my house and goods—remains confiscated, senselessly and illegally, does not thwart the Munich Finance Office in its desire for satisfaction; but on the other hand, the bann on the fee for my Jacob's tales has been lifted, and Bermann can pay me. In all this there is no logic or reason." [Letter to A. M. Frey, *Briefe I*]
The Tales of Jacob is well received in his circle of friends. There are letters and reviews from Rudolf Kayser, Stefan Zweig, Robert Faesi, Julius Meier-Graefe, A. M. Frey, Franz Werfel, Heinrich Mann, and others. There is divided reception in the German press. ". . . the critical response in the press of my native land was predominantly so miserable, so full of pompous obtuseness, that I was sometimes deeply hurt and felt disgusted. Almost every utterance that I have read inspires horror of the—no longer conscious—subjugation and emasculation of those souls." [Letter to A. M. Frey, *Briefe I*]
T.M. writes an article on Stifter's *Witiko* to be included in a memorial volume at Christmas.

WITIKO (DIE WELT IM WORT, Prague, Vienna, December 21, 1933)

He gives two readings from the Joseph novel to Zürich students in the auditorium of the Polytechnic Institute.

Christmas, 1933
"We passed Christmas in a quite pleasant manner with the children and some friends, Reisiger and Therese Giehse, who are actors from the Schauspielhaus. The darkness of the winter here might restore me somewhat, were I not aware of the continuing fiascos for which the fatherland is responsible. [Letter to Hermann Hesse, *Briefe I*]

January 1, 1934
Erika Mann reopens her cabaret, Die Pfeffermühle, in

Zürich. "With her literary cabaret, she has had, what is for Zürich, a quite unprecedented success, and it all comes from her energy and imagination and spirit, which is softly melancholy yet courageously enterprising. The little café, Zum Hirschen, formerly a rather dull place, is now overcrowded evening after evening . . ." [Letter to Ernst Bertram, *Briefe I*]

Jacob Wassermann dies in Alt-Aussee, Styria. "The news of his death did not take us unexpectedly, since we had seen him here several weeks ago and had to admit his decline, but it came to me, with my present sensitivity, as a heavy shock." [Letter to Ernst Bertram, *Briefe I*]

January 15, 1934

The second volume of the Joseph novel is prepared for publication. "In the meantime, I am reading the proofs of the second volume and writing rather distractedly on the third." [Letter to Karl Vossler, *Briefe I*]

JACOB MOURNS FOR JOSEPH From YOUNG JOSEPH (DIE NEUE RUNDSCHAU, January, 1934)

January 27, 1934

A lengthy correspondence begins between T.M. and Karl Kerényi, the mythologist and religious historian.

January 28 to February 9, 1934

T.M. makes a lecture tour through nine Swiss cities.

January 29, 1934

In Neuchâtel, he gives the *Sufferings and Greatness of Richard Wagner* before the Société des Belles Lettres.

January 31, 1934

In Solothurn, he gives the same lecture.

February 1–4, 1934

While in Bern giving the same lecture, he is with Professor Fritz Strich.

February 2, 1934

In Thun, he reads from Chapter IV of *Young Joseph (The Coat of Many Colours)*. "Yesterday toward evening, I went to Thun and had dinner with a Dr. Saurer, who had a German wife and whose car bore a German Eagle. The reading, in the aula of the Gymnasium before two hundred people, was harmless and effortless. The audience were as quiet as mice and courteous but obviously stupid." [Letter to Katja Mann, February 3, 1934, in the *S. Fischer Almanach 1964*]

February 3, 1934

In Bern, he gives a half-hour reading from *A Man and His Dog*.

February 5, 1934
In Glarus, he reads *The Coat of Many Colours.*
February 6, 1934
In Burgdorf, he reads to the Casino Gesellschaft.
February 7, 1934
In Olten, he reads to the Akademia.
February 8, 1934
In Aarau, he reads to the Literatur- und Lesegesellschaft.
February 9, 1934
In Baden, he gives the Wagner lecture.
February 26 to March 18, 1934
He goes to Arosa for a rest at the Neues Waldhotel. He works on Chapter One of *Joseph in Egypt (The Fort of Thel)*, which has obvious allusions to his life as an emigrant: " 'There are too many of you,' he went on reproachfully. 'Every day come some from here or there . . . and want to set foot inside . . . Above all, know ye how to live? I mean, have ye to eat and can be at your own cost so that ye come not as burden on the state or be driven to steal?' " [*Joseph in Egypt*]
He reads *Don Quixote* and Karl Kerényi's book about Greek/Oriental novels in the light of religious history, which was sent to him by the author.
March 21/22, 1934
In Basel he gives the Wagner lecture and attends Die Pfeffermühle Cabaret, which is giving a guest performance.
April, 1934
The second volume of the Joseph novel appears, *Young Joseph.*

DER JUNGE JOSEPH (Berlin: S. Fischer, 1934. 10,000 copies)
YOUNG JOSEPH (New York: Alfred A. Knopf, 1934. 428 pp.)

Easter, April 2, 1934
Annette Kolb visits T.M. in Küsnacht. He makes a request to the Ministry of Interior in Berlin and the Munich Police Department to have his passport extended and his house, library, and goods released to him. "While I have an inborn and natural aversion to the National Socialist system, I make now all the less concealment of this position, for I recognize and respect the contempt that victorious National Socialism has for servility . . ." [Thomas Mann Archives, Zürich]
April 5/6, 1934
He takes part in an international series of lectures in Locarno, where he gives the Wagner lecture. ". . . Reisiger was with me in Locarno and spoke on Whitman. I liked a French

Germanist, Vermeil from Strassburg, whom I heard speak on Goethe. Among others, the Italian socialist, Labriola, was there. The public made a lively response." [Unpublished letter to Ida Herz]

April 23, 1934

He gives a reading at the Schauspielhaus in Zürich.

April 30, 1934

In Basel, he gives the lecture *Goethe's Career as a Man of Letters*.

May, 1934

The Joseph novel progresses. "The Egyptian portion is taking up much space—already a few hundred pages—although I have really pressed no further along in the plot than the enchanted Joseph's first glimpses into Potiphar's house." [Letter to Käte Hamburger, *Briefe I*]

AT THE WELL [in English] (MENORAH JOURNAL, New York, April, 1934)

T.M.'s parents-in-law visit in Küsnacht.

May 17, 1934

When the American edition of *The Tales of Jacob* is to appear in a translation by Helen T. Lowe-Porter [first title: *Joseph and His Brothers*], T.M. takes his first trip to the United States at the invitation of the publisher, Alfred A. Knopf.

May 17–18, 1934

He goes to Paris, then to Boulogne.

May 19–29, 1934

He crosses on the R.M.S. *Volendam* of the Holland-American Lines. He reads *Don Quixote* and writes his impressions of an ocean voyage. "I have, quite simply, stage fright. And what wonder? My maiden voyage across the Atlantic, my first encounter with the mighty ocean, my first knowledge of it—and there, on the other side of the curvature of the earth, above which the great waters heave, New Amsterdam the metropolis awaits us!" [*Voyage with Don Quixote*]

May 29, 1934

He arrives in New York. "Ready for arrival, we await it on deck. Through the mist arises a familiar figure, the Goddess of Liberty with her crown, a naïve classistic symbol grown right strange to us today." [*Voyage with Don Quixote*]

He is received on the quai by Alfred Knopf, journalists, and reporters. In the evening there is a dinner at the Knopf home with guests Willa Cather, H. L. Mencken, and Henry Seidel Canby.

May 30, 1934

There is a reception by the New York PEN Club at the home of Henry Goddard Leach.

May 31, 1934

T.M. has lunch with the editors of *The Nation*.

June 1, 1934

He gives the Goethe lecture in the German Department at Yale.

June 4, 1934

He is made an honorary member of the Authors' Club at a dinner for ninety-five guests.

June 5, 1934

He has lunch with the Dutch Treat Club and in the evening goes to the Dodsworth Theater.

June 6, 1934

He has lunch with the editors of *The New York Times* and in the evening attends a testimonial dinner at the Plaza with three hundred guests. Here he is greeted by Mayor Fiorello La Guardia and others. He gives a speech in English: "The man who addresses you, ladies and gentlemen, is one who depends on solitude and seclusion, on a quiet and even attention to his own tasks; therefore not of a particularly social nature . . . For that reason, however, he loves people and knows, too, or rather hopes, to ally himself to them by means of the quietest and most personal pursuit of his calling." [*American Address*]

Among the guests are Nicholas Murray Butler, Willa Cather, Henry Goddard Leach, Sinclair Lewis, Dorothy Thompson, and Henry Seidel Canby.

June 7, 1934

He makes a speech on the radio and visits Rockefeller Center with Merle Crowell as a guide.

June 8, 1934

He is visited by friends and attends a farewell dinner at the Central Park Casino.

June 9, 1934

He leaves the United States on board the R.M.S. *Rotterdam*.

June 18, 1934

He is back in Küsnacht. "The adventure is behind me and

seems only a dream, rather confusing but very pleasant. I have experienced and harvested much that is good and gratifying which was sown in the past. The testimonial dinner on June 6, was a great success—three hundred people and the Mayor of New York." [Letter to Gottfried Bermann Fischer, *Briefe I*]

June 30, 1934

The Röhm Putsch takes place. Under the pretext of halting an uprising among the Storm Troops, the National Socialist regime eliminates some old and new opponents. T.M.'s sympathy for the victims is expressed in *Leiden an Deutschland.*

July, 1934

T.M. takes part in an international conference on art in Venice. "For me the greatest gain from the conference was the chance of seeing once again the city, which I have loved so long for deep and complex reasons, and the beach-island belonging to it, where a certain story—now twenty years old—took place. [Letter to Karl Kerényi, *Briefe I*]

The chapter excluded from *Young Joseph, Der Knabe Henoch*, is published by the Jewish periodical *Der Morgen.*

DER KNABE HENOCH (DER MORGEN, MONATSSCHRIFT DER DEUTSCHEN JUDEN, Berlin, July, 1934)

July 25, 1934

Austrian Chancellor Dollfuss is assassinated by the National Socialists.

August 2, 1934

Hindenburg dies. The "*Führer*" unconstitutionally unites the offices of president and chancellor. T.M., after his return from Venice, has great difficulty in concentrating on his work because of political events. "But I cannot describe how the atrocities of June 30, the Austrian horrors, and then that man's blows against the state, his further rise to power . . . have upset me. How these events excite me and draw me away from that which, were my heart firmer and cooler, I should look on as the only important and proper work for me. I ought to feel that world history does not affect me as long as it permits me to live and work. Yet I cannot think in such a way." [Letter to Karl Kerényi, *Briefe I*]

He plans to write a book about Germany. "The time seems to me ripe for a statement I have planned, and the moment could soon come when I shall regret having remained reluctantly silent during this respite." [Letter to Karl Kerényi, *Briefe I*]

September, 1934

He interrupts work on the Joseph novel. ". . . thus I am presently writing that article, called *Voyage with Don Quixote*, a chatty piece full of associations, which will serve to gain time as well as complete the volume of essays." [Letter to Ferdinand Lion, *Briefe I*] He is visited by Emil Preetorius: "aged, speaking softly, and shocked by what those out there are learning about their country." [Letter to Ferdinand Lion, *Briefe I*]

MEERFAHRT MIT DON QUIJOTE (NEUE ZÜRCHER ZEITUNG, November 5–15, 1934) *VOYAGE WITH DON QUICHOTE* (ESSAYS OF THREE DECADES)

October, 1934

He goes for a rest to the Villa Castagnola in Lugano.

October 15, 1934

The publisher, Samuel Fischer, dies at Freudenstadt in the Black Forest. "A part of me sinks into the grave with this old, tired man, and an epoch vanishes to which I feel intellectually and morally connected and which has only few representatives here and there who are bringing their life work to an end in a spiritual climate which is no longer theirs." [*In memoriam S. Fischer*]

IN MEMORIAM S. FISCHER (BASELER NACHRICHTEN, October 28, 1934)

October 22, 1934

T.M. speaks over the Swiss radio. "I give greetings and thanks to a land, a political entity, a culture which has been my home already now for one and a half years, since fate has not wished my return to the old and familiar." [*Gruss an die Schweiz*]

Beginning of November, 1934

After a long interruption, I am now again on the third volume, which offers me an almost boundless task . . ." [Letter to A. M. Frey, *Briefe I*]

JOSEPH IS SOLD FOR A SECOND TIME AND FLINGS HIMSELF UPON HIS FACE from JOSEPH IN EGYPT (DIE NEUE RUNDSCHAU, December, 1934)

November, 1934

Hans Reisiger visits in Küsnacht.

Christmas, 1934

"During the holidays, there was great tumult of children and guests; I am almost exhausted from it—calm and normality are the best for which the likes of us can wish . . ." [Letter to Karl Kerényi, *Thomas Mann/Karl Kerényi, Gespräch in Briefen*. Zürich: Rhein-Verlag, 1960] As a Christmas gift for the whole family, a German shepherd named Billi is purchased, "who is to guard the house and take walks with me. I think we shall be good friends; in any case, he will make the exile seem more like the old life, for I always had a com-

GRUSS AN DIE SCHWEIZ (SCHWEIZER SPIEGEL, Zürich, December, 1934)

panion like him in Munich." [Unpublished letter to Ida Herz]

January, 1935

"From Germany there continues to come—or comes once again?—much good will and friendliness. A student at Cologne only recently wrote me a kind of love letter. It seems that here and there the desire for 'something else' is appearing." [Letter to Ernst Bertram, *Bertram*]

The New York publisher, Alfred A. Knopf, visits T.M.

January 19 to about January 30, 1935

T.M. makes a tour with the Wagner lecture to Prague, Brünn, Vienna, Budapest, and again to Vienna. "I have not been to these cities for three years and am curious to see them under such altered circumstances. Also my daughter Erika is just now in Prague with her 'Pfeffermühle.'" [Letter to Rudolf Kayser, *Briefe I*]

January 25, 1935

He gives a lecture in Vienna.

January 27, 1935

GUTACHTEN ÜBER ERICH VON KAHLERS ISRAEL UNTER DEN VÖLKERN (Unpublished)

In Budapest, T.M. makes the personal acquaintance of Karl Kerényi, who several months later writes to T.M.; "And while I am talking of memories, I must say how pleasant it is to remember our meeting in Budapest. It was especially the youthful freshness in your character which impressed me. Thus from afar, you belong already to the classic writers of my youth."

January 28, 1935

LA FORMATION DE L'HOMME MODERNE (In ENTRETIENS: "LA FORMATION DE L'HOMME MODERNE, éd. par la Société des Nations. Paris Institut International de Coopération Intellectuelle, 1935)

In Vienna at the Urania, T.M. reads from the Joseph novel.

February, 1935

He is with Bruno Walter and his wife in St. Moritz at the Chantarella.

March, 1935

He reads Erich von Kahler's *Israel unter den Völkern* and recommends it to Gottfried Bermann Fischer for publication; however, since there is no question of publishing the book in Germany under the National Socialists, it appears in Zürich in 1936.

T.M. writes a paper for the conference of the Comité de la Coopération Intellectuelle which takes place in Nizza from April 3–5, 1935, although T.M. himself does not take part (published later in German under the title *Achtung, Europa!*).

"In all humanism there is an element of weakness, which in some circumstances may be its ruin, connected with its contempt of fanaticism, its patience, its love of scepticism; in short, its natural goodness. What is needed today is a militant humanism, conscious of its virility and inspired by the conviction that the principles of freedom, tolerance, and honest doubt shall not be exploited and destroyed by fanatics who have themselves no shadow of tolerance or doubt." [*Europe, Beware!*]

EUROPE, BEWARE! (ORDER OF THE DAY)

March 28, 1935

The volume of essays, *Leiden und Grösse der Meister*, appears. It is the last work by T.M. to be published in Germany until 1946. "The first edition has been quickly bought up. This, I must admit, I had expected." [Letter to Ferdinand Lion, *Briefe I*]

LEIDEN UND GRÖSSE DER MEISTER (Berlin: S. Fischer, 1935. 4,000 copies)

End of April to mid-May, 1935

The Pringsheims visit in Küsnacht. T.M. is ill with a spasm of the colon and has doubts about the plan of *Joseph in Egypt*. "Depression, fatigue, dullness, a paralysis of my productivity—or partial paralysis—dissatisfaction with the plan and style of the third volume, which has become ponderous and probably should have been something quite different—perhaps less than a novel, much lighter and dreamier . . . Have I not the endurance to give this work an ending worthy of its beginning?" [Letter to Ferdinand Lion, April 29, 1935, *Briefe I*]

Mid-May, 1935

T.M. travels to Nizza to visit Heinrich Mann and René Schickele. The French edition of *The Tales of Jacob* [*Les Histoires de Jacob*] appears. "If I am not deceived, you have solved the difficult problems of this translation with extraordinary tact and success, and I hope that the French public will grant you suitably rewarding thanks for it." [Letter to Louise Servicen, *Briefe I*]

May 26, 1935

There is an official celebration of T.M.'s sixtieth birthday sponsored by the Hottingen Lesezirkel at the Corso Theater in Zürich. A concerto grosso of Vivaldi is performed, and Robert Faesi gives the main address. A gift from the city of Zürich is awarded to T.M. by the vice president of the city counsel, J. Gschwend. T.M.'s reply: ". . . I am quite con-

DES DICHTERS DANK (NEUE ZÜRCHER ZEITUNG, June 2, 1935)

scious that my thanks will not be heard only by this assembly, but also by the whole city, that it will be reported throughout all of Switzerland, whose boundless peace I have enjoyed now for so long and where I have a feeling of happiness. 'Happiness' means essentially *harmony*, in concord with one's surroundings, and this same concord I have found in your land." [*Danksagung bei der Feier des sechzigsten Geburtstags*]

Fiorenza is performed.

June 6, 1935

At the family celebration there are numerous children, Hans Reisiger, Bruno Frank, and other friends. From the S. Fischer Publishing Company comes a chest containing handwritten greetings from almost all its authors and from other friends of T.M., among them, Albert Einstein, Bernard Shaw, Alfred Kubin, Knut Hamsun, and Karl Kerényi. He also receives through the mail greetings from René Schickele, Alfred Neumann, Ernst Bertram, and others. "There was great excitement. God knows when I shall read and answer all this. But the hundreds of letters from Germany, yes, from Germany, even from work camps—I must say, it does my heart good. It was a bright festive day in the circle of children and friends from morning til night . . ." [Letter to Alfred Neumann, *Briefe I*]

JOSEPH SPEAKS BEFORE POTIPHAR from JOSEPH IN EGYPT, (DIE NEUE RUNDSCHAU, June, 1935)

June 5, 1935

Julius Meier-Graefe, a close friend of René Schickele, dies in Vevey.

June, 1935

Erika Mann loses her German citizenship; she is married to W. H. Auden, thus becoming a British subject. She was divorced from Gustaf Gründgens in 1929.

June 9 to July 13, 1935

T.M. makes his second trip to the United States.

June 9, 1935

In Paris, he visits Annette Kolb.

June 10, 1935

He sails on the *Lafayette*.

June 20, 1935

Along with Albert Einstein, T.M. is awarded an honorary doctorate from Harvard.

June 22–29, 1935
He is guest of the Dutch–American writer Hendrik Willem van Loon at his country house in Riverside, Connecticut. "Only in Riverside, in the country, have I been able a few times to push my chapter a bit further." [Letter to Gottfried Bermann Fischer, *Briefe I*]

June 30, 1935
He is the guest of President and Mrs. Roosevelt at a private dinner in the White House. "I heard that my election [for the honorary doctorate], particularly mine, came about not without the support of President Roosevelt. He invited my wife and me privately, without consulting the German Ambassador naturally, to the White House in Washington, whither we traveled from New York by airplane in one hour and twenty minutes. It was my first flight, a technical adventure, otherwise not very exciting except for a time above the shining clouds, which reminded me of the view from the Rigi Pass." [Letter to Gottfried Bermann Fischer, *Briefe I*]
After a few days in New York, he returns on the *Berengaria* of the Cunard White Star Line.

July 12, 1935
He arrives in Cherbourg.

July 13, 1935
He is back in Küsnacht.

July, 1935
He works on *Joseph in Egypt*. "The third volume is indescribably difficult. Just now I am planning a great scene between Potiphar and his wife; Klaus thinks she has something of Proust in her. But then I must next rework and condense the beginnings of this volume. I believe I commenced it wrongly." [Letter to René Schickele, *Briefe I*]

About July 15–28, 1935
He visits his parents-in-law, Professor Pringsheim and his wife, who is celebrating her eightieth birthday.

August 17–29, 1935
He makes a trip to Salzburg.

August 17, 1935
He spends the night in Innsbruck.

August 19, 1935
He gives the Wagner lecture in Salzburg.

August 20, 1935
He reads from the Joseph novel at Bad Gastein, hears concerts and attends the theater: Gounod's *Faust*; Beethoven's *Fidelio* conducted by Arturo Toscanini with Lotte Lehmann in the title role; Verdi's *Falstaff* under Toscanini. He has several visits with Bruno Walter and Toscanini.

August 27, 1935
In the Mozarteum, T.M. reads the *Account of Mont-Kaw's Simple Passing* from *Joseph in Egypt*: "a case of a death from which I have gained strength." [Letter to René Schickele, *Briefe I*]

August 28, 1935
He attends Mozart's *Don Giovanni* conducted by Bruno Walter.

September 29, 1935
He reads Kerényi's treatise, *Gedanken über Dionysos*. "It comes to me at an unbelievably appropriate time, for I am just on the point of stylizing the passion of Potiphar's wife as dionysian, maenadic. You will certainly find traces of your study in the novel." [Letter to Karl Kerényi, *Thomas Mann/Karl Kerényi, Gespräch in Briefen*. Zürich: Rhein-Verlag, 1962]

October, 1935
He is visited by Otto Baseler, a teacher from Aarau, who carries on a voluminous correspondence with T.M.

T.M. writes a letter to the Nobel Prize Committee in Oslo, which has recommended the election of Carl Ossietzky for the Peace Prize. "It would be difficult to express the surge of joy and satisfaction which would go through the world, were the Committee to make a perhaps not so correct and not so easy choice but morally a very meaningful one, and award the Prize to a martyr for the principle of peace like Ossietzky, who for years has endured the concentration camp . . ." [*An das Nobel-Friedenspreis-Comité, Oslo*]

NOBELPRISET OCH CARL VON OSSIETZKY (GÖTEBORGS HANDELS-OCH SJÖFARTS-TIDNING, July 11, 1936)

October 10, 1935
He writes a foreword to Martha Karlweis' book on Jakob Wassermann.

ZUM GELEIT (In Martha Karlweis' JAKOB WASSERMANN: BILD, KAMPF, UND WERK. Amsterdam: Querido Verlag, 1935)

October, 1935
He reads Proust's novels, *Remembrance of Things Past*. "Presently the poor lady (Mut-em-enet) has much to suffer and in doing so may be slightly influenced psychologically by

Proust, who suddenly has me absorbed. He has a fantastic languidness, which disconcerts and attracts me. And things like 'The Death of My Grandmother' with the leech in her hair in *The Duchess of Guermantes* are simply unforgettable." [Letter to René Schickele, *Briefe I*]

Heinrich Mann's novel, *Die Jugend des Königs Henri Quatre,* appears in Amsterdam. "I have the greatest admiration for Heinrich's novel. Doubtless it is great literature, and today Europe has nothing better to offer, not to mention the mediocrity which has triumphed over the Germans within." [Letter to René Schickele, *Briefe I*]

November 8, 1935

In Winterthur, T.M. reads from *Joseph in Egypt* for the Winterthur Aid for the Children of Emigrants.

November 17, 1935

In Zollikon, he reads from the Joseph novel to the Young Zollikon Society.

November 20, 1935

The celebration of Eduard Korrodi's fiftieth birthday takes place at the Zürich "Zunfthaus." Korrodi is a literary historian and in charge of reviews and cultural news for the *Neue Zürcher Zeitung*. T.M. gives an extemporaneous speech. "There was an influential, memorable and important constellation at our table . . . I am also especially pleased at having given my pertly intruding speech, for I hear that in Germany no notice was taken of you on this day." [Letter to Eduard Korrodi, *Briefe I*]

End of November, 1935

T.M. is disappointed at hearing of Knut Hamsun's joining the Norwegian National Socialist Party under Quisling. "What incomprehensible crudeness! Doubtless he damages his image for the present and for the future with this unhappy move. His sympathy with this party rests partly on his confusing it with the real Germany, to which land he, like all great Scandinavians, owes much thanks." [Letter to René Schickele, *Briefe I*]

December, 1935

T.M. is visited by Gottfried Bermann Fischer, who hopes to establish his publishing company in Switzerland; he does not succeed.

December 11, 1935
In Solothurn, T.M. reads from *Joseph in Egypt* to the "Potters' Guild."

December 14, 1935
In Bern, he gives a reading before the Free Student Union, "where the audience in the town hall listened to a chapter from *Joseph* with such attention that one could have heard a needle hit the floor." [Letter to Otto Basler, *Briefe von Thomas Mann,* contributed by Otto Basler. *Blätter der Thomas Mann-Gesellschaft*, Zürich, No. 5, 1965]

January, 1936
The Bermann/Fischer publishing firm is established in Vienna.

January 10, 1936
In Basel, T.M. reads for the benefit of an aid fund for refugees with intellectual professions.

Mid-January to the beginning of February, 1936
He is in Arosa.

February 3, 1936
In an open letter to Eduard Korrodi, T.M. protests the former's article *Deutsche Literatur im Emigrantenspiegel*, in which Korrodi identifies the literature of the emigration as exclusively Jewish. Through this public declaration of his connection with the emigration, T.M. makes his final break with the National Socialist regime. "The deep conviction, nourished and supported daily from thousands of humanitarian, moral, and esthetic single observations and impressions, that nothing good can come from the present German leaders—nothing good either for Germany or the world—this conviction has caused me to flee that land in whose cultural tradition I have deeper roots than those who for three years have been hesitating as to whether they should dare deny my German identity before the whole world." [Letter to Eduard Korrodi, *Briefe I*]
His decision causes a strong reaction. "I had to follow suit in clear words for the sake of the world, in which there are many quite dubious feelings about my relationship to the Third Reich, and for my own sake, since I have needed spiritually to do this for a long time . . . I have saddened many people. The stream of letters proves this. But to many who are standing apart I have given an example that there is

such a thing as character and firm conviction." [Letter to Hermann Hesse, *Briefe I*]

February, 1936

He prepares the collection *Stories of Three Decades*, and writes a preface.

February 27, 1936

He writes a greeting for Bruno Walter on his sixtieth birthday, September 15. "I thank destiny that there is a contemporary of mine who was created and talented in quite a different way, as a mediator between my sphere and that in which he rules and governs—music. The love for this mysterious, strict, and boundless art was born in me and then deepened through definite cultural experiences . . . , and early it was my ambition and my desire, life, and occupation to interlace music with the word, to weave, imagine, and bind them into one genre—to give my tale a texture of theme and counterpoint like an harmonious architectural structure of ideas." [*Für Bruno Walter*]

March 13, 1936

He writes a greeting for his brother Heinrich on his sixty-fifth birthday, March 27. "What wish should I make for you on this day? Of course, the most natural and grandest, which includes everything: that in five years, by the time you are seventy, our people and our land may again be able to use us." [*Dem Fünfundsechzigjährigen*]

From April to the beginning of May, 1936

He works on the lecture *Freud and the Future* for Sigmund Freud's eightieth birthday. T.M. reads it, "for rehearsal," to several friends and neighbors, among them, Erich Kahler, Bernard von Brentano, Franz W. Beidler (Richard Wagner's grandson). "I was pleased with it." [Letter to Alfred Neumann, *Briefe I*]

Alfred Neumann dedicates his new novel, *Das Kaiserreich*, to "his great friend, Thomas Mann."

May 5, to about May 15, 1936

He makes a lecture tour to Vienna, Brünn, and Prague.

May 8, 1936

In Vienna, T.M. gives the Freud lecture as the main address at the celebration of Freud's eightieth birthday at the Academic Society of Medical Psychology. At a visit with Freud, T.M. presents him with a birthday greeting signed by numer-

PREFACE (In STORIES OF THREE DECADES. New York: Alfred A. Knopf, 1936. 567 pp.)

FÜR BRUNO WALTER (In BRUNO WALTER. Edited by Paul Stefan, with contributions by Lotte Lehmann, Thomas Mann, Stefan Zweig. Vienna, Liepzig, and Zürich: H. Reichner, 1936)

DEM FÜNFUNDSECHZIGJÄHRIGEN (DIE NEUE WELTBÜHNE, Paris, March 26, 1936)

SIGMUND FREUD UND DIE ZUKUNFT (IMAGO: ZEITSCHRIFT FÜR PSYCHOANALYTISCHE PSYCHOLOGIE, Vienna, Vol. 22, 1936)

ous scholars and writers including Romain Rolland, H. G. Wells, Virginia Woolf, Stefan Zweig, and T.M. T.M. repeats his lecture at the Masaryk Hochschule in Brünn and again in Prague.

FREUD AND THE FUTURE (In FREUD, GOETHE, WAGNER and ESSAYS OF THREE DECADES)

June 5–18, 1936

He travels to Budapest for a conference of the Comité de la Coopération Intellectuelle.

June 5, 1936

He departs for Vienna and travels from there by car with Lajos Hatvány to Budapest, where he is Hatvány's guest.

June 7, 1936

He gives the Freud lecture in Budapest.

June 8–12, 1936

At the conference of the Comité, T.M. gives a paper. After a lecture by an English member, T.M. makes an extemporaneous speech. "It was in the Hungarian capitol city where I forced myself in a public meeting to make an extemporaneous speech against the murderers of free people and about the necessity of a militant democracy. This utterance, with which I transgressed to the point of tactlessness against the academic character of the assemblage and, of course, against the fascist delegates, was answered, nevertheless, by the Hungarian audience with a lengthy demonstration of applause. The speech also earned me an enthusiastic embrace from Karel Čapek, the Czech poet, who, when the democratic countries betrayed his country, died of a broken heart." [*Sechzehn Jahre*]

HUMANIORA UND HUMANISMUS (In ALTES UND NEUES. Frankfurt on Main: S. Fischer, 1953)
DER HUMANISMUS UND EUROPA (PESTER LLOYD, June 11, 1936)

June 9, 1936

He gives a reading from the Joseph novel and attends the Budapest Opera.

June 13, 1936

In Vienna, he gives a reading from *Joseph in Egypt* and attends the opera. "After my . . . reading, we went to hear the third act of *Tristan* under Bruno Walter and entered a terribly bad-smelling house. The Nazis had thrown stink bombs, but the performance was carried on and, toward the end, only by the orchestra, for Isolde, who had vomited during the entire intermission, finally made a gesture signifying her incapacity and did not rise again from the body of Tristan . . .—it was all a blow directed against the summer festivals." [Letter to Heinrich Mann, *Briefe I*]

June 14, 1936
During a visit to Sigmund Freud, T.M. reads his Freud lecture "privately, to a little circle of friends," since Freud could not hear at the public lecture. "At the close, he had tears in his eyes . . ." [Unpublished letter to Ida Herz]

July, 1936
He works on the final chapters of *Joseph in Egypt*, which is to appear in October. "In the last few days, you were very close to my work and it to you. At the end of the third book of Joseph, I have written a magic scene, for which I have unabashedly helped myself to your explanation of Sophron's mime actresses . . ." [Letter to Karl Kerényi, July 15, 1936, *Briefe I*]
He reads Heinrich Mann's anthology, *Es kommt der Tag*. "I read uninterruptedly for two days in it, and after I had acquainted myself with all that was new to me, I reread that with which I was already familiar. It was a great pleasure and a great satisfaction." [Letter to Heinrich Mann, *Briefe I*]

End of July, 1936
He spends "a few days" in Sils-Baseglia. "For the first time, we came to know the Engadine Valley in the summer, for we had always been there before in the winter. It is a splendid landscape, and the air made the completion of the final chapter of *Joseph in Egypt* remarkably easier." [Unpublished letter to Ida Herz]

August, 1936
The essay *Freud and the Future* appears in a single edition.

FREUD UND DIE ZUKUNFT (Vienna: Bermann/Fischer, 1936. 4,000 copies)

August 23, 1936
Joseph in Egypt is finished. "In the evening, we had a little party with punch and a poem with best wishes composed by Erika and recited by Medi, as the youngest of us, and a closing lecture, which was very nice. The book is only a fragment—the work on it has been accompanied by many interruptions in these three and a half years of 'exile.' Oh, the old piece of rubbish has a hideously pedantic length, but I think it yet capable of bringing a bit of brighter cheerfulness into a country that can certainly use some cheerfulness." [Letter to Bruno Walter, *Briefe I*]

August 23 to September 23, 1936
T.M. travels by car to St. Cyr-sur-Mer for a visit with René Schickele and then on to Aiguebelle Le Lavandou on the

Côte d'Azur for a visit with Heinrich Mann and his daughter Leonie (Goschi). Here he falls ill with a throat infection. After his return home, he has erysipelas. "The thing takes its course moderately, without high fever, and the doctor is satisfied, but the swelling continues." [Letter to Heinrich Mann, *Briefe I*]

Kuno Fiedler, who baptized Elisabeth Mann and who has been in prison in Germany, escapes at Würzburg and stays temporarily in Küsnacht. "Like a ghost, Dr. Fiedler came out of our house and met us on our arrival yesterday." [Letter to Heinrich Mann, *Briefe I*]

Beginning of October, 1936

T.M. plans a new story—*The Beloved Returns: Lotte in Weimar*—". . . a tale that I intend to insert between the third and fourth volumes of my biblical novels . . . It is a project whose mastery will require much reading." [Letter to Frida Uhl-Strindberg, *Briefe I*]

JOSEPH IN ÄGYPTEN (Vienna: Bermann/ Fischer, 1936. 10,000 copies)

JOSEPH IN EGYPT (New York: Alfred A. Knopf, 1938. 664 pp.)

October 12, 1936

T.M. speaks at a program in memory of Jakob Wassermann in Zürich.

Mid-October, 1936

Joseph in Egypt appears.

End of October, 1936

He prepares to write *The Beloved Returns*. "I am working on the Goethe story, *The Beloved Returns*, in the mornings, but I stalk it day and night without finding its form clearly in my mind. In any case, it will be something special—so much I feel already—it will be a handsome little book." [Letter to Gottfried Bermann Fischer, *Briefe I*]

November 19, 1936

T.M. becomes a Czech citizen through the help of the merchant, Rudolf Fleischmann, in whose civil parish T.M. was accepted as a citizen. He swears the oath of citizenship before the Czech consul in Zürich.

December 2, 1936

He is deprived of his German citizenship under a law established July 14, 1933. Katja Mann and the four younger children are also included. The official reason is given in the German newspapers: "He has taken part repeatedly in proclamations issued by international organizations, mostly under Jewish influence, whose hostile position concerning

Germany is generally known. Recently his announcements have been openly connected with treasonous attacks against the Reich. On the occasion of a discussion in a well known Zürich newspaper on the valuation of the writings of German emigrants, he placed himself distinctly on the side of the treasonous emigration and expressed publicly the bitterest insults against the Reich, which were strongly contradicted in the foreign press. His brother Heinrich, his son Klaus, and his daughter Erika have already been deprived of their citizenship long ago because of their unworthy conduct outside of Germany." [*Völkischer Beobachter*, Munich, December 3, 1936]

T.M. replies to an official German information agency: "You wish a statement from me concerning the denial of my citizenship by the German government. First I should like to remark that this act has no legal meaning because my having become a citizen of Czechoslovakia two weeks ago automatically deprives me of German citizenship. There is no necessity of speaking of any emotional meaning that this official move might have for me. I have already explained at an earlier time that I have deeper roots in German life and tradition than the temporary, though subtly penetrating, figures who at the present are ruling in Germany." [*Berner Tagwacht*, December 10, 1936]

He writes to his publisher concerning his move: "The response is great—almost as it was after I received the Nobel Prize—and on my part, I feel the clarification of my position was right." [Unpublished letter to Gottfried Bermann Fischer, December 5, 1936]

December 19, 1936

The philosophical faculty of the University of Bonn revokes T.M.'s honorary doctorate.

December 29, 1936

Erika Mann's cabaret show, Die Pfeffermühle, opens in New York "in a pretty little theater but without much atmosphere. It was on the top floor of a skyscraper, the Chanin Building, near Grand Central Station . . . in New York the cabaret caused relatively little excitement . . ." [*Der Wendepunkt* by Klaus Mann]

DIE PFEFFERMÜHLE (In the program notes for the American tour)

After the return of Therese Giehse and the musician Magnus Henning to Switzerland, the cabaret is closed. Erika Mann begins her career as lecturer. "Her specialty, however, remains direct appeal and spoken commentary, the talk interspersed with anecdotes, the chat which is seemingly improvised but in reality carefully prepared, which is fascinating and convincing partly because of the charm of the speaker and partly because of the solid substance discussed. Erika could be one of the most sought-after lecturers on the North American continent—because she has something of value to say ('She has a message!'), and because of the charming intensity with which she says it ('She has personality!')." [*Der Wendepunkt* by Klaus Mann]

December 31, 1936

T.M. replies to the Dean of the Philosophical Faculty of Bonn University (Professor Karl Justus Obenauer) concerning the withdrawal of his honorary doctorate on December 19: "I could never have dreamed, it could never have been prophesied of me at my cradle, that I should spend my later years as an émigré, expropriated, outlawed, and committed to inevitable political protest. From the beginning of my intellectual life I had found myself in happiest accord with the temper of my nation and at home in its intellectual traditions. I am better suited to represent those traditions than to become a martyr for them; far more fitted to add a little to the gaiety of the world than to foster conflict and hatred in it. Something very wrong must have happened to make my life take so false and unnatural a turn. I tried to check it, this very wrong thing, so far as my weak powers were able—and in so doing I called down on myself the fate which I must now learn to reconcile with a nature essentially foreign to it." [*An Exchange of Letters*]

EIN BRIEFWECHSEL (NEUE ZÜRCHER ZEITUNG, January 24, 1937. Zürich: Verlag Oprecht, Zürich, 1937. 20,000 copies) *AN EXCHANGE OF LETTERS* (New York: Alfred A. Knopf, 1937. 12 pp.)

January, 1937

Translations of this exchange of letters appear in almost all major nations of the world.

January 7–15, 1937

T.M. makes a reading tour to Prague, Budapest, and Vienna.

January 7, 1937

He visits Katja and Golo Mann in Proseč, where they have been living since the family became Czech citizens. T.M. signs his name in the parish guest book. In Prague, he reads to the Urania Society from *The Beloved Returns* and the Joseph novel. In a short greeting, he introduces himself as a new Czechoslovakian compatriot.

January 12, 1937
In Budapest, on an evening in honor of T.M. at the Hungarian Theater, he gives a reading.

January 14, 1937
In Vienna, he gives a reading and pays a visit on Sigmund Freud.

January 22 to February 20, 1937
In Arosa, he works on *The Beloved Returns.*

February, 1937
Negotiations take place concerning the founding of the periodical, *Mass und Wert.* T.M., Konrad Falke, and Ferdinand Lion are to be editors, and the publisher is Emil Oprecht. "A rich lady, with literary sympathies, who, by the way, wishes to remain in the background, has provided us with the necessary means . . ." [Letter to Hermann Hesse, *Briefe II*]

T.M. advocates the awarding of the Nobel Prize to Sigmund Freud and is supported by Romain Rolland.

February 23, 1937
The establishment of *Mass und Wert* is decided upon. T.M. asks Hermann Hesse to join the staff.

March, 1937
Erika Mann speaks in the United States to the American Jewish Congress. T.M. cables her: "Best wishes on your appearance before the American Jewish Congress. You speak there as an independent individual but at the same time to a certain extent in my place as my daughter and a child of my spirit . . ." [Cable to Erika Mann, *Briefe II*]

March, 1937
In his introductory words to a reading before the Kadimah Jewish Union in Zürich, T.M. speaks of the Joseph novel and of the problem of anti-Semitism. "Anti-Semitism is an appurtenance and watchword for all dark, confused, and bestial mass-humanity and mass-mystique of today. It is neither thought nor word, has no human voice; it is a cacophony. And in a cacophony the intelligent man, who is firm with himself, cannot harmonize. He only waits until it pauses for a moment and then pronounces in the silence his 'No.'" [*Zum Problem des Antisemitismus*]

ZUM PROBLEM DES ANTISEMITISMUS (ALLGEMEINE WOCHENZEITUNG DER JUDEN IN DEUTSCHLAND, Düsseldorf, December 18, 1959) [first printing]

April 6–29, 1937
T.M. makes his third voyage to the United States at the invitation of the New School for Social Research in New York.

April 7, 1937
He boards the *Normandie* at Le Havre.

April 12, 1937
Arriving in New York, he spends some time with Aldous Huxley. He stays at the Bedford Hotel and meets there the physician and writer Martin Gumpert.

April 13, 1937
In New York he gives the lecture *The Sufferings and Greatness of Richard Wagner.*

April 15, 1937
He gives the main address at a banquet of the New School of Social Research to celebrate the fourth anniversary of the founding of the Graduate Faculty of Political and Social Sciences. "Four years ago, when the disastrous character of the new German government stood revealed, it was Alvin Johnson who took up the idea, which was probably stirring in many minds at the time, but was generally regarded as too visionary for fulfilment.—That idea was to preserve the institution of the German University, in spite of the inevitable dispersal of the German intellectuals all over the world, and to refound it here, beyond the seas." [*The Living Spirit*]
The sum of one hundred thousand dollars is appropriated for the "University in Exile" that T.M. has so strongly supported.

THE LIVING SPIRIT (SOCIAL RESEARCH. New York, Volume 4, August, 1937)

About April 20, 1937
T.M. gives a speech at a dinner of the American Guild for German Cultural Freedom for the founding of the Deutsche Akademie in New York. "Thus a comprehensive organization is to be established which will include all the intellectual life active outside of Germany today, not only the scholarly and scientific but also the creative, so that literature, research, music, and the plastic arts will find their places in it . . . But beyond the merely representative, immediate and practical efforts through the Academie are to encourage a German cultural life outside the German borders." [*Zur Gründung der 'American Guild for German Cultural Freedom' und der 'Deutschen Akademie'*]
T.M. has his first personal meeting with Joseph W. Angell, Lecturer at Yale and later military historian. The plan for a Thomas Mann Library at Yale is discussed.
T.M. meets the publisher of the *Washington Post*, Eugene

ZUR GRÜNDUNG DER AMERICAN GUILD FOR GERMAN CULTURAL FREEDOM UND DER DEUTSCHEN AKADEMIE (In GESAMMELTE WERKE IN ZWÖLF BÄNDEN. Volume XI. Frankfurt: S. Fischer, 1960)

Meyer, politician and philanthropist, and his wife, Agnes E. Meyer. In the following years, T.M. has a close friendship with them. With Agnes E. Meyer, who is herself active as a writer, T.M. carries on a lengthy correspondence, which reveals detailed information about T.M.'s years in the United States. He also makes the acquaintance of Caroline Newton, who is a great admirer and collector of his works, and they begin an interesting correspondence.

April 21, 1937

In the Mecca Temple in New York City, T.M. gives a speech at a memorial program for the victims of Fascism. "Freedom must be strong. She must believe in herself and in her right to defend herself. She must be a freedom with authority—masculine—who will not allow herself to be seduced through the intellect to doubt weakly her rights in the world. She must know how to defend herself against a malice that will abuse her again and again in order to kill her." [*Bekenntnis zum Kampf für die Freiheit*]

BEKENNTNIS ZUM KAMPF FÜR DIE FREIHEIT (DAS WORT, Moscow, July, 1937)

April 24, 1937

He sails on the *Ile de France* from New York.

April 30, 1937

He spends a short time in Paris, then returns to Küsnacht. "My contact with America, where I have many friends, has grown closer. We are thinking seriously of spending a part of the year there. Such a separation from Europe would be infinitely beneficial for my spiritual freedom and serenity." [Letter to Karl Kerényi, *Thomas Mann/Karl Kerényi, Gespräch in Briefen*. Zürich: Rhein-Verlag, 1960]

May, 1937

T.M. becomes painfully ill with sciatica contracted during his trip. He prepares for an issue of *Mass und Wert* and writes the introduction for it. "I have now written a comprehensive, programmatic introduction . . ." [Letter to Hermann Hesse, May 21, 1937, *Briefe II*]

EINLEITUNG (In MASS UND WERT Zürich, September/ October, 1937)

MASS UND WERT (ORDER OF THE DAY)

June 6, 1937

Erika Mann comes from the United States to visit her father on his birthday.

June 10–30, 1937

T.M. goes to Ragaz for the cure. "Thanks to the baths in Ragaz and some vitamin injections, I am almost free from my sciatica, which was in no way a pleasure." [Letter to Martin Gumpert, September 6, 1937, *Briefe II*]

August, 1937

The chapter on Riemer in *The Beloved Returns* is finished.

September, 1937

The first issue of *Mass und Wert* appears.

Karl Kerényi visits T.M. in Küsnacht.

The President of Czechoslovakia, Thomas Masaryk, dies. T.M. writes a eulogy.

The fourth chapter of *The Beloved Returns*, the conversation with Adele Schopenhauer, is written.

September 15 to October 7, 1937

T.M. takes a rest in Locarno with Hans Reisiger at Hotel Reber.

Emil Ludwig is often with T.M., who works on the fifth chapter (*Adele's Tale*) of *The Beloved Returns*.

October 9, 1937

Back in Küsnacht, T.M. finishes the chapter begun in Locarno and prepares a new Wagner lecture.

November, 1937

"In the last week, I have worked like a horse. Because of a complete production of Wagner's *Ring des Nibelungen* at the Stadttheater, I had very suddenly to write an essay. *On revient toujours*—" [Letter to Stefan Zweig, November 14, 1937, *Briefe II*]

November 16, 1937

He gives the lecture *Richard Wagner and the Ring* in the aula of the University of Zürich.

December, 1937

T.M. writes a "Message" for artists that Erika is to read at a rally in New York City. For his coming spring tour to the United States, he prepares a lecture, *The Coming Victory of Democracy*. He also works on an address to be given at Yale and on the introduction to an American edition of Schopenhauer in the series, "The Living Thoughts Library." "I am writing so much about politics for my lecture that half of the rubbish will have to be thrown away afterwards. It is a fearful waste, but, once I am set free, no one will be able to check me." [Letter to Erika Mann, *Briefe II*]

He attends a concert directed by Bruno Walter in Zürich ("the performance of Bruckner which was for me epochal"). Afterward he spends the evening with the conductor.

ZU MASARYKS GEDÄCHTNIS (DAS NEUE TAGEBUCH, Paris, September 25, 1937)

RICHARD WAGNER UND DER RING DES NIBELUNGEN (MASS UND WERT, Zürich, January/February, 1938)

RICHARD WAGNER AND THE RING (ESSAYS OF THREE DECADES)

VOM KÜNFTIGEN SIEG DER DEMOKRATIE (Zürich: Europa Verlag Oprecht, 1938. 3,000 copies)

THE COMING VICTORY OF DEMOCRACY (Transl. Agnes E. Meyer. London: Secker Warburg, 1938. 104 pp. ORDER OF THE DAY)

December 18, 1937
He is awarded Czechoslovakia's Herder Prize for exiled writers.

December 25, 1937
Christmas is celebrated with the four younger children (Erika and Klaus are in America). Michael becomes seriously ill with an infection of cerebral and ocular membranes that demands particular care from his parents.
After Christmas, T.M. resumes work on *The Beloved Returns*. "I am stealing this short interval to push 'Lotte' a bit further. At the moment I am at the scene between Lotte and young August, the son of the Mamsell." [Letter to Alfred Neumann, December 28, 1937, *Briefe II*]

THE BELOVED RETURNS: CHAPTER THREE (MASS UND WERT, Zürich, November/ December, 1937)

December 29, 1937
T.M. attends an evening of music in the home of Willem de Boer, concertmaster of the Zürich Tonhallenorchester. The program includes compositions by the host for his favorite instrument, the viola d'amore. "Your art and virtuosity have won me over completely to the viola . . . What richness of register—which you knew so well how to use, so that immediately the words 'string-organ' came to my lips." [Letter to Willem de Boer, *Briefe II*]

January 10–31, 1938
T.M. goes for a rest to the Neues Waldhotel in Arosa. He works on *The Beloved Returns* and then on the Schopenhauer essay. "By the way, I am now writing about Schopenhauer." [Letter to Fritz Strich, January 12, 1938, *Briefe II*]

February 10 to the beginning of July, 1938
T.M. makes his fourth trip to the United States for the purpose of making a lecture tour through fifteen American cities. The tour is organized by the literary agent, Harold Peat of New York City. T.M. plans to give his lecture *The Coming Victory of Democracy*. "I stand at the beginning of a lecture tour through the United States in which I intend to speak in numerous cities, in universities and town halls, about democracy. I intend to speak of its timeless, human youthfulness. I shall defend it against current counter tendencies which make false claims of youthfulness and of the future. I shall proclaim my belief in the coming victory of democracy." [*Zur Gründung einer Dokumentensammlung in Yale University*]

February 12, 1938
T.M. embarks on the *Queen Mary*.
February 21, 1938
He arrives in New York City.
February 25, 1938
The official opening of the Thomas Mann Library at Yale University takes place with a speech by T.M. "An American university establishes an archive, a library, where the works of my solitude are brought together and clearly ordered—works as they appear in German and in translation, manuscripts, rough drafts, outlines, letters and studies, as well as critical remarks by my contemporaries about my efforts. This collection will give those interested an insight into a mental workshop of our time, and to studious young people it will present a view of a life that was born with the drive to express itself in word, image, and thought—to extract from the past the permanent, from chaos, form—to make appearance clear to the soul, to that which Goethe calls 'des Lebens Leben.'" [*Zur Gründung einer Dokumentensammlung in Yale University*]

REDE BEI DER ERÖFFNUNG DER THOMAS MANN LIBRARY AN DER YALE UNIVERSIT (MASS UND WERT, Zürich November/ December, 1938)

T.M. begins his lecture tour, accompanied by Katja and Erika Mann.
March 1, 1938
He is at Northwestern University, near Chicago. "Interest is great; Chicago, for example has been sold out long in advance . . . But the shameless manager takes one thousand dollars for the evening, and I receive only half of that." [Letter to Ida Herz, *Briefe II*]
March 3, 1938
He lectures at the University of Michigan, Ann Arbor.
March 9, 1938
He speaks at the Institute of Arts and Sciences in Brooklyn during the afternoon, and at Constitution Hall in Washington, D.C. that evening. He visits Eugene and Agnes E. Meyer.
March 11, 1938
German troops march into Austria (the *Anschluss* ensues on March 13). "The shock of what happened to Austria came to us while on the lecture tour, and we truly believed we should never see Europe again . . ." [Unpublished letter to Félix Bertaux, Thomas Mann Archives, Zürich]

March 14, 1938
T.M. is in Philadelphia.

March 18, 1938
He is in Tulsa.

March 21, 1938
While at the University of Utah, Salt Lake City, for a lecture, T.M. considers taking up residence in the United States. [Unpublished letter to Agnes E. Meyer, Yale Library]

March 29, 1938
He stops at the Clift Hotel in San Francisco.

April 1, 1938
In Los Angeles, T.M. spends some weeks in Beverly Hills, while writing the *Tagebuchblätter*—personal remarks about the loss of his homeland and an ironic characterization of Hitler, which is later published under the title *A Brother*. "How often have the scenes of my first sally in the cheerful struggle against transitoriness changed since my school days, when joy and sorrow began to cool down as I expressed them in words. Some of these scenes seemed firmly established, and I often looked back on them from my provisional position and called them 'at home.' But they also proved provisional; they disappeared, hid away, and only loosely and incidentally did the memory of their reality remain, and even here recalling them was always connected with my labor of writing . . . But what is it to be without a home? In the works which I write is my home. Engrossed in them I feel all the familiarity of being at home. These works are language, German language and thought form, my personal development of the tradition of my land and my people. Where I am is Germany . . ." [*Tagebuchblätter* from Herbert Lehnert, *Thomas Mann in Exile, 1933–1938*, in *The Germanic Review* (New York, November, 1963)]

TAGEBUCH-BLÄTTER (Unpublished typed copy at Yale University)

April 29, 1938
At the University of Illinois, Urbana, T.M. is given the Cardinal Newman Award.

May 5, 1938
T.M. immigrates officially to the United States via Canada. The formal steps were initiated by Agnes E. Meyer.

May 2–31, 1938
He stays at the Bedford Hotel in New York City.

May 6, 1938

He gives a lecture at Carnegie Hall.

May 7, 1938

He writes a foreword to Erika Mann's *Zehn Millionen Kinder*, on the education of the youth in the Third Reich.

GELEITWORT—ERIKA MANNS ZEHN MILLIONEN KINDER. DIE ERZIEHUNG DER JUGEND IM DRITTEN REICH (Amsterdam: Querido-Verlag, 1938)

While in New York, T.M. is approached by President Harold W. Dodds of Princeton University with the offer of a chair as "Lecturer in the Humanities," in which he would hold a seminary on *Faust*, and a seminar on *The Magic Mountain*, and also give three public lectures. Because of the situation in Austria, T.M. decides to remain in the United States. "You may see what an impression the outrage in Austria—that it were possible, that it was tolerated—has made upon me by the fact that I have decided . . . not to return to Europe from this trip to America. I am giving up my home in Switzerland and intend to take up residence in a university town in the American East." [Letter without name and address, May 21, 1938, *Briefe II*]

May 27, 1938

T.M. accepts the position at Princeton.

June 1, 1938

He is awarded an honorary doctorate by Columbia University.

End of May to June 19, 1938

T.M. stays in a country house belonging to Caroline Newton, in Jamestown, Rhode Island. Here he finishes the Schopenhauer essay and resumes work on *The Beloved Returns.* "After the wanderings of the last three months, we have come to a temporary resting place in a little borrowed house here on the sea, and I am again taking up the dormant threads of *The Beloved Returns* as I should do in Küsnacht, were I there." [Letter to Erich von Kahler, *Briefe II*].

T.M. makes several trips to Princeton in search of a suitable dwelling.

He gives a speech at a meeting of the American Committee for Christian German Refugees.

CHRISTENTUM—DEMOKRATIE—BARBAREI (PARISER TAGESZEITUNG, July 10, 1938)

Erika and Klaus Mann are in Madrid, Barcelona, and Valencia, as newspaper reporters on the Spanish civil war.

June 29, 1938

T.M. returns to Europe on the *Washington* of the United

States Lines. "Life on this ship is more pleasant than I have ever met it on ships of other nations, and we were even blessed with unusually good weather for the greater part of the trip. Only in the Irish Sea was there a proper storm, which made us seriously late." [Letter to Agnes E. Meyer, *Briefe II*]

July 11, 1938
He is back in Küsnacht.

July, 1938
"I am quite involved in *The Beloved Returns*." [Letter to Agnes E. Meyer, July 18, 1938, *Briefe II*]
He prepares for the course in *Faust* at Princeton and does editorial work on *Mass und Wert*.

August, 1938
Heinrich Mann finishes his novel *Die Vollendung des Königs Henri Quatre* [Henry IV, King of France], and T.M. invites him for a few days to Küsnacht. "The forests and lake shore are so beautiful to journey through by car, and you would come into a land whose position against that infamous scoundrel is of the most gratifying firmness since the events in Austria." [Letter to Heinrich Mann, *Briefe II*]

Mid-August, 1938
He spends a week at Sils Baseglia, in the Engadine Valley, with Erika, who has returned from Spain.

September, 1938
He prepares for the move to the United States.

September 13, 1938
T.M. gives a farewell reading (from *The Beloved Returns*) at the Zürich Schauspielhaus.

September 14, 1938
T.M. leaves for Paris.

September 16, 1938
Political affairs in Europe are heading for a crisis as Prime Minister Chamberlain talks with Hitler at Berchtesgaden in a vain effort to curb the threat of war over Czechoslovakia.

September 17, 1938
T.M. sails from Boulogne on the *Nieuw Amsterdam*. He will not see Europe again for fifteen years.

1938–1941
AT PRINCETON

September 25, 1938
T.M. arrives in New York.

September 26, 1938
He speaks at a mass assembly of the Committee for the Rescue of Czechoslovakia in Madison Square Garden. "Yesterday I arrived from Europe on a steamer that was overcrowded with Americans and citizens of other lands. For forty-eight hours, these people were in a mood of deepest spiritual depression. They declared they could neither eat nor sleep when they considered the news coming out of Europe." [*Ansprache auf einer Versammlung in New York*]

September 28, 1938
He is in Princeton at the Mitford House, 65 Stockton Street. "Our house, the property of an Englishman, is very comfortable and an improvement over all our earlier dwellings. . . . The landscape is cultivated and pleasant for taking walks. There are astonishingly beautiful trees, which now in the Indian summer are aglow with the most splendid colors." [Letter to Erich von Kahler, *Briefe II*]
The desk he used in Munich and Küsnacht is placed in his study. ". . . thus am I determined to continue my life and work with the greatest steadfastness just as before, unchanged by the events that injure me but cannot divert or humble me." [Letter to Erich von Kahler, *Briefe II*]

DIESER FRIEDE (Stockholm: Bermann/Fischer, 1938. 9,000 copies. "Printed in the USA")
THIS PEACE (New York: Alfred A. Knopf, 1938. 38 pp. Also in ORDER OF THE DAY)

September 29, 1938
At the conference in Munich, Chamberlain and Daladier agree to Hitler's demand that the German-speaking area of Czechoslovakia (Sudentenland) become a part of the Reich; thus by yielding to Hitler, they temporarily preserve the peace.

ACHTUNG, EUROPA! AUFSÄTZE ZUR ZEIT (New York: Longmans, Green & Co. Alliance Book Corporation, 1938—Stockholm: Bermann/Fischer, 1938. 3,000 copies)

October 1, 1938
German troops march into Czechoslovakia. In deep despair over the political situation, T.M. writes the essay *This Peace*. "You can imagine what it has been for me: first my days of uncertainty in Paris, then the week of dejection on the ship with tormentingly faulty reports, the hours of tense hope after my arrival, culminating in a mass meeting in Madison Square Garden, where I spoke and witnessed horrifying

testimonies. Now comes 'Munich' and my ultimate comprehension of the filthy game that was being played all the time, the climax of it all being the betrayal of their own people by the 'democratic' nations because of Hitler's extortion tactics. . . . The shame, the disgust, the loss of all hope. For days I was truly ill with despondency yet under these circumstances had to take up my position here." [Letter to Erich von Kahler, *Briefe II*]

The essay, *This Peace* (under the title, *Die Höhe des Augenblicks*), serves as a foreword to the collection of political essays entitled *Achtung, Europa!*. The excerpt from the *Tagebuchblätter* entitled *A Brother* was left out of the collection at the request of Gottfried Bermann Fischer. "It grieved me that *A Brother* had to be withdrawn, and I have taken it somehow as a defeat, for this was the first time that I could not present my sadness, hate, and scorn before the world. But I have seen the necessity of removing it, and you are, of course, right that the foreword is incomparably more important than that ironic jest." [Letter to Gottfried Bermann Fischer, *Briefe II*]

BRUDER HITLER (DAS NEUE TAGEBUCH, Paris, March 25, 1939)
THIS MAN IS MY BROTHER (ESQUIRE, March, 1938)
A BROTHER (ORDER OF THE DAY)
SCHOPENHAUER (Stockholm: Bermann/Fischer, 1938—Schriftenreihe "Ausblicke." 4,000 copies)
SCHOPENHAUER (ESSAYS OF THREE DECADES)

At the same time as the collection, *Achtung, Europa!, This Peace* appears in English in a separate edition. The Schopenhauer essay appears in the series, "Ausblicke," and later in English as the foreword to the selection entitled *The Living Thoughts of Schopenhauer*.

October 1, 1938

T.M. takes up his position as Lecturer in the Humanities at Princeton.

November 9, 1938

He gives a speech at a Book and Author Luncheon at the Waldorf Astoria Hotel in New York.

November 28 and 29, 1938

On two evenings he gives a public lecture on Goethe's *Faust*, in Alexander Hall at Princeton.

AUS DEM PRINCETONER KOLLEG ÜBER FAUST (MASS UND WERT, Zürich, May–June, 1939)

Autumn–Winter, 1938

Of the social life at Princeton, Klaus Mann writes: "Guests rarely came en masse but rather singly or in little groups—friends from New York, like Martin Gumpert, W. H. Auden, Tom Curtiss; or Princeton neighbors, among them, Albert Einstein with his beautiful silver mane, domed forehead, and wily piercing glance. . . . Also Erich von Kahler was there again. . . . With him came Hermann Broch, the Austrian. . . ." [*Der Wendepunkt* by Klaus Mann (also written in English as *The Turning Point*, but here translated from German)]

The Mann home becomes more and more the center for aid and advice to German and Austrian emigrants. T.M. and Katja write countless letters to influential people, sign affidavits, support the various committees, help in securing money. "My correspondence . . . has swollen alarmingly, until no less than three people must help me with it: my wife, an English lady living here (Mrs. Molly Shenstone), and Dr. Meisel, who did such a marvelous translation of the book by Borgese and who now also lives in Princeton." [Letter to Gottfried Bermann Fischer, *Briefe II*]

T.M. makes fruitless efforts to obtain immigration papers for endangered members of the Thomas Mann Society in Prague (which already has been dissolved). Some of the members eventually succeed in reaching England.

December, 1938

He again resumes work on *The Beloved Returns*. "Only now have I actually got to work on 'Lotte' and pursue her every morning a bit further, as far as the demands permit which this country, in its naïve enthusiasm, places upon me." [Letter to Gottfried Bermann Fischer, December 6, 1938, *Briefe II*]

December 5, 1938

He gives a speech on the "Deutscher Tag" in New York, sponsored by the "Deutsch-amerikanisches Kulturbund." "Yesterday, I had the opportunity to spread some propaganda for German books. I made a warm plea to German-Americans for the Alliance Book Corporation as well as the Forum Collection. After all, there were four thousand listeners present." [Letter to Gottfried Bermann Fischer, *Briefe II*]

REDE AUF DEM DEUTSCHEN TAG IN NEW YORK (VOLKS-ECHO, New York, December 10, 1938)

Mid-December, 1938

He reads to Erich von Kahler from the seventh chapter of *The Beloved Returns*. "Kahler was so impressed with the first twenty-five pages, which I recently read to him, that he went so far as to use the word 'magnificent'. I said that it depended on circumstances, but if one venture into it, he is trapped in 'magnificence.' He laughed about the 'trapped in' [*geraten*], and yet that is the right word. I am writing very slowly on the chapter and enjoying the intimateness, not to mention the *unio mystica*, which is indescribable." [Letter to Ferdinand Lion, *Briefe II*]

End of December, 1938

T.M. writes a "manifesto" that "should, so to speak, be supported by the whole moral and intellectual world through its most prominent representatives and bring some degree of solace and strength into a world that has been plunged into deep moral confusion by the latest triumphs of injustice and force." [Letter to Harry Slochower, *Briefe II*]

The text is sent also to James T. Farrell, who writes an article in the *New York Herald Tribune* denouncing the still unpublished manifesto. Because of Farrell's indiscreet act, T.M. withdraws the document.

T.M. writes the foreword to *Escape to Life*, a book about the German emigration by Erika and Klaus Mann.

LETTER in ESCAPE TO LIFE by Erika and Klaus Mann (New York: Houghton Mifflin & Co., 1939)

January 4, 1939

He visits Stefan Zweig, who has only recently arrived from England.

January 17, 1939

In Alexander Hall at Princeton, T.M. gives a public lecture on Richard Wagner.

He makes an effort to obtain a subsidy in the United States for the periodical, *Mass und Wert*. ". . . I am persisting in the effort to continue this one important free German periodical. It is the only one of its kind, and its downfall, in every sense, would be a sad affair." [Letter to Emil Oprecht, *Briefe II*]

February 13, 1939

He gives a public lecture at Princeton on Sigmund Freud. "For the lecture in English, I have used essentially the same one that I gave three years ago at Freud's eightieth birthday." [Letter to Albert Einstein, *Briefe II*]

February 28, 1939

Ludwig Hardt reads at the Mann house before guests.

Beginning of March, 1939

T.M. reads Heinrich Mann's novel *Die Vollendung des Königs Henri Quatre* [*Henry IV, King of France*]. "I am reading it day and night—during the day, in every free half hour and at night in the quiet before I put out the light, which, under the present circumstances, I do very late. As I read this book, the feeling of a truly exciting uniqueness never leaves me—the feeling that it has to do with the best, the proudest, and the most intelligent which this epoch has to offer." [Letter to Heinrich Mann, *Briefe II*]

March 6, 1939

Michael Mann marries Gret Moser, a friend from his school years in Switzerland.

March, 1939

Monika Mann marries the Hungarian art historian and well-known Donatello scholar, Jenö Lányi, in London.

March 8 to mid-April, 1939

Accompanied by Katja and Erika Mann, T.M. goes on tour with his *The Problem of Freedom* lecture.

March 8, 1939

In Boston, Ford Hall Forum.

March 9, 1939

New York, McMillan Theater.

March 11, 1939

Detroit, Masonic Auditorium.

March 13, 1939

Cincinnati.

March 15, 1939

Chicago.

March 18, 1939

St. Louis.

March 22, 1939

Fort Worth.

March 25, 1939

Lincoln, Nebraska, Central High School.

March 29, 1939

Seattle, Meany Hall.

T.M. goes on to Beverly Hills and spends some time at the Beverly Hills Hotel. "We are charmed once more by this landscape. Its slight absurdity is outweighed by the manifold charms of nature and life. Perhaps we shall someday build a hut here." [Letter to Agnes E. Meyer, *Briefe II*]

April 3, 1939

He gives a speech at a meeting of the American Committee for Christian German Refugees in Beverly Hills. "There is no doubt that charity, active sympathy, has today taken on a

CHAPTER SIX of *THE BELOVED RETURNS* in German [Lotte's conversation with August von Goethe] (MASS UND WERT, March April, 1939)

THE PROBLEM OF FREEDOM (BULLETIN OF THE ASSOCIATION OF AMERICAN COLLEGES, Washington, D.C., 1939)

AN DIE GESITTETE WELT (written at Princeton on November 24, 1938, not published)

militant meaning, for it is an essential part of Christianity—this new moral and spiritual power that was born of the meeting of Jewry and Greece and two thousand years ago entered civilization and gave it law." [*An die gesittete Welt*, Thomas Mann Archives, Zürich]

April 10, 1939

He repeats the speech at a similar meeting in Chicago.

April 12, 1939

He visits Eugene and Agnes E. Meyer in Washington.

April 15, 1939

A tribute dinner is given for T.M. at the Hotel Astor in New York by the American Committee for Christian German Refugees.

April 16, 1939

In Baltimore, T.M. gives the lecture on *The Problem of Freedom.*

About April 20, 1939

He resumes his duties at Princeton with a conference for the course Modern Languages 310.

April 28, 1939

At Rutgers, he lectures on *The Problem of Freedom* and is awarded an honorary doctorate.

May 8, 1939

He speaks at the World Congress of Writers in New York. "I declare again and again: before the situation in Germany turns for the better, the Germans will have to go through so much that they will only need hear the word 'freedom' to break into tears." [*Ansprache auf dem Weltkongress der Schriftsteller*]

May 10, 1939

At a conference on *The Magic Mountain* for students at Princeton, T.M. gives the lecture *Einführung in den Zauberberg.*

May 18, 1939

Princeton awards T.M. an honorary doctorate before the end of the semester because he plans to make a trip to Europe. He gives his speech of thanks in English. "This is a fine moment, for it is a moment for thanks, and I know of no finer feeling than that of gratitude. Happily, gratitude is a character trait and a talent which one may attribute to himself and take pride in without appearing arrogant. Thus

THE PROBLEM OF FREEDOM (New Brunswick: Rutgers University Press, 1939. 16 pp.)

ANSPRACHE AUF DEM WELTKRONGRESS DER SCHRIFTSTELLER (Summary in LITERATURNAJA GAZETA, Moscow, June 10, 1939)

EINFÜHRUNG IN DEN ZAUBERBERG FÜR STUDENTEN DER UNIVERSITÄTAT PRINCETON (Stockholm: Bermann/Fischer Verlag, 1939. 142 printings)

nothing hinders me from saying again with gratitude that bounteous nature has furnished me plentifully with at least this talent, which has perhaps been the greatest help in making my life happy." [*Ansprache in Princeton*. In Herbert Lehnert, *Thomas Mann in Princeton. The Germanic Review* (January, 1964)]

ANSPRACHE IN PRINCETON (THE GERMANIC REVIEW, January, 1964)

May 19, 1939

Albert Einstein and T.M. speak in the chapel at Princeton "for the theologians."

May 29, 1939

He lectures on *The Problem of Freedom* at Dubuque University in Iowa, and is awarded an honorary doctorate.

June 2, 1939

He takes part in a meeting of the League of American Writers. In his speech *Writers in Exile* T.M. speaks of the early death of Ernst Toller. T.M. is made honorary president of the organization.

WRITERS IN EXILE TWICE A YEAR, New York, 1939)

June 4, 1939

He is awarded an honorary doctorate by Hobart College, Geneva, New York.

President Harold W. Dodds of Princeton offers T.M. the same position at Princeton for the second half of the first semester, 1939–1940. "I believe that I shall probably accept . . . Presently a European vacation is beckoning me—hopefully full of productive labor—first to Switzerland, then to a Swedish spa . . ." [Letter to Agnes E. Meyer, *Briefe II*]

June 6 to mid-September, 1939

T.M. makes his first trip back to Europe with Katja and Erika Mann.

June 6, 1939

He departs on the *Ile de France*.

June 13, 1939

He arrives in Le Havre.

June 14, 1939

Heinrich comes from Nizza to meet T.M. in Paris. "Then let it once more be said how admirably pleasant it all was in Paris and what a joy this prompt meeting gave all three of us." [Letter to Heinrich Mann, *Briefe II*]

June 16 to the beginning of August, 1939

He goes to Nordwijk aan Zee in Holland, where he stays at the Grand Hotel and at the spa hotel Huis ter Duin. "We have made a proper choice with this place. The hotel is excellent, the beach splendid, and the air has the approximate effect of the Engadine Valley. Thus we hope to be strengthened again after a winter in which at least I felt that too much was demanded of me." [Letter to Heinrich Mann, *Briefe II*]

He writes an introduction to an American edition (Random House) of Tolstoy's *Anna Karenina* and a foreword to a new edition of *Royal Highness* for Alfred Knopf.

ANNA KARENINA (MASS UND WERT, Zürich, May/June/July, 1940)
ANNA KARENINA (ESSAYS OF THREE DECADES)

July, 1939

Golo Mann takes over as editor for the third (and last) year of *Mass und Wert*. "In his seriousness and his zeal—which still do not prove his ability—I put great trust, and he has helpful friends and advisors." [Letter to Ferdinand Lion, *Briefe II*]

Erika Mann travels to Switzerland. Klaus Mann's novel about the German emigrants, *Der Vulkan*, appears. T.M. writes him: "Again and again there will be those who will attempt the great and painful task [of writing about the emigration], but as for your light, good, spoiled character, 'Kikjou-Weis,' no one will be able to imitate you in creating her—she is yours. And whoever has a feeling for this method of giving life to sadness and fantasticness and grace and depth (for my part, I declare that I have a feeling for this), will pause at your paintings and panorama—a picture of German tradition and migration, seen and painted à la Cocteau." [Letter to Klaus Mann, *Briefe II*]

T.M. is visited by the publishers Gottfried Bermann Fischer, Emil Oprecht, and Emanuel Querido. On July 21, the Dutch painter Paul Citroen makes sketches of T.M.

T.M. continues work on *The Beloved Returns*. "Here I had to write an introduction to *Anna Karenina* for an American edition, which is quite successful. Now every morning in my beach hut, I write on *The Beloved Returns* and have seized the fantastic hope of bringing out the book in the fall. It is already being set up for printing in Stockholm." [Letter to René Schickele, July 29, 1939, *Briefe II*]

About August 7, 1939

He travels to Zürich and stays at Waldhaus Dolder. "During this entire trip, I have not ceased working and pressing the novel toward its conclusion. Now I am deep in the eighth chapter, which is again quite like a social comedy, and the ninth is to be only a light ending . . ." [Letter to Louise Servicen, August 13, 1939, *Briefe II*]

August 18, 1939

He flies to Stockholm as German delegate to the proposed band, Jenö Lányi.

August 21, 1939

He flied to Stockholm as German delegate to the proposed meeting of the PEN Club Congress with the intention of lecturing in German on *The Problem of Freedom*. The Congress does not take place. *Das Problem der Freiheit* appears in the Fischer series, *Ausblicke*. T.M. discusses with Gottfried Bermann Fischer the edition of his works that is later called the *Stockholmer Gesamtausgabe*. In this two-volume edition, *The Magic Mountain* is to receive its one hundred forty-second and one hundred forty-third printings.

DAS PROBLEM DER FREIHEIT (Stockholm: Bermann/Fischer Verlag, 1938. Ausblicke Series)

T.M. visits the Swedish publisher Karl Otto Bonnier, at whose home T.M. also meets the President of the Swedish PEN Club, Prince Wilhelm of Sweden, and Gottfried Bermann Fischer.

T.M. flies back to London from Malmö via Amsterdam.

September 1, 1939

German troops march into Poland, and World War II begins.

September 9, 1939

From Southampton, T.M. returns to the United States on the *Washington* of the United States Lines, "in a crowd of two thousand people, who spent the nights on improvised beds in the social area, metamorphosed into a concentration camp." [Letter to Heinrich Mann, *Briefe II*]

September, 1939

He decides to continue the publication of *Mass und Wert* throughout the war. "There was only a hesitation and brief consideration. We have reached our decision: this periodical shall continue to exist. . . . There can only be one purpose to this war: to achieve for Europe a peace which her name deserves; . . . a peace which does not merely provide atavistic heroes with protection for their historic deeds but rather a peace born of a firmly founded union of free peoples who are, however, responsible for each other under a

ZU DIESEM JAHRGANG (MASS UND WERT, Zürich, November–December, 1939)

common moral law." [Foreword to the third year of *Mass und Wert*]

Mid-October, 1939

"Recently again for the first time, I have spoken publicly, but it was only before a not very large audience of the Town Hall Education-Organization. It was *The Problem of Freedom* lecture but quite changed and brought up to date. They found that I had improved in speaking." [Letter to Agnes E. Meyer, *Briefe II*]

October, 1939

"Now I am writing the last pages of *The Beloved Returns*. The day is near when I shall again write the words, 'The End,' and on the following morning, if I know myself, the first lines of Joseph IV will be put down on paper." [Letter to Agnes E. Meyer, *Briefe II*]

End of October, 1939

The Beloved Returns is finished. T.M. dictates a recommendation to the Guggenheim Foundation for the purpose of helping Hermann Broch obtain a grant for his mass-psychology studies at Princeton.

November 2, 1939

T.M. reads his introduction to *The Magic Mountain* [*Einführung in den Zauberberg*] to Professor John H. H. Lyon's seminar at Columbia University.

November 3, 1939

He prepares a lecture on Goethe's *Werther* for Professor Harvey W. Hewett-Thayer's students at Princeton.

GOETHES WERTHER (In CORONA: STUDIES IN CELEBRATION OF THE EIGHTIETH BIRTHDAY OF SAMUEL SINGER, PROFESSOR EMERITUS, UNIVERSITY OF BERNE, ed. by Arno Schirokauer and Wolfgang Paulsen. Durham, N.C.: Duke University Press, 1941)

Caroline Newton gives T.M. a poodle. "For a dew days now, we have had a charming black poodle of French background—a gift from the biographer Caroline. We call him Nico. He disturbs me terribly, but I loved him at first sight. He lies on my feet under the desk." [Letter to Agnes E. Meyer, *Briefe II*]

Katja Mann's parents, the Pringheims, emigrate to Switzerland. "Katja is calmed by the fact that her ancient parents have actually succeeded in reaching Switzerland. This was finally accomplished through the particular aid of the House of Wahnfried, and the old former millionaires may at least now live out the time that is still given to them." [Letter to Heinrich Mann, November 26, 1939, *Briefe II*]

November, 1939

Heinrich Mann marries his companion of many years, Nelly Kröger, from Niendorf on the Baltic. "That is a good, beautiful, and comforting settlement. It blesses a well-proven relationship, which is no longer very pressingly in need of a blessing . . ." [Letter to Heinrich Mann, *Briefe II*]

Professor Giuseppe Antonio Borgese (1882–1952), Professor of Italian Literature at the University of Chicago, marries Elisabeth Mann. "Yes, we have also had a wedding. Medi has married her antifascist professor, who, with his fifty-seven years, would never have thought of winning so much youth. But the child wanted it and has prevailed. It must be admitted that he is a witty, charming, and well-preserved man and the bitterest hater of his Duce . . ." [Letter to Heinrich Mann, *Briefe II*]

Beginning of December, 1939

T.M. refuses the honorary presidency offered him by the League of American Writers because of the Communist tendencies within the organization. *The Beloved Returns* appears as the second work in the *Stockholmer Gesamtausgabe*. T.M. writes the essay, *This War*. "I have written something vigorously pro-British which came from the heart and is now appearing in translation. It will shortly be printed over there." [Letter to Stefan Zweig, January 4, 1940, *Briefe II*]

January 5, 1940

He begins work on *The Transposed Heads*. "Just imagine. I am now writing something Indian, a Maya-grotesque concerning the cult of the magna mater, for whose sake the people cut off their heads—a game of separation and identity, not very serious. At the most, it will be a curiosity, and I do not know at all whether I shall finish it." [Letter to Agnes E. Meyer, *Briefe II*]

Mid-January to the beginning of February, 1940

He makes a lecture tour in Canada, speaking on *The Problem of Freedom* and *This War*. Among other cities, he goes to Ottawa, finally back to Toledo, Ohio. "Canada was quite interesting, even the monstrous cold—according to our thermometer, it was 22 degrees below zero, Fahrenheit—that never happened to me before. The new ambassador from the United States was attentive enough to come to my lecture, and we were his first luncheon guests. My pro-British addi-

LOTTE IN WEIMAR (Stockholm: Bermann/Fischer, 1939. 10,000 copies)

THE BELOVED RETURNS (New York: Alfred A. Knopf, 1940. 453 pp.)

DIESER KRIEG (Stockholm: Bermann/Fischer, 1940. Printed in Holland and confiscated when German troops marche[d] in and destroyed all but a few copies)

THIS WAR (Trans. Eric Sutton. New York: Alfred A. Knopf, 1940. 68 pp.)

tion was very gratefully received." [Letter to Agnes E. Meyer, *Briefe II*]

February 3, 1940

"In spite of everything, my Indian story is making good progress. Yesterday I read aloud the first twenty-five pages." [Letter to Agnes E. Meyer, *Briefe II*]

February 4, 1940

Bruno Walter and his wife visit T.M. Erika Mann is back from a lecture tour.

February, 1940

T.M. makes a lecture tour of several weeks through the Midwest and the South, speaking on *The Problem of Freedom*. "The travel that is ahead of me will be quite strenuous. I am a bit afraid of it. At the end of the tour lies the Gulf of Mexico, and it will be sensible, perhaps also pleasant, to rest a few days there." [Letter to Agnes E. Meyer, *Briefe II*]

February 7, 1940

Dover, Delaware, at Gary Chapel.

February 9, 1940

In Dubuque, Iowa, he is awarded an honorary doctorate.

February 12, 1940

In Chicago, he visits the Borgeses.

February 15, 1940

Minneapolis, University of Minnesota, in Northrup Hall.

February 17, 1940

Topeka, Kansas.

February 19, 1940

Dallas, Texas.

February 21, 1940

Houston, Texas.

February 22 to the end of the month, 1940

He interrupts a few days of rest in San Antonio, Texas to give a lecture (February 26) at Texas State College for Women in Denton. ". . . a few days of rest in San Antonio near the Gulf of Mexico, where it is already very summerlike. The population there is heavily Mexican, an often very attractive type and a relief after the eternal Yankee." [Letter to Heinrich Mann, *Briefe II*]

DIE KUNST DES ROMANS (ALTES UND NEUES. Frankfurt on the Main: S. Fischer, 1953)

Beginning of March, 1940

On returning to Princeton, he works on his lectures, among others, *Die Kunst des Romans*. "I have much to do—preparing lectures for the 'boys' on the art of the novel, in which my main effort is to see that the lectures are not too good." [Letter to Heinrich Mann, *Briefe II*]

March 19, 1940

He writes a letter to Kuno Fiedler thoroughly praising his controversial theological writings. The letter appears as a review in *Mass und Wert.*

KUNO FIEDLER, GLAUBE, GNADE UN[D] ERLÖSUNG NACH DE[M] JESUS DER SYNOPTIKER (MASS UND WERT, Zürich. May/June/July, 1940)

March, 1940

He gives a public lecture at Princeton on Goethe's *Werther.*

April 10, 1940

He gives another lecture on the art of the novel at Princeton.

End of April, 1940

He visits Eugene and Agnes E. Meyer in Washington. Among the guests are the Scandinavian and British ambassadors and the Republican Senator Robert A. Taft.

May 2 and 3, 1940

He gives two lectures in Professor Hans Jaeger's seminar on German literature in the nineteenth and twentieth centuries. The first, *On Myself*, is entitled in the manuscript *Von Kinderspielen bis zum 'Tod in Venedig'* [From Child's Play to *Death in Venice*]. The second lecture, untitled, is a continuation up to 1940. ". . . the double lecture *On Myself* . . . was held yesterday and the day before. The classroom was even fuller yesterday than on the day before, although it was 'Home Party Day,' and the town was teeming with girls, which ordinarily brings a yawning emptiness to the auditoriums—however, this was not the fact in our case, so that I may speak of a triumph over the fair sex." [Letter to Agnes E. Meyer, *Briefe II*]

VORLESUN[G] ÜBER AUT[O]BIOGRAPH[I]SCHES (Unpublished manuscript in the Thomas Mann Archiv[e], Zürich)

After the conclusion of his academic duties, T.M. determines to dedicate himself only to completing his own work. "I do not believe that, even if we remain here, I shall give myself once again to these amusements. I must be completely free for Joseph IV, which is to be finished by my seventieth birthday (if not a few years sooner)." [Letter to Agnes E. Meyer, March 22, 1940, *Briefe II*]

May, 1940

The German army marches into Holland, Belgium, and France. After they take Tournai, the northern French army is surrounded. "You know the mood I am in. All this is only the crowning and fulfillment of seven years of grief—

years full of presentiments and full of despair that the others did not know and did not want to know. . . . What could be the plan of destiny in giving the most monstrous triumph to the vilest and most evil which the world has ever seen? Time will tell." [Letter to Agnes E. Meyer, May 25, 1940, *Briefe II*]

Golo Mann volunteers for service as a truck driver for the Red Cross in France. "I am the last to censure his decision, which I find humanely both understandable and proper. But the uselessness of his sacrifice would make his loss even more painful." [Letter to Emil Oprecht, *Briefe II*]

There is uncertainty about the fate of Professor Peter Pringsheim, who has remained in his position in Brussels since 1933.

June 6, 1940

On T.M.'s sixty-fifth birthday, the editor of the *Neue Volkszeitung* in New York, Gerhart Seeger, sponsors a "Birthday Symposium." Participating are professors from Princeton and from the University in Exile, as well as friends (among them, Bruno Walter).

June 12, 1940

In a circle of friends, T.M. reads from *The Transposed Heads* the chapter "which deals with an ascetic in an Indian forest." "I can tell you, . . . that we laughed ourselves to tears over it, the reader and writer not excepted." [Letter to Agnes E. Meyer, *Briefe II*]

End of June, 1940

After the French armistice with the Third Reich, the Emergency Rescue Committee is established, under the direction of Dr. Frank Kingdon, president of Newark University, and with the assistance of T.M. and Erika Mann, later joined by Hermann Kesten. The committee works in close cooperation with the President's Advisory Committee on Political Refugees.

About June 28, 1940

T.M. visits Eugene and Agnes E. Meyer at their country place in Mount Kisco, New York. "Objectively seen, we had a few days in Mount Kisco, which were pleasant but rather too social, although at least distracting. The Busch Quartette was there, along with Serkin, and I made the acquaintance of a very magnificent quintette of Brahms—rather more symphonic than chamber music—a memorable impression." [Letter to Erich von Kahler, *Briefe II*]

July 5 to October 6, 1940

T.M. takes a vacation in Brentwood near Los Angeles, 441 North Rockingham. On the way, he spends a day in Chicago with the Borgeses.

"Here we have an almost splendid, spacious house set in a hilly landscape strikingly similar to that of Tuscany. I have what I wanted—the light and the dry, always refreshing warmth, the pleasant spaciousness in contrast to Princeton—the oak, eucalyptus, cedar, and palm trees and the ocean promenade, which I can reach in only a few minutes by car. Also some good friends are here; mainly, the Walters and the Franks with their eldest children . . ." [Letter to Erich von Kahler, *Briefe II*]

July, 1940

There is continuing uncertainty about the fate of Heinrich and Golo Mann, as well as Professor Peter Pringsheim, after the occupation of France by German troops.

July 26, 1940

T.M. attends a Bruno Walter concert in the Hollywood Bowl.

Although ill with a catarrh, T.M. works on the ending of *The Transposed Heads*. "The climate here thins the blood, so I am told, and at the beginning makes one very tired, which explains the unusual difficulty I have had in completing *The Transposed Heads*. It is no important work or major political undertaking—only a divertissement and intermezzo." [Letter to Agnes E. Meyer, *Briefe II*]

July 28, 1940

ADDRESS BEFORE THE EMER GENCY RESCUE COMMITT (ORDER OF T DAY)

The Manns have a tea for the Emergency Rescue Commitee, with speeches by President Frank Kingdon and T.M. "It is a great, urgent, bitterly necessary work, that of saving the hounded and frightened people who sought refuge from barbarism in France, once the land of light and liberty, and who now with dazed eyes look forword to being surrendered to a cruel and bestial enemy." [*Address before the Emergency Rescue Committee*]

July 31, 1940

T.M.'s first grandchild, a boy, Fridolin Mann, is born to Michael and Gret Mann, who live in Carmel, California.

Beginning of August, 1940
The Transposed Heads is finished. "The Indian tale is still in its copied form . . ." [Letter to Agnes E. Meyer, August 8, 1940, *Briefe II*]
T.M. begins work of the fourth volume of the Joseph novel. "I am writing on Joseph, if you are interested. A theological chapter forms the beginning." [Letter to Agnes E. Meyer, August 12, 1940, *Briefe II*]

About August 22, 1940
Erika Mann flies via Portugal to England "at the wishes and urgings of the British Ministry of Information." [Letter to Agnes E. Meyer, *Briefe II*]
T.M. makes stronger efforts to help Heinrich and Golo Mann, as well as other endangered emigrants, to escape from France. "But these months were so occupied, so full of business—mostly current, grievous affairs. There was the effort to free Golo and my brother, which has still not succeeded, and the never-ending steps and labors to free others there who are in danger . . ." [Letter to Erich von Kahler, *Briefe II*]

September, 1940
Publication of the periodical *Mass und Wert* ceases with the September issue.
With the help of a young American, Heinrich Mann and his wife, Golo Mann, and Franz Werfel and his wife cross the Pyrenees by secret paths, and reach Lisbon on September 20.

About September 23, 1940
The British evacuation ship, *City of Benares,* carrying women and children for the most part, is sunk en route to Canada by a German U-boat. Monika and her husband, Jenö Lányi, are on board. Monika is saved and taken to Scotland, but she has seen her husband drown before her eyes.

End of September, 1940
T.M. buys a piece of land to build a house. "We are returning to Princeton for the winter, but we have bought a piece of ground [in California] with seven palms and a number of lemon trees and shall probably build there . . ." [Unpublished letter to Ida Herz]

October 3, 1940
He gives the lecture *War and Democracy* before the Friends of the Colleges of Claremont, Los Angeles. "Yesterday in

WAR AND DEMOCRACY (Los Angeles: Adcraft Press, 1940. 25 pp. por.)

Los Angeles, I gave a speech before four hundred people who were not pro-British and who have not only accepted America's position since September, 1939, but have often applauded it loudly. That is only a symptom. I believe, whether with Wilkie or Roosevelt, we shall have this land at war by early next year." [Unpublished letter to Ida Herz, October 4, 1940]

October 5, 1940

T.M. leaves Brentwood and spends one day in Chicago with the Borgeses.

October, 1940

He begins making monthly radio broadcasts to Germany over the B.B.C. "GERMAN LISTENERS: A German writer speaks to you whose work and person have been outlawed by your rulers, and whose books, even if they deal with the most German matters, with Goethe, for example, can only speak to foreign, free nations, in their language, while for you they must remain silent and unknown. . . . In war-time there is no way left for the written word to pierce the wall which the tyrants have erected around you. Therefore I am glad to take the opportunity, which the English radio service has offered me, to report to you from time to time about all that I see here in America, the great and free country in which I have found a homestead." [*Listen, Germany!*]

T.M. contributes the amount of the honorarium which would have been paid to him for the radio programs to the Princeton Committee of the British War Relief Society.

The Transposed Heads appears as a single edition.

October 13, 1940

German emigrants who have been rescued from France arrive in New York on the Greek ship *Nea Hellas*. Among them: Alfred Döblin and Franz Werfel with their wives, Fritz von Unruh, Leonhard Frank, and Konrad Heiden. "A grand reception at the harbor, with Mielein and the Magician [T.M. and Katja] also making their appearance. Frank Kingdon, who had worked especially for the rescue, naturally is there. I come with Hermann Kesten, who has already been in New York some time. A festive mood, much handshaking with Alfred Polgar, Hermann Budzislawski, etc. . . . At lunch in the Bedford, Heinrich . . . reports on his

DEUTSCHE HÖRER!: 25 RADIO-SENDUNGEN NACH DEUTSCHLAND (Stockholm: Bermann/ Fischer, 1942)

LISTEN, GERMANY!: TWENTY-FIVE RADIO MESSAGES TO THE GERMAN PEOPLE OVER B.B.C. (New York: Alfred A. Knopf, 1943. 112 pp.)

DEUTSCHE HÖRER!: 55 RADIO-SENDUNGEN NACH DEUTSCHLAND [second, extended edition] (Stockholm: Bermann/ Fischer, 1945. 4,000 copies)

DIE VERTAUSCHTEN KÖPFE EINE INDISCHE LEGENDE (Stockholm: Bermann/ Fischer, 1940. 4,000 copies)

THE TRANSPOSED HEADS A LEGEND OF INDIA (New York: Alfred A. Knopf, 1941. 196 pp.)

nocturnal flight across the French–Spanish border. The steep mountain path that had to be climbed was, as the narrator stated with mild disapproval, 'actually designed for goats and not for a writer of ripe age. And anyway, how does one come to this? I am, after all, no criminal!'" [*Der Wendepunkt* by Klaus Mann]

A celebration is organized by the Emergency Rescue Committee to greet the rescued writers. T.M. gives a speech. "Ladies and gentlemen, allow me to give expression to my feeling that our present meeting is a victory celebration—the celebration of that victory of which Winston Churchill spoke in solemn sincerity and described as not the winning of wars but as a deed that is certain to be a valiant memory. We are celebrating a retreat that was so difficult and successful as to merit the name of victory—a civilian Dunkirk . . ." [*Ansprache auf der Festveranstaltung des Emergency Rescue Committees*, unpublished, Thomas Mann Archives, Zürich]

Erika Mann returns from England by plane via Portugal with an English passport. Monika, with her Hungarian passport, must go by boat. "But Moni must board a ship . . . and will naturally be awaiting every moment the explosion to which she is already accustomed. There are trying demands." [Unpublished letter to Ida Herz]

November 5, 1940

Franklin D. Roosevelt is elected president for the third time.

November 15–27, 1940

In Chicago, T.M. visits the Borgeses and stays at Hotel Windemere. He gives readings at Northwestern University and the University of Chicago. He attends the Chaplin film, *The Great Dictator*; a performance of Strauss' opera, *Salome*, on Thanksgiving Day; and a performance of *Life with Father*.

T.M. and Katja Mann await their second grandchild, which is late in arriving. "It is good that, here in our comfortable hotel apartment, I have worked just as at home. A new message to Germany for the London radio has been sent off, a new Joseph chapter finished and another begun. I am now on those two humorous-mythological figures, the chief baker and the head butler (*The Two Fine Gentlement*)." [Letter to Agnes E. Meyer, November 26, 1940, *Briefe II*]

November 30, 1940
T.M.'s second grandchild, Angelica Borgese, is born.
Christmas, 1940
"We had a nice Christmas Eve with four children and German and British friends. It is always charming to see once again the lighted tree and the gifts spread about. After dinner we heard some lovely new records, and finally, like a proper paterfamilias, I read from the Bible about the two courtiers who had to go to prison, and we laughed a bit." [Letter to Agnes E. Meyer, *Briefe II*]
End of December, 1940
In Chicago, T.M. visits the Borgeses again. "We are here for a few days on a visit to our second grandchild, the four-week-old Angelica Borgese, who makes a very satisfying impression—no wonder, since she came into the world with second papers [American citizenship]." [Letter to Hendrik van Loon, *Briefe II*]
December 18, 1940
At the celebration for the twenty-fifth anniversary of the Alfred A. Knopf Publishing Company, T.M. gives a speech in honor of Blanche W. Knopf. "I think that our guest of honor is a wonderful example of that American type of woman who combines all the charm of the fair sex with admirable energy and capacity in the realm of social and cultural activity. Far be it from me to minimize or to underestimate the share of my friend Alfred in building up the famous institute. After all he is the spirit, the spiritus rector of it. But Blanche is its soul. And where spirit and soul are working together, there is creation." [*Remarks*]

REMARKS (READ AT A LUNCHEON GIVEN BY F. HURST, A. O. MACCORMACK, AND H. L. MENCKEN TO B. W. KNOPF DECEMBER 18, 1940. Norwood, Mass.: Plimpton Press, 1941)

Klaus Mann establishes the periodical *Decision* in New York. T.M. contributes *The War and the Future* to the second issue.

THE WAR AND THE FUTURE (DECISION, New York, February, 1941. Also in ORDER OF THE DAY)

Beginning of January, 1941
In Washington, T.M. visits Eugene and Agnes E. Meyer. "What delightful days you again prepared for us in Washington, and how grateful I am for your receptivity to my writer's humor." [Letter to Agnes E. Meyer, *Briefe II*]
January 12, 1941
He gives *The War and the Future* in the Town Hall in Washington.

January 14–15, 1941
T.M. and Katja Mann are guests of President Roosevelt at the White House for two days, "where we were received with astonishing distinction. The dizzying peak was a cocktail in his study . . . 'He' again made a strong impression on me or, at least, aroused anew my sympathetic interest. This mixture of wisdom, friendliness, a desire to please, along with his having been pampered and his honest belief, is difficult to characterize, but something like a blessing is on him, and I am confident that he is, so it seems, the born opponent to That which must fall." [Letter to Agnes E. Meyer. *Briefe II*]

January 15–21, 1941
From Washington, T.M. goes on a lecture tour to Georgia and North Carolina. He gives *The War and the Future* in Atlanta and Athens, Georgia. At Duke University, he gives the lecture on *The Magic Mountain*. He returns to Princeton but leaves again almost immediately for New York, where he stays at the Bedford Hotel.

January 22, 1941
At the Federal Union Dinner, he gives the speech *The Rebirth of Democracy*. "The greatest thing that is going on today, and of which the beginnings are shaping themselves, is the growing unification of the entire English-speaking world—a development on which all the hopes for a peace of freedom and common sense are pinned." [*The Rebirth of Democracy*]

THE REBIRTH OF DEMOCRACY (VITAL SPEECHES, New York, March, 1941)

January 23, 1941
He attends a concert under Bruno Walter, at which Mahler's *Das Lied von der Erde* is performed. ". . . a vital work, as it seems to me, while so many works of that time are conceived in a pale dying away. Tomorrow at noon, we return to Princeton. Joseph is on the point of being summoned to court by a breathless messenger." [Letter to Agnes E. Meyer, *Briefe II*]

January 30, 1941
T.M. has "worries about Joseph." "Perhaps it might have been smarter to create a fictitious, indefinite Pharaoh instead of Echnaton, who might bring the book in danger of charges concerning historical authenticity. The political and religious elements cannot be completely folded into the dialogue, the

description, or some other indirect device. Again, some examining, reporting, so to say, instructive insertions are necessary, and no matter how I try to guard against dryness, the work remains poetically questionable and open to criticism. Along with my scruples there is also simple exhaustion and a certain boredom working against me." [Letter to Agnes E. Meyer, *Briefe II*]

Mid-February, 1941

He spends two days in New York.

Buddenbrooks is recorded by the American Foundation for the Blind, and T.M. records a foreword to it.

He attends a performance of *Fidelio*, conducted by Bruno Walter at the Metropolitan Opera.

He gives the address *I am an American* on radio, sponsored by the Immigration and Naturalization Service of the United States Department of Justice.

MUSIK DES LEBENS (NEUE LITERARISCHE WELT, Darmstadt, March 25, 1952)

I AM AN AMERICAN (I AM AN AMERICAN, BY FAMOUS NATURALIZED AMERICANS. ed. by Robert Spiero Benjamin. New York: Alliance Book Corporation, 1941)

March 10–11, 1941

Agnes E. Meyer visits him at Princeton.

From March 12, 1941

He begins packing to move to California.

1941–1953
IN CALIFORNIA AND THE JOSEPH NOVEL [CONTINUATION]

Mid-March to mid-April, 1941

He makes a lecture tour of the West, giving the lecture *The War and the Future* in a revised form.

About March 20, 1941

He visits the Borgeses in Chicago. "Chicago with Medi, Borgi, and the baby was peaceful and intimate. Erika joined in. The anti-Papist [Borgese] read forcefully from his Mexican opera-poem (English), and I presented as best I could the chapter on the interpretation of the dream, about which the children laughed themselves to tears." [Letter to Erich von Kahler, *Briefe II*]

March 23, 1941

He gives a lecture in Colorado Springs, at the Broadmoore Hotel.

March 24, 1941

He gives a lecture in Denver.

March 26, 1941

In Los Angeles after a lecture, he meets with Heinrich Mann and Bruno Frank at his hotel. "It was late, and we had to rise at five the next morning to make the plane for San Francisco. The two-hour flight, with an excellent breakfast above the clouds and the magnificent mountains, was a great experience. Another was the reception at the airport, under police protection, with the howl of sirens as we raced through the traffic lights. This had also never happened to me before." [Letter to Erich von Kahler, *Briefe II*]

March 27, 1941

At Berkeley, T.M. is awarded an honorary doctorate and initiated into Phi Beta Kappa. At the banquet he gives a lecture in German, *Thinking and Living*. "The ceremony on the campus—probably the most beautifully landscaped campus in the world—was blessed with unusually fine weather. With the sun shining, the great amphitheater offered a delightful and colorful view from the stage, where we met with Katja's brother. Thus I became a Doctor of Laws, again something new, but I shall pay no further heed to it. Also the Free-Mason-like initiation into Phi Beta Kappa (*Philosophia biou kubernētēs*) was quite dignified. Afterwards came a great banquet, and only then, when it would have been sensible to go to bed, did we come to my lecture, in two overcrowded halls—one in which I gave the lecture and the other in which one merely listened. I had altered the text appropriately and spoke of the responsibility of the thinker to life, a responsibility in which Germany had failed, and about Nietzsche, who, if he were living today, and in spite of his romantic sins, would be accepted—through American tolerance—into Phi Beta Kappa. This excited some merriment." [Letter to Erich von Kahler, *Briefe II*]

T.M. spends some time at Berkeley and at Del Monte Lodge in Pebble Beach, and gives a lecture at Stanford University.

Mid-April, 1941

He settles in Pacific Palisades, 740 Amalfi Drive. "I greet you from our new temporary home in California—a nice, pleasantly situated, and practical little house in which we hope to remain for the time being." [Letter to Joseph Angell, *Briefe II*]

End of April, 1941

He makes progress on the Joseph novel in spite of other duties, such as an article for *The Virginia Quarterly* ("to be written in German and printed in German"), a birthday greeting for Heinrich Mann, and a radio message for Germany. ". . . the great scene between Pharaoh and Joseph, which leads to an investigation of the latter, is making unceasing progress in spite of everything, and it is quite truly the *scène à faire*. The Hermes motif—the moon, rogue, and intermediary motif—appears now in all fullness of detail and instrumentation." [Letter to Agnes E. Meyer, *Briefe II*]

DENKEN UND LEBEN (VIRGINIA QUARTERLY REVIEW, Charlottesville, Va., 1941)
THINKING AND LIVING (ORDER OF THE DAY)

May 2, 1941

Heinrich Mann's seventieth birthday is celebrated in a private home with a speech by T.M., in which he compares the "nonsense of the total state" to the "total man." [Thomas Mann Archives, Zürich]

REDE ZUM 70. GEBURTSTAG VON HEINRICH MANN (written for the periodical, DECISION, but not published)

May, 1941

T.M. gives a speech at the Federal Union Dinner at the Beverly Hills Hotel in Los Angeles.

TISCHREDE AUF DEM FEDERAL UNION DINNER (written for the periodical, DECISION, but not published)

May 25, 1941

"Erika is with us, and quite a comfort she is, an invigorating, entertaining, helpful, dear, strong child. She is only very worried, as are we, about Klaus, who is having threatening and tiring difficulties with his periodical." [Letter to Erich von Kahler, *Briefe II*]

T.M. visits Pomona College, Claremont, to give support to Golo Mann's application for a position.

Beginning of June, 1941

At a meeting of the Emergency Rescue Committee in San Francisco, speeches are given by Frank Kingdon and T.M. "My speech is already finished and describes quite drastically what we emigrants have had to put up with in the past eight years from a world of stupidity, evil, and unwillingness to accept the inevitable." [Letter to Erich von Kahler, May 25, 1941, *Briefe II*]

VOR DEM AMERICAN RESCUE COMMITTEE (ALTES UND NEUES. Frankfurt on Main: S. Fischer, 1953)

June, 1941

T.M. carries on a conversation with Professor John T. Frederick in the radio series "Of Men and Books," about *The Transposed Heads*.

June 17, 1941
Erika Mann flies to England again at the request of the British Ministry of Information.
T.M. writes an article for *Decision* and several forewords to American publications.

GERMANY'S GUILT AND MISSION (DECISION, New York, July, 1941)
PREFACE (to Martin Niemöller's GOD IS MY FÜHRER. New York, 1941. Also in ORDER OF THE DAY)
HOMAGE (in Franz Kafka's THE CASTLE. New York: Alfred A. Knopf, 1941)
PREFACE (to Martin Gumpert's FIRST PAPERS. New York: Duell, Sloan, Pearce, 1941)

July, 1941
Professor Alfred Pringsheim dies in Zürich at the age of ninety. Work begins on T.M.'s house. "Where the house is to be built, numerous lemon trees have been felled, and the foundation of the little house appears in the form of a trellis on the ground. Thus at my visit yesterday, I saw the space for my future study, in which my books and my desk from Munich will stand and where I shall presumably finish *Joseph*. Strange. The group of chapters dealing with the great conversation between J. and Pharaoh, which leads to J.'s elevation, has now become clear to me and is reaching its conclusion." [Letter to Agnes E. Meyer, July 16, 1941, *Briefe II*]

July 25, 1941
T.M. attends a private showing of Dieterle's film *The Devil and Daniel Webster*. Among the other guests are Max Reinhardt and Brahmane Krishnamurti.

July 26, 1941
He prepares to write the "fourth main piece" of the Joseph novel. "At the moment I am preparing for much to come, actually the whole second half of the work . . . It cannot be lacking in highly dramatic, touching, and gripping scenes, which, at the same time will amuse. It is the victory of a sly kindness over a time of stupid human extortion which, with foolish conceit, admires its historical stature in the mirror." [Letter to Agnes E. Meyer, *Briefe II*]

October, 1941
T.M. worries about the German authors who had made contracts with American film companies to facilitate their coming to the United States. The contracts are soon to expire, and writers like Alfred Döblin, Alfred Neumann, Alfred Polgar, Wilhelm Speyer, Walter Mehring, as well as Heinrich Mann, will be left without means of support. "It is simply lasting too long. What are those German writers around me to do when their emergency contracts with the

film companies run out . . . ?"[Letter to Oskar Maria Graf, *Briefe II*]

October 3, 1941

". . . I have just finished the marriage of Joseph to Asnath, the daughter of the priest of the Sun . . ." [Letter to Agnes E. Meyer, *Briefe II*]

October, 1941

The Michael Mann family, with T.M.'s grandson Fridolin, visit in Pacific Palisades. ". . . the house is somewhat overcrowded, but I am quite foolish about the beautiful, always friendly little boy, radiant with health. Certainly, he will have a good journey on this earth." [Letter to Agnes E. Meyer, *Briefe II*]

October 14 to the end of November, 1941

He makes a long lecture tour (*The War and the Future*) to the South, the East, and the Midwest.

October 16, 1941

Austin, Texas.

October 18, 1941

New Orleans.

October 20, 1941

Birmingham, Alabama.

October 25–27, 1941

Mobile, Alabama, at the Admiral Semmes Hotel. "It is unsettled, and our lodgings change almost daily, so that the calmness of mood necessary for letter-writing cannot appear, even though the actual 'work' of reading *The War and the Future* in English has become quite mechanical." [Letter to R. J. Humm, *Briefe II*]

October 28, 1941

Greenville, South Carolina.

October 29, 1941

Greensboro, North Carolina.

October 31 to November 1, 1941

In Washington, T.M. visits Eugene and Agnes E. Meyer, who has interceded in T.M.'s behalf to have him named Consultant in Germanic Literature for the Library of Congress. T.M. thanks her. "Your 'refined' gift of invention is a cause for my honest amazement. I cannot imagine a better solution to my problem, and I am artist enough to rejoice almost more in the form you were able to give to it than in the 'remuneration.'" [Letter to Agnes E. Meyer, *Briefe II*]

November 3, 1941

In Chicago, he stays at the Hotel Windemere. "I have a symposium here this evening with Norman Angell [author of *The Great Illusion*] and Borgese." [Letter to Agnes E. Meyer, *Briefe II*]

November 4, 1941

Indianapolis.

November 7 to about November 16, 1941

He stays at the Bedford Hotel in New York, except for a two-day trip (November 11–12) to Amherst College.

November 17, 1941

Philadelphia. "A day at Princeton [where he visits Erich von Kahler] will follow. Then I go via Chicago directly to San Francisco, because the last lecture is to be at Stockton University." [Unpublished letter to Agnes E. Meyer]

November 20, 1941

He goes to New York and from there returns to the West.

November 22, 1941

In San Francisco, he visits Michael Mann. In Stockton, California, he gives the last lecture of the tour.

About November 27, 1941

He returns to Pacific Palisades.

December 1, 1941

Archibald MacLeish, the Librarian of Congress, names T.M. Consultant in Germanic Literature to the Library. This honorary title carries with it a salary of $4,800, which T.M. receives in 1941–1944.

December 6, 1941

Committee meeting of the German–American Congress for Democracy.

December 7, 1941

The Japanese attack Pearl Harbor by sea and air.

December 8, 1941

The United States declares war on Japan.

December 11, 1941

Germany and Italy declare war on the United States. "The strike at Pearl Harbor has moved me frightfully. Were it only ships! But so many precious young human lives! How

was it possible that there was so little watchfulness at this moment?" [Letter to Agnes E. Meyer, *Briefe II*]
The residence status of German immigrants who still have not received American citizenship becomes that of "enemy aliens."

December, 1941
T.M. works on the chapter about Tamar. "Now it is time for the story of Tamar, a large insertion, which is also a novella. Do you remember? She is a remarkable wench who will use any means to fit herself into the passion story." [Letter to Erich von Kahler, December 31, 1941, *Briefe II*]

Christmas, 1941
"During the holidays our little house was noisily full. Besides Golo, Erika—enlivening as always—and my brother-in-law [Professor Peter Pringsheim] from Berkeley were also here. Added to these was our little grandson, whom we brought back with us from San Francisco for a few weeks to relieve his mother . . ." [Letter to Erich von Kahler, *Briefe II*]

January 1, 1942
T.M. officially becomes Consultant in Germanic Literature of the Library of Congress. "Actually, I should be living in Washington, for since January 1, I have belonged to the staff of the Library of Congress . . ., and I have even sworn the oath of office . . ." [Unpublished letter to Ida Herz]

January, 1942
Erika Mann is working in the office of the Coordinator of Information in New York.

January 16–20, 1942
In San Francisco for four days, T.M. gives *How to Win the Peace*. "The human adjustment between freedom and equality, the reconciliation of individual values and the demands of society, is called *democracy*. But this adjustment is never completely and finally attained; it remains a problem that humanity must solve again and again. And we feel today that in the relationship of freedom and equality the center of gravity has moved toward the side of equality and economic justice, away from the individual and toward the social. *Social democracy* is now the order of the day. If democracy is to hold its own, it must be done through a socially established freedom that rescues individual values by

HOW TO WIN THE PEACE (ATLANTIC MONTHLY, February, 1942)

friendly and willing concession to equality." [*How to Win the Peace*]

"The lecture itself was held in the afternoon. The theater was sold out beyond the limits of the place, and the stage was completely filled, so that I could not be present for the introduction. There was simply no place for me. It was sponsored by the Town Hall, and as usual, I had to speak for eighty minutes, which is no small matter, and afterwards there were questions, which I hold to be a proper vice of your great nation. A lunch at the hotel followed, and with the coffee, the questions continued on their joyful way." [Letter to Agnes E. Meyer, *Briefe II*]

End of January, 1942

Klaus Mann volunteers for military service. After the January/February issue, the publication of *Decision* ceases. He begins writing his memoirs in English, *The Turning Point*. T.M. continues work on the Joseph novel. "The story of Tamar has, I believe, succeeded quite well. She is a good character. Now begin the lean years in Canaan and Egypt. But there is grain in Egypt." [Letter to Agnes E. Meyer, *Briefe II*]

Beginning of February, 1942

The Mann family moves into the new house at 1550 San Remo Drive. T.M., Guiseppe Antonio Borgese, Albert Einstein, Bruno Frank, Count Sforza, Arturo Toscanini, and Bruno Walter send President Roosevelt a telegram with the request that those classified as "enemy aliens" be designated as declared opponents of National Socialism and Fascism. "We, therefore, respectfully apply to you, Mr. President, . . . to utter or to sanction a word of authoritative discrimination, to the effect that a clear and practical line should be drawn between the potential enemies of American democracy on the one hand, and the victims and sworn foes of totalitarian evil on the other." [Telegram to Franklin D. Roosevelt, *Briefe II*]

February 21, 1942

T.M. mentions for the first time a plan for a Faust novel. ". . . my study is tolerably in order, and now my thoughts sometimes go on past Joseph, which only needs finishing, to an artist-novel, which will be perhaps my most daring and mysterious work." [Letter to Agnes E. Meyer, *Briefe II*]

He is involved in furnishing the new house. "The completing of our little nest is making very slow progress, and we might have done it quite differently had we known everything in advance. What, for example, is the purpose of the large livingroom (which is still a vast emptiness) and so many children's rooms. Our social life will subside; the children are not visiting us, they have to lead their own lives. When Golo takes a job, which we must cordially hope for him, then with the poor monk in our troublesomely arranged splendor, we shall grow old and sigh . . . My study is the most finished and the prettiest that I have ever had. The library fits into it incomparably better than at Princeton, and with the radiant double view through the Venetian blinds, I shall actually send my Joseph away. But I am depressed and distracted, and what I write is 'of uneven quality,' as Munker has already said; nevertheless, the volume is supported to a certain extent by the Tamar novella. You should hear the second half. It is perhaps the strangest and best written that I have done." [Letter to Erika Mann, *Briefe II*]

February 22, 1942

Stefan Zweig commits suicide in Brazil. "And when it was evident that even this land would be pulled into war, he departed this life." [Letter to Friederike Zweig, *Briefe II*]

March 7, 1942

T.M. is called before the Tolan Committee from Washington for a hearing concerning those Germans who had been declared enemy aliens. "The hearing yesterday before the Washington committee in Los Angeles was extraordinarily interesting. It was a proper public legal process and one of the most instructive American experiences for me since I have been here . . . the studied courtesy with which we Germans were treated—it was quite charming and democratic." [Letter to Agnes E. Meyer, *Briefe II*]

March 28–29, 1942

The "Buddenbrook House" in Lübeck as well as the house on Breite Strasse in which T.M. was born and the family house on Beckergrube are all destroyed during a British bombing raid.

May, 1942

Heinrich Mann visits T.M. for two weeks.

May 4, 1942
In the evening, T.M. is at Max Reinhardt's home, "which is decorated with the true art of the theater." Plans are discussed for a Reinhardt Theater in New York.

May 5, 1942
"I am writing now of Joseph and Benjamin. While at the table Joseph fans the hand of the little one as he had done long before when they strolled about hand in hand. Naturally, Benjamin's heart throbs . . . Since there must always be some humor in the telling, I explain the state of Benjamin's soul as indescribable but then go on to describe it. Thus I entertain myself with this kind of thing, while in Russia everything is at stake." [Letter to Agnes E. Meyer, *Briefe II*]

Mid-May, 1942
He reads Theodor Fontane's *Effi Briest*—"He has an artistic charm which moves me to the point of enchantment . . ."—and Verdi's letters—"The letters of an artist have always held great delight for me, and particularly these." [Letter to Agnes E. Meyer, *Briefe II*]

May 14, 1942
"Writing *Joseph* is so much pleasure for me that I can hardly wait until the next morning. Toward the end, the book is becoming ever lighter, more dramatic, fantastic, and amusing, all of which is good for the reader. The cup has just been taken from the sack. The brothers rage, but Benjamin is silent." [Letter to Agnes E. Meyer, *Briefe II*]

June 2, 1942
He prepares the collection of speeches and essays entitled *Order of the Day* and writes a foreword. "I have finished the recognition scene and am taking an intermission to write a foreword for the political essays . . . What do you think of the title, 'The Order of the Day?' It occurred to me recently and seemed not bad." [Letter to Agnes E. Meyer, *Briefe II*]

FOREWORD to ORDER OF THE DAY (Nation, 1942.)

June 27, 1942
He works on the chapter, "Telling the News." "What am I reading? Fontane's *Stechlin* (thoroughly charming and quietly sublime!), the Psalms of David, Goethe's poems—this in connection with the scene from *Joseph*, which I am writing at the moment, as the brothers return to Canaan and do not know how they are to tell their father the news that

Joseph is alive and 'lord of all Egypt.' Thus they take with them the little girl, Serach, daughter of Asher, a musically gifted child, to sing Jacob the miracle to the lute—an extra-biblical and old Jewish tradition, which I have taken and framed humorously." [Letter to Agnes E. Meyer, *Briefe II*]

Beginning of July, 1942

Lotte Lehmann invites T.M. to Santa Barbara. "After tea, she sang some Brahms lieder, accompanied by Walter. In this she is master, and I was very happy. The German *Lied* could make one a patriot. There is nothing else in the world like such songs as 'Wann der silberne Mond' and 'Wie bist du, meine Königin.'" [Letter to Agnes E. Meyer, *Briefe II*]

July 11, 1942

The chapter "Telling the News" is finished. "Yesterday afternoon after dictating letters, I brought the Serach chapter to a close, the point where Jacob learns that Joseph is alive. Whether I have succeeded is another question—enough that I have given a problem its right and wrong solution and have brought the whole a step further toward its conclusion." [Letter to Agnes E. Meyer, *Briefe II*]

In the evening, T.M. is at the home of Bruno Walter with the Werfels and the Korngolds. ". . . Walter, who is completely involved in the *St. Matthew Passion*, which he will soon conduct, demonstrated splendidly at the piano the astonishing variation and the untiring invention in the means of expression, so entertaining in its diversity, which old bewigged Bach employed in that gigantic work. 'Well,' I said to myself, 'you do it approximately the same way in your own work. Although it's not as good, at least you have made the effort.'" [Letter to Agnes E. Meyer, *Briefe II*]

July, 1942

Franz Werfel's *The Song of Bernadette* is an unusually successful book. The film rights are sold for $100,000. "To see amid so much suffering by the emigrants this blooming success is gratifying, even though somewhat shameful." [Letter to Agnes E. Meyer, *Briefe II*]

July 20, 1942

Anthony (Toni), Michael Mann's second son, is born in San Francisco.

August 18, 1942

T.M. interrupts work on the Joseph novel in order to prepare a lecture on it for the Library of Congress. He makes plans with the film director, Reinhold Schünzel, to make a film about Greece, through which T.M. hopes to avoid the strain of another lecture tour, but the plan is never carried our. For *Reader's Digest*, T.M. writes his memories of Katja Mann's grandmother, Hedwig Dohm, but the article, *Little Grandma*, is not accepted.

LITTLE GRANDMA A Story (THE NASSAU LIT. Princeton, N.J., September, 1942)

August 20, 1942

T.M. works on the lecture about *Joseph and His Brothers*. "I have thrown myself into the Library lecture and write on it daily. It will serve as a means for me to show my gratitude and, at the same time will be something good and worthwhile." [Letter to Agnes E. Meyer, *Briefe II*]

September, 1942

Klaus Mann's autobiography, *The Turning Point*, appears. "It is an unusually charming, affectionately sensitive, intelligent, and sincerely personal book—personal and direct, even in your adopted language, which, I should think, is handled with ease, certainty, and naturalness." [Letter to Klaus Mann, *Briefe II*]

T.M. visits Michael Mann and his family. "Bibi and Gret are here with Anthony, who is very brown with dark-blue eyes and an anxious expression; indeed, he looks like his father and me." [Letter to Klaus Mann, *Briefe II*]

September 15, 1942

He writes a foreword to his first twenty-five radio broadcasts to Germany. "More people listen than one might expect, not only in Switzerland and in Sweden, but also in Holland, in the Czech 'Protectorate,' and in Germany proper, as has been frequently proved by the most strangely coded replies from these countries. By roundabout ways such replies, indeed, come even from Germany. Evidently there are people in this occupied territory whose hunger and thirst for free speech are so great that they brave the dangers connected with listening to the foreign broadcasts." [*Listen, Germany!*]

ORDER OF THE DAY: POLITICAL ESSAYS AND SPEECHES OF TWO DECADES (New York: Alfred A. Knopf, 1942)

October, 1942

Alfred A. Knopf publishes a collection of T.M.'s essays, which have already been translated into English.

October 15, 1942

"*Joseph* has only been held up a few weeks by the interlude [the lecture]. I am now in the last chapters, and if it were all up to me, the book might easily appear in the spring. But Mrs. Lowe is far behind, and I do not like to push the old lady with too great haste. More likely, it will be autumn '43 before the book appears." [Letter to Agnes E. Meyer, *Briefe II*]

T.M. gives a radio speech on the *German–American Loyalty Hour* concerning why he left Germany.

WARUM ICH DEUTSCHLAND VERLIESS (AUFBAU, New York, November 20, 1942)

End of October, 1942

With the exception of Monika, all T.M.'s children have left home. Erika is on a lecture tour through fifty cities. Klaus is in New York, where his book is being well received. Golo has a position in a college in Olivet, Michigan. ". . . [Golo] is so busy that he must rise at three in the morning in order to prepare himself." [Letter to Agnes E. Meyer, *Briefe II*]

The Negro couple who have been the Mann servants give notice when the husband is drafted; Katja Mann manages the household alone.

November 8 to mid-December, 1942

T.M. travels to Washington and New York.

November 8, 1942

He leaves for Chicago to visit the Borgeses. "The days in Chicago had been overshadowed by news of the war in North Africa, perturbing accounts of the march of the German troops through unoccupied France, Pétain's protest, the transhipment of the Hitler Corps to Tunis, the Italian occupation of Corsica, the recapture of Tobruk." [*The Story of a Novel*]

November 12, 1942

Giuseppe Antonio Borgese's sixtieth birthday is celebrated.

November 14, 1942

"The sight of Washington on a war footing was new and remarkable to me. A guest once more of Eugene Meyer and his beautiful wife in their palatial home on Crescent Place, I gazed in astonishment at the heavily militarized district around the Lincoln Memorial, with its barracks, office buildings, and bridges, and at the trains laden with war materials that incessantly rolled into the city." [*The Story of a Novel*]

At a dinner with the Meyers, T.M. is present along with the Czech and Brazilian ambassadors. "After dinner we heard the radio address of Wendell Willkie, who had just returned from his One-World tour. Communiqués on the important naval victory off the Solomons cheered the gathering." [*The Story of a Novel*]

November 17, 1942

In the Coolidge Auditorium of the Library of Congress, T.M. gives the lecture *The Theme of the Joseph-Novels*. He is introduced by Vice-President Henry A. Wallace. "Faust is a symbol of humanity, and to become something like that in my hands was the clandestine tendency of the Joseph story. I told about beginnings, where everything came into being for the first time. That was the attractive novelty, the uncommon amusement of this kind of fable telling—that everything was there for the first time, that one foundation took place after the other, the foundation of love, of envy, of hatred, of murder, and of much else. But this dominant originality is at the same time repetition, reflexion, image, and the result of rotation of the spheres which brings the upper, the starlike, into the lower regions; carries, in turn, the worldly into the realm of the divine so that gods become men, men in turn become gods. The worldly finds itself pre-created in the realm of the stars, and the individual character seeks its dignity by tracing itself back to the timeless mythical pattern giving it present-day relevance." [*The Joseph Novels*]

THE JOSEPH NOVELS (Translated by Konrad Katzenellenbogen. THE ATLANTIC MONTHLY, February, 1943)

"I gave a lecture in the Library of Congress—what about? Quite simply about my own Joseph novel. This is what they wanted, and a thousand people in two auditoriums (one with a loudspeaker) listened gladly to what I had to say about '*die ernsten Scherze*,' as Goethe said of Faust. It was a festive evening. The Vice-President of the United States Henry A. Wallace himself introduced me—a great honor—and afterwards I was brought back to speak with this excellent, charming man again." [Unpublished letter to Ida Herz]

Afterwards there is a reception at the home of Eugene Meyer. Among the guests is Attorney General Francis Biddle. "Biddle, with whom I had corresponded about the restrictions imposed upon 'enemy aliens,' particularly the German exiles, told me of his intention to remove these limitations very soon." [*The Story of a Novel*]

Eugene Meyer and his wife arrange further personal meetings for T.M. with the Swiss ambassador, Dr. Bruggmann, and his wife, who is the sister of Vice-President Wallace, as well as with the Soviet Ambassador Maxim Litvinov. "Our hosts had invited him [Litvinov] and his charming British wife to lunch." "In hours free of social obligations I tried to push forward on the current chapter of *Joseph the Provider*—already one of the last, the chapter on the blessing of the sons." [*The Story of a Novel*]

While traveling, T.M. reads the memoirs of Igor Stravinsky and biographical works about Nietzsche. "Music, then, and Nietzsche. I would not be able to explain why my thoughts and interests were turning in this particular direction at that time." [*The Story of a Novel*]

End of November, 1942

In New York at the Bedford Hotel, T.M. discusses with the agent, Armin Robinson, the foreword to a book which is to be entitled *The Ten Commandments*, to which ten world-famous writers are to contribute.

"The shocking war news that the commanders and crew of the French fleet had sunk their ships outside Toulon came in the midst of our days filled with going to concerts and to the theater, with invitations and meetings with friends . . . The usually quiet pages of my notebook, which I still had from Switzerland, were now sprinkled with names. The Walters and Werfels, Max Reinhardt, the actor Karlweis, Martin Gumpert, the publisher Landshoff, Fritz von Unruh figured into it; also charming old Annette Kolb, Erich von Kahler, Molly Shenstone, our British friend from Princeton, and American colleagues of the younger generation, such as Glenway Wescott, Charles Neider, and Christopher Lazare. In addition there were our children." [*The Story of a Novel*]

T.M. spends Thanksgiving Day at the country house of his publisher, Alfred A. Knopf, in Purchase, New York, along with some South American guests.

Beginning of December, 1942

". . . I once again saw Princeton and the friends belonging to that period of my life when I lived there: Frank Aydelotte, Einstein, Christian Gauss, Helen Lowe-Porter, Hans Rastede of the Lawrenceville School and his circle, Erich von Kahler, Hermann Broch, and others." [*The Story of a Novel*]

December 10, 1942
At a Nobel Prize anniversary dinner, T.M. gives the speech *The Peace of Washington*. Among those present are Pearl S. Buck, Sigrid Unset, and Sir Norman Angell.

THE PEACE OF WASHINGTON (in THE WORLD WE FIGHT FOR AND AMERICAN UNITY Ed. by the Common Council for American Unity, New York, 1942)

About December 12, 1942
"This morning I again took up *Joseph* with some hesitation and unfamiliarity. I must finish it by New Year's Day, so that I have January free for the thousand dollar novella." [Letter to Agnes E. Meyer, *Briefe II*]
He worries about Michael, who is in the hospital with locked bowels, but the planned operation proves to be unnecessary. On December 19, "The situation has improved, and the doctors offer a good hope that the—always precarious—operation will be avoided." [Letter to Agnes E. Meyer, *Briefe II*]

December 19, 1942
T.M. begins the last chapter of *Joseph the Provider*. "Adieu, I am beginning the last chapter of *Joseph*. It is not easy—*tout est dit*, and I am searching, really without any substance, for a final cadence." [Letter to Agnes E. Meyer, *Briefe II*]

Christmas, 1942
The Borgese family spends three months visiting in Pacific Palisades.

December 28, 1942
Klaus Mann begins his service in the American Army.

January 4, 1943
Joseph the Provider is finished. "Yesterday afternoon, I wrote the last lines. They are friendly, human words of the hero to his brothers, who, after the death of the father, are afraid Joseph may still take revenge on them. I have even taken in this motif from the Bible. It permitted me to end the whole with Joseph's splendid voice—to allow him to *speak* once again. Thus it is done and may stand as a monument to perseverance and endurance, for I see much more of this in the work than as a monument to art and thought." [Letter to Agnes E. Meyer, *Briefe II*]
The completion of the novel is celebrated in his family circle with the Borgeses. "We drank champagne. Bruno Frank, informed of the event of the day, telephoned to congratulate me, his voice vibrant with feeling." [*The Story of a Novel*]

January 5, 1943
He prepares for the new work by reading the Pentateuch,

Goethe's essay *Israel in the Desert*, and Freud's essay on Moses, among others. Instead of a foreword to the book, T.M. plans to write a novella. "I had long been asking myself why I should contribute only an essayistic foreword to the book of stories by distinguished writers—why not rather an 'organ prelude,' as Werfel later put it? Why not a tale of the issuance of the Commandments, a Sinai Novella? That seemed very natural to me as a postlude to the Joseph story; I was still warm from the epic. Notes and preparations for this work required only a few days." [*The Story of a Novel*]

January 24, 1943

T.M. sends a radio message to Germany on the tenth anniversary of Nazi rule. "The Nazis are not in the least concerned about Germany: they are acting to save their own skins. Will you protect them to the last—let it all come to an end for you and for Germany and not put an end to these mad ones before they, at the eleventh hour, outdo all their shameful deeds to the last straw and make finally impossible a fair peace born of a spirit of reconciliation? Goebbels warns. The warning is for you, people of Germany!" [*Deutsche Hörer!: 55 Radiosendungen nach Deutschland*]

January 25, 1943

T.M. begins to write *The Tables of the Law*.

January 28, 1943

He attends a lecture "given by an experienced but simple-minded stage-hyena" concerning *Order of the Day* and *Listen, Germany!* at a little theater in Hollywood. Afterwards, T.M. autographs his books. "What one will not do to further his popularity!" [Letter to Agnes E. Meyer, *Briefe II*]

February 11, 1943

". . . it happened to be our wedding anniversary—there drew round for the tenth time the day we had left Munich with scanty baggage, without suspecting that we would not return." [*The Story of a Novel*]

He is working on the eleventh chapter of *The Tables of the Law*.

February 17, 1943

"Along with the simoon, which we had to endure for a week, I took a cold in the evening after the frying heat of the day and for a time was truly suffering. I am still coughing, but it is going better now. I did not have to interrupt my work at all, so that Moses has made his steady progress. I am on page 52 and have the little folk at the Kadesch oasis near volcanic Mount Horeb, thus coming to the essential, the Giving of the Law, which I am treating as a kind of Michelangelesque sculptural work with a body of people as raw material." [Letter to Agnes E. Meyer, *Briefe II*]

March 18, 1943

The German resistance group of the brother and sisters Scholl and Professor Huber—the *"Weisse Rose"*—are captured in Munich after distributing leaflets at the University and are sentenced to death two days later. T.M. hears of this only in June. "Now the world is moved to its depths at the happenings at Munich University, the reports of which came through to us from Swiss and Swedish papers, first only vaguely, then with ever more affecting details. We know now of Hans Scholl, the survivor of Stalingrad, and his sister, of Christoph Probst, Professor Huber, and all the others, of the Easter students' uprising against an obscene speech by a Nazi party boss, of the martyrdom of these people by the axe, of the leaflet they had distributed in which there were words that say much about the sins committed against the spirit of freedom at German universities in certain unfortunate years." [*Deutsche Hörer!: 55 Radiosendungen nach Deutschland*, broadcast of June 27, 1943]

Beginning of March, 1943

Klaus Mann's book *André Gide and the Crisis of Modern Thought* appears. T.M. writes his son, who is now in basic training, about the book. "First I know how important it is to you to receive mail, and second, I should like to express my thanks for the Gide book, which I read with the happy consciousness that the greatest part, if not all of it, was written here in our midst. It fascinated, entertained, and taught me very much, for you certainly know exactly and intimately this soul and this art while loving it . . ." [Letter to Klaus Mann, *Briefe II*]

March 13, 1943

The Tables of the Law is finished. "In not quite two months —a short span for me, with my way of working—I wrote the story down almost without corrections. . . . During the writing, or perhaps even before, I had given it the title of *Das Gesetz (The Law)*, by which I was referring not only to the Decalogue but also to the moral law in general, man's civilization." [*The Story of a Novel*]

March 14, 1943

". . . all the mythological and Oriental material that had accumulated in the course of the *Joseph*—pictures, excerpts, drafts" is cleared away and packed.

1943–1947
THE YEARS OF *DOCTOR FAUSTUS*

March 15, 1943

T.M. begins work on *Doctor Faustus*. "And only one day later—March 15, to be exact—my evening notes contained the curt jotting: 'Dr. Faust.' This is its first mention, and in only the briefest of references: 'Looking through old papers for material on "Dr. Faust."''" [*The Story of a Novel*]

March 17 (not March 27), 1943

An old plan is revived. "'Going through old notes in the morning,' I have down for the 27th. 'Dug up the three-line outline of the Dr. Faust of 1901. Association with the Tonio Kröger period, the Munich days, the never realized plans for *The Lovers* and *Maya*.' [in reality a nine-line outline that was not entered in the notebook dated 1901 until 1905, at the time of the conception of the *Maya* novel] . . . Forty-two years had passed since I had set down something about an artist's pact with the devil as a possible subject for a piece of writing, and the seeking and finding of these notes was accompanied by a degree of emotion, not to say inner tumult, which made one thing very clear to me: that the meager and vague nucleus had been surrounded from the beginning by a belt of personal concern, a density of biographical feeling, which from the first destined the long short story for a novel . . ." [*The Story of a Novel*]

March 18, 1943

T.M. attends a concert conducted by William Steinberg in Los Angeles, at which he heard Mozart's *Overture to Don Giovanni*, Brahms' Piano Concerto in B flat played by Vladimir Horowitz, and Tshaikovsky's *Symphonie Pathétique*.

He cannot decide in the next weeks whether to study the

Faust material or to take up again the fragment of *Felix Krull*.

March 21, 1943

Along with his reading for the Faust novel, there is a "mention of the *Confidence Man*" in the notes for *The Story of a Novel*. [Thomas Mann Archives, Zürich]

March 27, 1943

He borrows the German chapbook of Faust *(Das Volksbuch des Doktor Faustus)* from Professor Arlt and reads Hugo Wolf's letters sent from the Library of Congress.

March 29, 1943

For his Faust studies, T.M. reads the *Gesta Romanorum*, Stevenson's *Dr. Jekyll and Mr. Hyde*, Paul Bekker's history of music, and parts of other writings.

End of March, 1943

The Borgeses leave Pacific Palisades. "The Borgeses, who were here three months (we had a good time with them), have been in Chicago now for a long time. Little Angelica, an original child who chatters English, German, and Italian all mixed together, has developed splendidly in our climate, and even Medi finally looked less like a cabbage butterfly." [Letter to Caroline Newton, *Briefe II*]

April, 1943

Erika goes as a correspondent to England, Egypt, Palestine, and Iran.

April 5, 1943

T.M. makes a confidential mention of his Faust plan to Bruno Frank. "What was that—was I already announcing this plan of mine to old friends, unclear though I was in my own mind concerning form, plot, manner of presentation, even time and place?" [*The Story of a Novel*]

April 10, 1943

"One day, in spite of everything, I set about untying the bundles of material on the *Confidence Man* and rereading the preliminary studies—with a result that was passing strange. It was 'insight into the inner kinship of the Faust subject with this one (the motif of loneliness, in the one case mystic and tragic, in the other humorous and roguish); nevertheless my feeling is that the Faust, if I am capable of shaping it, is more appropriate for me today, more topical, more urgent . . .' The balance had been swung. The *Joseph* business was not to be followed by a preliminary 'something else' in the form of my novel about a rogue." [*The Story of a Novel*]

April 11, 1943

T.M. reads "On German urban life in Luther's region."

April 12, 1943

He writes Paul Tillich at Union Theological Seminary about how one studies for the German ministry.

Mid-April, 1943

As further preliminary study, he reads Luther's letters, examines Dürer pictures, reads Ernest Newman's *Hugo Wolf*, and reads the *Witches' Hammer*.

April 28, 1943

He writes a letter to Alexey Tolstoy "as a contribution to a Russian–American exchange." [*The Story of a Novel*]

LETTER TO ALEXEY TOLSTOY (THE NEW REPUBLIC)

May, 1943

"Amid such surveys and studies the month of May 1943 began, a month in which the tenderest, most delicate impressions and feelings were coupled with a striving, testing, inventing which had already become the dominant factor in my life and which arrogated for its own purposes all that reality brought my way." [*The Story of a Novel*]

Beginning of May, 1943

Michael Mann's children visit T.M. from San Francisco. "with the two boys, who look fine and strong. Moved, as always, by Frido's beautiful eyes . . . Much jesting with the little fellow, who is just beginning to talk." [*The Story of a Novel*]

May 6, 1943

T.M. writes a detailed letter about his eldest grandson [Frido] to Bruno Walter, who suggests that the child be taken into the novel about a musician [*Doctor Faustus*] in an "allegretto moderato" episode.

While often with his neighbors—the Werfels, the Bruno Franks, the Alfred Neumanns, and the composer Arnold Schönberg—T.M. discusses music, the life of a composer, and Friedrich Nietzsche.

Mid-May, 1943

"A sizable pile of notes had accumulated, testifying to the complexity of the plan. I found I had some two hundred half-quarto sheets: a wild medley of disordered, boxed-in notes from many fields—linguistic, geographic, politico-social, theological, medical, biological, historical, and musical." [*The Story of a Novel*]

May 23, 1943 (Sunday morning)

T.M. begins to write *Doctor Faustus.*

June 2, 1943

"I am *writing* again—on the novel, for which the war in Europe will unfortunately lend me the time. The matter is difficult, gloomy, sad like life, even more so than life, for thought and art always go beyond life and exaggerate it. To be enjoyable, the story needs a brightness and, for that, cheerfulness. But up until now, this has not come from me even in worse times." [Letter to Agnes E. Meyer, *Briefe II*]

June 18, 1943

At a mass demonstration in San Francisco as protest against the National Socialists' atrocities committed on the Jews, T.M. gives the speech *The Fall of the European Jews.*

THE FALL OF THE EUROPEAN JEWS (AUFBAU, New York, July 9, 1943)

He attends the film *Mission to Moscow*, based on the memoirs of the former ambassador to Moscow, Joseph E. Davies.

June 21, 1943

The first idea for a title to the new novel appears. "The title goes *Doctor Faust. The Strange Life of Adrian Leverkühn as Told by a Friend*. The difficult story, permeated with the German Middle Ages, is narrated through the medium of a thoroughly rational, humanist scholar and thus attains the brightness which it, and I, require." [Letter to Agnes E. Meyer, *Briefe II*]

June 28, 1943

The first four chapters finished, T.M. reads them for the first time in his family circle. "The Franks for supper. Later in my study, read aloud from *Doctor Faust*, the first three chapters. Was deeply moved, and the hearers proved receptive to the aura of excitement that emanated from it all." [*The Story of a Novel*]

July, 1943

In the evening, T.M. visits Lion Feuchtwanger. Franz Werfel reveals his plans for the utopian fantasy, *Stern der Ungeborenen* [*Star of the Unborn*]. "[brotherly feelings filled me.*] Here was a comrade—one who had also let himself in for

*This phrase is not included in the translated *Story of a Novel* but is in the original of *A Chronicle*.

something insane, probably impossible . . ." [*The Story of a Novel*]

The philosopher and music scholar Dr. Theodor Wiesengrund-Adorno, whose book *Zur Philosophie der modernen Musik* [On the Philosophy of Modern Music] has made a great impression on T.M., becomes the latter's "helper, adviser, and sympathetic instructor" in questions of music. "The manuscript he brought me at the time, whose startling pertinency to the world of my novel instantly arrested me, dealt largely with Schönberg, his school, and the twelve-tone technique. . . . The analysis of the row system and the criticism of it that is translated into dialogue in Chapter XXII of *Faustus* is entirely based upon Adorno's essay." [*The Story of a Novel*]

July 24, 1943

Katja Mann has her sixtieth birthday. "Many a pensive recollection came to mind of the first period of our exile, in Sanary-sur-Mer, where we had celebrated her fiftieth, of the since deceased friend who had been with us then, René Schickele. [*The Story of a Novel*]

Erika Mann goes to Cairo as a war correspondent.

End of July, 1943

T.M. interrupts work on the novel. "The Kretschmar chapter was well along, but my diary notes of those days speak of fatigue and depression, of my decision to put the novel aside now, for I had been forcing its pace, and work instead on a lecture I had promised to give in Washington in the fall." [*The Story of a Novel*]

August 14, 1943

He sends a hand-written greeting to Alfred Döblin on his sixty-fifth birthday and attends the celebration at the Play House on Montana Avenue, where Heinrich Mann gives the speech. "His words of thanks were noteworthy. He said that relativism had caused the ruin, that today we should recognize 'the Absolute.' Afterwards in conversation with me, he went further and said, 'The difficulty of speaking about God is driven from us!' Thus it is. I attempted to suppress my protestant-humanistic background and said that Catholics and Jews had it easier. But thus it is." [Letter to Wilhelm Herzog, *Briefe II*]

AN ALFRED DÖBLIN (in ALTES UND NEUES. Frankfurt on Main: S. Fischer, 1953)

August 19, 1943

He writes *The War and the Future.* "I have been making notes for several days and am now dictating for my wife to take down in shorthand. Many times I utter horrifyingly 'leftish' things, but I hope to protect myself from any scandalous effect by sprinkling it all with rather a lot of conservative and traditional powdered sugar." [Letter to Konrad Kellen, T.M.'s secretary from 1941 to 1943, now in service, *Briefe II*]

THE WAR AND THE FUTURE (Washington: U.S. Government Printing Office, 1944)

Golo Mann is called for basic training.

August 27, 1943

T.M. finishes the lecture. "Now the thing is ready for copying and must then be translated. It is certainly too long for one hour, but I have done this intentionally so that several different titles will suit it, and I can use it, so to speak, *à deux mains*—sometimes one part and another time, another. A lecture one could hardly call it; it presents an exalted chat concerning Germany, Wagner, Europe, the coming humanism, the similarity of our fear of social changes to the ever recurring resistance of the ear to musical progress—and still more." [Letter to Agnes E. Meyer, *Briefe II*]

In the evening at Arnold Schoenberg's home in Brentwood, T.M. talks with the composer about romantic music and Wagner.

August 28, 1943

T.M. visits Franz Werfel and is with Igor Stravinsky. "Comically enough, I do not rightly know how I am to dispose of my Adrian musically." [Letter to Agnes E. Meyer, *Briefe II*]

September 13, 1943

He gives the lecture *The Problem of Humanity in our Time,* before the Jewish women's organization Hadassah in the Wilshire Ebell Theater, Los Angeles. He is at a buffet dinner at Arnold Schoenberg's for his sixty-ninth birthday. Among the guests are Professor of German Gustave Arlt from the University of California at Los Angeles, Otto Klemperer, and Frau Else Heims-Reinhardt.

THE PROBLEM OF HUMANITY IN OUR TIME (unpublished)

September, 1943

"At this period, too, we began to see much of Artur Rubinstein and his family . . . Courted and hailed for his enormous talent, which overleaps all difficulties; possessed of a flourishing household, marvelous health, all the money he wants . . .—everything conspires to make him one of the happiest persons I have ever met." [*The Story of a Novel*]

About September 20, 1943

For the present, T.M. finishes work on Chapter VIII, the Kretschmar lectures, without being finally satisfied with it. He begins Chapter IX.

End of September, 1943

Adorno visits T.M. They discuss Chapter VIII.

Beginning of October, 1943

T.M. visits Adorno. "Then Adorno sat down at the piano and, while I stood by and watched, played for me the entire Sonata Opus 111 [of Beethoven] in a highly instructive fashion. I had never been more attentive. I rose early the following morning and for the next three days immersed myself in a thoroughgoing revision and extention of the lecture on the sonata . . ." [*The Story of a Novel*]

October 3, 1943

At a program sponsored by Writers in Exile in the Education Building of Westwood University, there are speeches by T.M., Lion Feuchtwanger, Professor Gustave Arlt, and others.

October 9 to December 8, 1943

T.M. makes a lecture tour of the East and Canada.

October 9, 1943

He leaves from Los Angeles. "However, I did not part with the manuscript [of *Doctor Faustus*]; the as yet meager pages come along with me in a briefcase which also contained my lecture notes and which I never left in the care of a porter." [*The Story of a Novel*]

October 12, 1943

"In Washington we stayed, as always, with our oldest American friends and patrons, Eugene and Agnes Meyer . . . The news of Italy's coming over to the side of the Allies, her declaration of war against Germany, reached us there." [*The Story of a Novel*]

October 13, 1943

He gives *The War and the Future* in the Coolidge Auditorium of the Library of Congress, where he is introduced by Archibald MacLeish, the librarian.

October 16, 1943
In New York, he gives the same lecture at Hunter College. "The audience was large. Hundreds had had to be turned away, and the utterly quiet attentiveness of those who listened to my one and a quarter hour reading had, as always, something overwhelming about it for me." [*The Story of a Novel*]

October 17, 1943
In Boston, he is introduced by Gaetano Salvemini of Harvard and gives the same lecture under the title *The Order of the Day*.

October 18, 1943
In Manchester, New Hampshire, he gives his lecture *The New Humanism*. ". . . as a stopgap, agents will sometimes sell one to a place where one has no business being and cuts the oddest figure. That was how it was in a small industrial town where some sort of provincial public meeting was being held in the good cause of collecting money for aid to the war-torn countries. The whole affair took place with doors open, amid the coming and going of the crowd, with plenty of band music, rousing speeches, and popular jokes. My lecture, completely out of place as it was, was evidently the windup of the variegated program. At short notice I cut it down to half an hour in manuscript, and in speaking condensed it to twenty minutes . . . At the end the chairman assured me that the whole thing had been very amusing. I thought so, too." [*The Story of a Novel*]

October 22, 1943
In New Bedford, he gives *The New Humanism*. He stays in Boston at the Copley Plaza Hotel.

October 22–27, 1943
He goes on to Canada.

October 25, 1943
In Montreal, he gives *The New Humanism* twice, once to the Canadian Women's Club. "In Montreal, the police had to be called because the crowd refused to give way and threatened to knock down the doors . . . I ask myself each time: 'What do these people expect? I am not Caruso! Will they be completely disappointed?' But they are not. They assure me that it is the most magnificent thing they have ever heard . . .

Then it must all be true." [Letter to Agnes E. Meyer, *Briefe II*]

October 30, 1943

In New York, T.M. stays at the Bedford Hotel. He sends a radio message to Germany at the B.B.C. office.

Max Reinhardt dies. "Because of a severe cold, I was unable to take part in the New York memorial meeting." [*The Story of a Novel*]

November, 1943

T.M. refuses to cooperate or take part in the Free Germany Movement, which is encouraged by Reinhold Niebuhr and Bert Brecht among others. He travels in behalf of the movement to Washington and in conversation with Assistant Secretary of State Adolph Berle finds that the government of the United States would not support such a movement,—would not, that is, recognize a German government in exile. "With mixed feelings—for despite all my respect for what my fellow countrymen were trying to do, this denouement was a relief to me—I reported the failure of my mission at a second meeting." [*The Story of a Novel*] [In the previously noted review of the first German edition of the present work (*Modern Language Notes*, 1967, p. 515), Herbert Lehnert maintains, on the basis of a personal letter from Adolph Berle and a State Department memorandum, that "Mr. Berle advised against Thomas Mann's participation on personal grounds, namely Mann's application for citizenship and his non-partisan stature."—*trans. note*]

He attends concerts and the theater: Shakespeare's *Othello* with Paul Robeson, a matinee in the Town Hall of the Busch Quartette playing Beethoven's String Quartette Opus 132, "that supreme work which, by what might be called the kindness of providence, I had the chance to hear at least five times during the years I was working on *Faustus*." [*The Story of a Novel*]

November 7, 1943

In Chicago, he gives *The New Humanism*.

November 11, 1943

Lewiston, Maine.

November 16, 1943

At Columbia University, he gives his *War and the Future* lecture. "A thousand people listened to me, but strangely there was not a single genuine German among all those to whom I pleadingly spoke about uniting the German Hitler opposition in exile. One would have thought that at least one or two of them might be interested in the publicly presented political thoughts of a man whom they feel called, even particularly called, to bring about that union." [Letter to Bert Brecht, *Briefe II*]

He prepares a speech for the occasion of the seventieth birthday of Alvin Johnson, President of the New School for Social Research. He makes an experiment with the "osmotic growths," for which his brother-in-law Peter Pringsheim in Chicago has sent a solution of water glass and crystals. "And one evening in our New York hotel, after a supper at Voisin's, with many a mock shudder, we had a crack at the pseudobiological experiment. By we, I mean ourselves and a group of our friends, among them dear Annette Kolb, Martin Gumpert, Fritz Landshoff, and our Erika. I had just read aloud the first chapters of *Doctor Faustus* and now we actually watched the muddy water sprouting those colored shoots which Jonathan Leverkühn had found so melancholy . . ." [*The Story of a Novel*]

November 27, 1943

At Daylesford near Philadelphia, T.M. gives the lecture *Alvin Johnson—World Citizen* at the birthday party for Alvin Johnson and also the celebration of the twenty-fifth year of the New School for Social Research. "The affair from beginning to end could not have been more successful or run more harmoniously, and for this we have to thank your excellent direction and prudent adroitness." [Letter to Caroline Newton, *Briefe II*]

ALVIN JOHNSON—WORLD CITIZEN (in ALVIN JOHNSON. Ed. by New School for Social Research, New York, 1943)

November 30, 1943

At the University of Ohio, he gives *The War and the Future*, then goes on to St. Louis.

December 4–5, 1943

In Kansas City, he stays at the Hotel Muehlebach. At the home of the president of Kansas City University, Clarence R. Decker, T.M. has a meeting with Klaus Mann who is about to leave "for the European theater of war" and Erika, who has come from her lecture tour in Dallas. ". . . she, too, was determined to return to Europe to resume her activity as war correspondent. So we were together with these dear children for one last time before a parting that, presumably, might be for very long." [*The Story of a Novel*]

December 5, 1943

He returns in two days and three nights to Los Angeles on the "Pony Express."

December 8, 1943

He arrives in Pacific Palisades.

December, 1943

Joseph the Provider appears.

December 15, 1943

At a memorial meeting for Max Reinhardt at the Wilshire Ebell Theater, T.M. gives his address. ". . . I knew him early—the inner, calm manliness of his character, the discreet, sculptured way of speaking, his intelligently listening manner—in short, his personality impressed me as it impressed everyone who came in touch with its characteristic magnetism. And to see him at work, perhaps at rehearsals in Berlin—which he permitted me to attend, though I know not why, since they were especially strongly forbidden to the curious—belongs to the most interesting experiences of my life." [*Gedenkrede auf Max Reinhardt*]

Christmas, 1943

"We had expected to spend yesterday evening alone, for without our children or children's children, we did not wish to have any more or less good friends in. But Golo had a furlough and arrived at noon. He traveled in the coach four days to be with us four days. He is perhaps the most devoted of our children, although they all have strong 'home ties.'" [Letter to Agnes E. Meyer, *Briefe II*]

End of December, 1943

T.M. makes new changes in the eighth chapter and continues to write on the ninth. "In the novel I had much to rework, and I am writing slowly onward—much more slowly than the first hundred pages went in the rush of newness." [Letter to Agnes E. Meyer, *Briefe II*]

January 5, 1944

T.M. and Katja Mann take the examination for American citizenship in Los Angeles. The witnesses are Professor Max Horkheimer and his wife. "But the examinations were no joke, especially not mine, for, unlike Katja, I had not studied. With the form of government, the constitution, and

JOSEPH DER ERNÄHRER (Stockholm: Bermann/Fischer, 1943. 5,000 copies)
JOSEPH THE PROVIDER (New York: Alfred A. Knopf, 1944. 608 pp.)

GEDENKREDE AUF MAX REINHARDT (in ALTES UND NEUES. Frankfurt on Main: S. Fischer, 1953)

the departments of government I was relatively familiar, but when the lady examining us came to speak of the power and legislation of the single states and cities, I had no idea and could only express my great astonishment at the individual authority of these units, since I had to say something." [Letter to Agnes E. Meyer, *Briefe II*]
Klaus Mann is in Italy. Erika is back from her trip through the Near East and is now on a lecture tour through the United States as her agent Colston Leigh's "big horse."

January, 1944
"My worries are for Adrian Leverkühn and the problem of making readable the musical details that obtrude, such things as polyphony in modern, essentially homophonic harmonic music like Brahms' or even Bach's . . . With such problems, Adrian occupies himself excellently." [Letter to Agnes E. Meyer, *Briefe II*]

February 16, 1944
"Now, for the time being, the young adept has broken with music and is studying theology at Halle—a broad, peculiar field." [Letter to Agnes E. Meyer, *Briefe II*]
T.M. writes a tribute to Bruno Walter who celebrates his fiftieth year as a conductor.

MISSION OF MUSIC TRIBUTE TO BRUNO WALTER (NEW YORK TIMES MAGAZINE, March 19, 1944)

Beginning of March, 1944
Chapter XIII, with Schleppfuss' colleague and the witch story, is finished.

March 6, 1944
Dominica Borgese, T.M.'s fourth grandchild, is born.
Hermann Hesse's *Magister Ludi* arrives, of which T.M. has already read the introduction. "Now, seeing the whole thing, I was almost alarmed at its kinship with the task I had elected: the same idea of fictional biography—with the dashes of parody that this form necessarily involves; the same connection with music. Also, a criticism of culture and our era, although from the point of view of a visionary cultural utopia and theory of culture rather than of a passionate and telling dramatization of our tragedy." [*The Story of a Novel*]

About March 22 to April 5, 1944
T.M. visits the Borgeses in Chicago. "The visit was for Medi and the new grandchild, Domenica . . . We had snowstorms, hail, winter squalls, and murderous winds there, and

I am happy to be home again all in one piece except for the obligatory cold, which the sun here will soon cure. Of my younger friends, one after the other is doing poorly: Werfel, Lubitsch, Speyer, Schoenberg—all with severe heart trouble. And now, in our absence, Bruno Frank almost died of coronary thrombosis . . ." [Letter to Annette Kolb, *Briefe II*]

April, 1944

T.M. sends a handwritten greeting to Lion Feuchtwanger on his sixtieth birthday, July 7. It is to be sent through the editor of the magazine *Aufbau*, in New York. "Let me make it short and cordial . . . It can hardly have escaped your notice that you are dear to me and that I seek out your company with preference when we come together in a group. That is easy to explain: you are a dear, cheerful, open, and—excuse the phrase—true-hearted man, whose talk reminds me of Munich and makes me feel comfortable. Besides this, you are a knowledgeable, experienced man, from whom one can learn something, and behind your very human personality, there is your vast and lively work, historically accurate, clear and sharp in its criticism of our epoch—a fortunate work, which, since its inception, has won a broad appeal . . ." [Letter to Lion Feuchtwanger, *Briefe II*]

Mid-April, 1944

Chapter XIV is finished, and Chapter XV is written in ten days. "That chapter contains the correspondence between Adrian and Kretschmar and, in Adrian's letter, the undeclared reproduction of the third *Meistersinger* prelude, which gave me great pleasure." [*The Story of a Novel*]

May–June, 1944

"Work on the novel, in spite of many a weary hour, many a spell of depression springing from the 'consciousness of writing falsely,' had now regained something of its initial impetus. Was this because 'my season' had come—May and June, the season of my birth, when there was usually an upswing in my vital forces? Chapter XVI, with Adrian's letter from Leipzig, which introduces in montage Nietzsche's adventure in the Cologne bordello, and Chapter XVII, in which the letter is analyzed by his anxious friend, followed one another in quick succession. I had escaped from the tangle of motifs in the expositional part of the book and saw clear action before me." [*The Story of a Novel*]

End of May, 1944

T.M. refuses to sign the manifesto of the Council for Democratic Germany or to take a public position with respect to it. Instead, he publishes his radio message to Germany of May 1, 1944. ". . . I want to publish my most recent B.B.C. broadcast to Germany in the original. It has to do with the Council in as much as it protests the slogan for the German people's enslavement—the slogan which has been invented [by some anti-Hitler Germans in exile] to become the new shibboleth for nationalistic revenge and to play the part which the words 'Dolchstoss' [dagger-thrust] and 'Schandfrieden' [infamous peace] played in 1918." [Letter to Clifton Fadiman, *Briefe II*]

PLAIN WORDS TO THE GERMAN PEOPLE (ROTARIAN, Chicago, October, 1944)
WHAT IS GERMAN? (ATLANTIC MONTHLY, May, 1944)

June 6, 1944

D–Day, the British and Americans land in Normandy. "On the morning of June 6, my sixty-ninth birthday, Agnes Meyer telephoned from Washington, before I had even glanced at the newspapers, not only to bestow her congratulations but to tell me the news that the invasion of France had begun. She had received gratifying reports directly from the War Department. It was a moment of great emotion, and looking back upon the adventures of these eleven years I could not help but see a meaningful dispensation, one of the harmonies of my life, in the fact that the longed-for, the scarcely-thought-possible event, was taking place on this day, my day. Naturally thoughts of the invasion, and the earnest hope that it would continue to go well, overshadowed all the festive gaieties the day brought me." [*The Story of a Novel*]

"On that day, we were without our children and grandchildren and only had a few good friends [the Werfels and the Franks] in for supper." [Letter to Caroline Newton, *Briefe II*]

June, 1944

T.M. becomes ill with "stomach and intestinal flu, which is going around here now." In spite of this, he continues to work on *Doctor Faustus*. "During my illness, I wrote something good—Adrian's relations with the prostitute; from whom, although warned, he takes the disease, whereupon two physicians to whom he turns are done away with by the Devil. It is very exciting and mysterious. Bruno Frank thinks it grand. The early motif of the tropical butterfly (Hetaera Esmeralda) enters again for the episode." [Letter to Agnes E. Meyer, *Briefe II*]

June 23, 1944

After taking the oath in Los Angeles, he receives American citizenship. "So were we now American citizens, and I am glad to think . . . that I became one under Roosevelt, in *his* America." [*The Story of a Novel*]

July 1, 1944

Joseph the Provider is selected by the Book-of-the-Month Club, which assures it of wide distribution. T.M. celebrates his golden anniversary as a writer. "*The Chicago Sun*, unnaturally well-informed, was even able to announce that, with the appearance of the *Provider*, I celebrate my golden anniversary as a writer, for it is exactly fifty years since my first story was printed in the Leipzig *Gesellschaft*. This had really slipped my mind, but it is true." [Letter to Agnes E. Meyer, *Briefe II*]

July, 1944

Of Chapter XX: "The next thing to do in the novel was the portrait of Rüdiger Schildknapp. It turned out an artistically successful bit, and at the time I was not even conscious of its recklessness in human terms—for it was a portrait, though a highly stylized one which differs in essential details from its model. Moreover, Europe, Germany, and all who lived there —or no longer lived—were separated by too deep and ultimate a gulf, were too submerged, belonged too much to the past and to dreams . . ." [*The Story of a Novel*]

T.M. is involved in a controversy with Professor Henri Peyre of Yale, who accuses T.M. of having pled for a "soft peace" with Germany in the essay *What is German?*. "Professor Peyre sees in it [the essay] a plea for the granting of a 'soft peace' to Germany. That, to be sure, is a misunderstanding. The sole purpose of my article was to identify, objectively and psychologically, certain traits of German character with which I am only too familiar and which have become disastrous for Germany and the world." [*In My Defense*]

IN MY DEFENSE (ATLANTIC MONTHLY, October, 1944)

July 20, 1944

The plan to assassinate Hitler fails. "Terrible reports came through on the growing massacre of the Jews; then accounts of the generals' attempt to assassinate Hitler, of the failure of the coup, the mass execution of army officers, the complete Nazification of the army, and a kind of general mobilization of the people—Goebbel's 'total war.'" [*The Story of a Novel*]

July 29, 1944

In a letter to President Beneš, T.M. explains why he is rejecting his Czech citizenship to become an American citizen. "I received the kindliest of replies." [*The Story of a Novel*]

He receives a visit from Ernst Křenek and his wife. "The summer weeks . . . brought us a visit of importance to me. Ernst Křenek and his wife came to stay, and I was able to thank him for *Music Here and Now*. On our walk under the palm trees of Ocean Avenue, and afterwards at our house, I was able to learn a great deal of value from him on the fate of music in the past forty years, its present status, the relationship of the public and various types of soloists and conductors to its new forms." [*The Story of a Novel*]

August, 1944

T.M.'s portrait is painted by William Earl Singer. Michael Mann's family from San Francisco and Katja Mann's brother, Peter Pringsheim, from Chicago visit at Pacific Palisades. "Michael has brought much music into our house, which suits me very well. The string quartette made a return visit along with guests and a buffet dinner conjured up by Katja. There were some excellent players—Temianka and van den Burg—and Bibi did quite well on the viola. There were wonderful piece to hear: above all a quartette by Mozart arrested me—one of the six he dedicated to Haydn and with which, so it seems, he took especial pains; thus it must be something just right. For the second or third time, I got to hear Beethoven's Opus 132, a colossal work, colossal especially in the lyrical movement and the indescribable last one." [Letter to Bruno Walter, *Briefe II*]

End of August, 1944

After finishing Chapter XII, about twelve-tone music, T.M. pauses in his work on *Doctor Faustus* and writes some short articles: a foreword to Bruno Frank's *Cervantes* and a foreword to a Swedish edition of Grimmelshausen's *Simplicius Simplicissimus*. He plans to give a lecture at the Library of Congress about Germany and the Germans.

VORWORT ZU BRUNO FRANKS CERVANTES (unpublished)
FÖRETAL (In Hans Jakob Christoffel Grimmelshausen's DEN ÄVENTYLIGE SIMPLICISSIMUS. Stockholm: 1944)
DAS GESETZ (Los Angeles: Pazifische Presse, 1944. 500 numbered copies)

October, 1944

The story, *The Tables of the Law* appears.

T.M. visits Professor Gerhard Albersheim, "a musician and musicologist of conservative cast," and meets "rising instrumentalists and singers, 'stars in the making,' in for concerts." He visits the violinist, Henry Temianka, who lives in downtown Los Angeles. He meets Charles Laughton, "the uncannily amusing and slyly deep actor." [*The Story of a Novel*]

THE TABLES OF THE LAW (New York: Alfred A. Knopf, 1945. 63 pp.)

EIN REICHES LEBEN (printed separately in AUFBAU, New York, February 9, 1944)

He again takes up work on the novel, Chapter XXIII. "*Faustus* is at the moment in a novel-of-manners phase. Adrian is now playing in Munich, and I am cramming in my memories of Munich social life in 1910. The atmosphere of this simple Capua, which was to become the 'cradle of the movement,' naturally suits Adrian very little." [Letter to Agnes E. Meyer, October 11, 1944, *Briefe II*]

Golo Mann is in London with the American Broadcasting Section. Klaus is ill with malaria in an Italian hospital. Erika is in Paris, Brussels, Antwerp, Aachen, and London.

October 15, 1944

T.M. writes congratulations to Max Osborn on his seventy-fifth birthday in the form of an introduction to his memoirs, *Der bunte Spiegel*.

October 20, 1944

The title for the Faust novel is definitely decided upon: *Doctor Faustus: The Life of the German Composer Adrian Leverkühn as Told by a Friend* [*Doktor Faustus. Das Leben des deutschen Tonsetzers Adrian Leverkühn, erzählt von einem Freunde*.]. "That is the title as it is now firmly fixed, and yet I think it does not indicate paralytic megalomania. The word 'German' has forced itself in willy-nilly as symbol of all the sorrow and misery of loneliness with which the book is concerned and for which the book itself is a symbol." [Letter to Erich von Kahler, *Briefe II*]

October 29, 1944

T.M. makes a campaign speech for F.D.R. "The gathering took place on the afternoon of October 29 in a private garden in the Bel Air residential section. Only about two hundred persons came, but in spite of the fog and cold that set in toward evening they stuck it out for hours on chairs set up on the lawn, for everybody was 'having a good time.'" [*The Story of a Novel*]

November 1, 1944

At an evening party at the home of Eddy Knopf with Ernst Lubitsch, Count Ostheim and his American wife, and Salka Viertel, T.M. starts to become ill with influenza, which is to keep him in bed several days.

November 7, 1944

F.D.R. is elected president for the fourth time. "I was out of bed in time for election day, November 7. But the infestion, as it often is with me, was hard to expel. It continued to smoulder in the organism and produced unpleasant after-effects: a troublesome sore throat, then violent facial pains and pseudo toothache from the 'triplex nerve,' pains that gave me bad days and worse nights." [*The Story of a Novel*]

November, 1944

T.M. reluctantly prepares a lecture for Washington. ". . . something about Germany, about the character and destiny of the German people. And amid all kinds of reading about German history, the Reformation, and the Thirty Years' War, and also dipping into Croce's *History of Europe*, I began making preliminary notes on this subject, although all the while I felt no real desire or resolve to continue with it." [*The Story of a Novel*]

Having become seriously ill with intestinal influenza and a high fever, T.M. spends a week in bed.

November 16, 1944

He notifies his agent Colston Leigh and also Archibald MacLeish that he will not go on the lecture tour.

About November 26, 1944

He resumes work on *Doctor Faustus*. "I have even begun to write a little again in the early morning hours. Adrian is now in Italy, in Palestrina amid the Sabine Hills, well-known to me. There is the stone hall where he lives, he is to have his conversation with the 'Angel of Poison' (that is the meaning of Sammael, Samiel)." [Letter to Agnes E. Meyer, *Briefe II*]

Mid-December, 1944

He begins Chapter XXV, the conversation with the devil. "'Wrote away at conversation with the devil,' now remains for two months, past Christmas and a good way into the new year, the standing entry for my day's activity . . ." [*The Story of a Novel*]

About December 18, 1944

Heinrich Mann's wife, Nelly, née Kröger, commits suicide. "The unfortunate woman had made repeated attempts to escape from life by an overdose of sleeping pills. This time she had succeeded. We buried her on December 20 in the cemetery of Santa Monica, and a host of mourners offered their sympathy to the bereaved." [*The Story of a Novel*]

Heinrich Mann works on his "brilliantly fantastic novel," *Empfang bei der Welt* (Reception in the World), "taking place everywhere and nowhere." His memoirs, *Eine Epoche wird besichtigt* (Sightseeing an Era) are just finished and appear in part in the Moscow *Internationale Literatur*.

December 22, 1944

Tonio Mann and Domenica Borgese are baptized in the Unitarian Church in Los Angeles.

December 24, 1944

"We had a proper children's Christmas, just as you see it in books, for along with the Italian grandchildren, we had the Swiss ones, and thus there were four pairs of eyes dazzled with the lights and presents. Our living room is a desert of toys and will have to be thoroughly cleaned." [Letter to Ida Herz, *Briefe II*]

End of December, 1944

"The year ended amid a number of very real political anxieties. The Rundstedt offensive, a last bold act of desperation and a well-prepared attempt by the Nazis to alter the course of destiny, was in full swing and was having alarming success. . . . But the adventure petered out." [*The Story of a Novel*]

Erika Mann is back from Europe.

January 1, 1945

T.M. again takes up the radio messages to Germany interrupted in the previous May.

January 6, 1945

T.M. is visited for several weeks by Heinrich Mann. T.M. reads *The Tables of the Law* in German before an emigrant society whose members have bought war bonds as entrance fee. "The audience stood up altogether at my entrance, listened like children, and at the end stood again and applauded for minutes." [Letter to Agnes E. Meyer, *Briefe II*]

Mid-January, 1945
He continues to work on the devil's conversation in Chapter XXV. "During those depressing days I had gone on working on the current chapter, and at a gathering in our house shortly after the middle of January I read aloud at one stretch almost all that I had written of the central dialogue—some thirty pages or so. Erika was present and was immediately able to suggest cuts that lightened the text considerably." [*The Story of a Novel*]

February, 1945
He writes *The End*, an article requested by the periodical *Free World*. ". . . a kind of obituary of National Socialism, which I believe has succeeded quite well. I used entrances from my notebook at the time of the beginning of my emigration, and they show how my personal distraction and fear were outweighed by a feeling of sympathy for the unfortunate German people . . ." [Letter to Agnes E. Meyer, *Briefe II*]

THE END (FREE WORLD, New York, March, 1945)

Klaus Mann is on the staff of the American soldiers' newspaper, *Stars and Stripes*.

February 20, 1945
He finishes Chapter XXV with the devil's conversation and interrupts his work on the novel. "It was, I noted, February 20 when I finished the dialogue and felt relieved that it was done. It comprised fifty-two pages of manuscript. Only now was half the book really written, exactly half by page count. It was now all right to permit an interruption . . ." [*The Story of a Novel*]

February 21, 1945
He begins working out the lecture *Germany and the Germans*. "The writing of this took up the next four weeks." [*The Story of a Novel*]

DEUTSCHLAND UND DIE DEUTSCHEN (DIE NEUE RUNDSCHAU, Stockholm, October, 1945)
GERMANY AND THE GERMANS (Washington: Library of Congress, 1945. 20 pp.)

March 7, 1945
After the success of the article *The End*, which is accepted by *Reader's Digest*, T.M. decides to publish more of his notebook entries of the years 1933–1934. The title is to be *Leiden an Deutschland*.

Between March 20 and 30, 1945
He prepares to continue *Doctor Faustus*. "I drew up a chronological table and survey of the events and mental processes that were to take place from 1913 to the end, and revised certain items for the book which I had had tucked into my

journal, concerning the end of the First World War." [*The Story of a Novel*]

End of March, 1945

The culmination of the German catastrophy is imminent. "The rush of events in Germany that followed hard upon the crossing of the Rhine and the forcing of the Oder proved to be a serious distraction, without lifting my spirits. 'Victorious but hopeless' is the phrase I find in my journal; I seem to have disbelieved in the capacity of the victors to win the peace after the war." [*The Story of a Novel*]

April 2, 1945

He writes congratulations to Berthold Viertel, the Austrian stage director, lyric poet, and translator, on his sixtieth birthday.

GLÜCKWUNSCH (AUFBAU, New York, April 27, 1945)

April 12, 1945

F.D.R. dies. "We stood distracted, feeling that the world all around us was holding its breath . . . We worked out a telegram to the widow of the deceased president, and listened to the radio all evening, deeply moved by the tributes and mourning from all over the world." [*The Story of a Novel*]

T.M. gives a speech in tribute to F.D.R. at the memorial service in the Municipal Building in Santa Monica.

MACHT UND GÜTE (AUFBAU, New York, April 20, 1945)

April 22, 1945

T.M. gives a speech at the inauguration of the Interdependence Movement, which was founded by Will Durant, at the Hotel Roosevelt in Hollywood, with Theodore Dreiser present.

TISCHREDE AUF DER GRÜNDUNGSFEIER DER INTERDEPENDENCE-BEWEGUNG (unpublished)

April 25, 1945

The San Francisco Conference convenes and the United Nations is founded.

T.M. writes the article *Die Lager* (The Camps), at the request of the Office of War Information, following the discovery by American forces of the horrors in the German concentration camps.

THOMAS MANN ÜBER DIE DEUTSCHE SCHULD (later *DIE LAGER*, BAYERISCHE LANDESZEITUNG, newspaper of the Allied Sixth Army for the German civilian population, Munich, May 18, 1945)

End of April, 1945

Dr. Faustus is resumed. "Events came thick and fast now, a daily hail of fantastic reports . . . Amid all this I had, to use the expression of my journal, 'shouldered' the novel again and was writing—'fluently,' in fact—Chapter XXVI, Adrian's installation at Pfeiffering." [*The Story of a Novel*]

May 7 and 8, 1945

Germany capitulates.

May, 1945

Klaus Mann is in Munich as a special reporter for *Stars and Stripes*. As to the Mann house on Poschingerstrasse, "The outer structure of our house, repeatedly struck by bombs, still stood; the inside, which even before had undergone a good many changes, was altogether destroyed." [*The Story of a Novel*]

T.M. works on Chapter XXVII, Adrian's compositions for poems of Keats and Klopstock. "I proceeded with considerable assistance from Adorno, whose interest in the book grew the more he learned about it and who was beginning to mobilize his musical imagination in its behalf." [*The Story of a Novel*]

Symptoms of a gnawing, serious illness pile up. T.M. loses weight and is in a weak condition.

May 24 to July 4, 1945

He makes a trip to the East. "I set out on the twenty-fourth of the month, together with my loyal wife, supported as I have always been, beyond all gratitude I can express, by her unwavering, loving care. I put my trust in the reserves of strength which are usually released by such enterprises, in the benefits of a change of air and type of life directed entirely outward." [*The Story of a Novel*]

He visits the Borgeses in Chicago. ". . . I tried out the Germany lecture on them. It proved to be still too long." With the aid of Erika, he works over the lecture on the train to Washington. ". . . once again guests in the house on Crescent Place, we enjoyed pleasant holidays." [*The Story of a Novel*]

May 29, 1945

He gives *Germany and the Germans* in the Coolidge Auditorium of the Library of Congress, where he is introduced by Archibald MacLeish. At a reception afterwards in the Meyer home, the guests include Attorney General Francis Biddle and his wife, Antonio Borgese, Gottfried Bermann Fischer, and Walter Lippmann, to whom "my explanation that the bad was at the same time also the good, the good gone astray and in a condition of doom, greatly appealed . . ." [*The Story of a Novel*]

May 30, 1945

T.M. visits the Library of Congress, guided by Luther Evans, the successor to Archibald MacLeish. At a dinner at the home of the columnist Drew Pearson, T.M. talks with Sumner Welles about the plans for the future shape of Germany. He visits the National Gallery, guided by the director, David E. Findley. He has breakfast with Elmer Davis in the Social Security Building.

June 3–12, 1945

He stays at the St. Regis Hotel in New York City.

June 6, 1945

T.M.'s seventieth birthday is celebrated throughout the free world. "As my friend, you will be happy to hear that my birthday was celebrated cheerfully and honorably over the whole earth, so to speak, as far as South Africa. Everywhere there are articles and events and from everywhere greetings." [Letter to Agnes E. Meyer, *Briefe II*]

The Bermann/Fischer Publishing Company in Stockholm dedicates the first issue of the reestablished *Neue Rundschau* as a special issue for T.M. on his seventieth birthday. He is especially pleased with Heinrich Mann's contribution to it, *Mein Bruder* (My Brother). "Your article is naturally the greatest piece in Bermann's issue—charmingly personal, moving especially in the memories of Papa, whom I have thought of often in life—and a wonderful document in its presentation of our brotherly differences in our relations to things German." [Letter to Heinrich Mann, *Briefe II*]

For the occasion, Karl Kerényi publishes his correspondence with T.M. entitled *Romandichtung und Mythologie* [Novel-Writing and Mythology].

T.M. and Katja Mann spend the evening with Bruno Walter. "Hubermann was there; after dinner a number of other friends came, and the two masters played Mozart together—a birthday present such as is not offered everyone." [*The Story of a Novel*]

T.M.'s three daughters are present. "Eri, animated, warm-hearted, helpful . . . Poor Mönchen, fadedly lovely, her eyes swimming in tears as we talked; little deadpan Medi, who had managed to leave her children somewhere (she is without help) and come to New York for the day, enjoying everything in a charming manner and inspiring warmth. Once the three sisters went out alone in a carriage through the city—something which had never happened before." [Letter to Klaus Mann, *Briefe II*]

June 8, 1945

At Hunter College, T.M. gives *Germany and the Germans.*

June 9, 1945

The *Tribüne für freie deutsche Literatur und Kunst* [German language weekly published in New York in the 1940's] celebrates T.M.'s birthday. Christian Gauss from Princeton is among the guests. Afterwards T.M. has wine with Paul Tillich and Heinrich Eduard Jacob.

June 13–24, 1945

He spends ten days with Katja and Monika Mann at Mountain House on Lake Mohawk in Ulster County.

June 21, 1945

T.M. receives news of Bruno Frank's death. "Liesl [Frank] telegraphed that toward morning he passed away in his sleep. We are naturally very sad. For thirty-five years he was a good friend, a good neighbor, and one with whom we had much in common! He was a dear, cheerful, truly devoted companion who accepted life with his whole heart." [Letter to Klaus Mann, *Briefe II*]

June 24, 1945

". . . the New York German weekly *Aufbau* urgently wanted a memorial article." [*The Story of a Novel*]

IN MEMORIAM BRUNO FRANK (AUFBAU, New York, June 29, 1945)

June 25, 1945

T.M. is honored by a testimonial dinner of the Nation Associates at the Waldorf-Astoria. Robert Sherwood is toastmaster. There are speeches by the editor of *The Nation* (Freda Kirchwey), Justice Felix Frankfurter, the former Spanish prime minister Juan Negrin, the journalist William L. Shirer, and Secretary of the Interior Harold Ickes. T.M. makes a speech of thanks. "I should never have agreed to the plan for this meeting if I had not been able to see in it from the beginning a meaning and purpose wholly above the personal—the purpose of honoring a position in favor of American liberal thought which finds its clearest and most outstanding expression in the periodical which we are here to thank this evening: *The Nation* under the intelligent and exciting leadership of a typically American and, at the same time, rare and unusual woman Freda Kirchwey." [*Address*]

ADDRESS (in ADDRESSES IN HONOR OF DR. THOMAS MANN. New York: The Nation Associates, 1945)

June 26, 1945

T.M. reads several chapters from *Doctor Faustus* at the St. Regis to a group of friends, among them Hedwig Fischer,

Gottfried Bermann Fischer and his wife, Fritz Landshoff, Martin Gumpert, Kadidja Wedekind, and Joachim Maass.

June 29, 1945

"There was another well-arranged celebration in Chicago, which I owed to the university and, personally, to a kind friend, James Frank, the great physicist." [*The Story of a Novel*]

July 4, 1945

He is back in Pacific Palisades.

July, 1945

He writes the essay about Dostoyevsky for the Dial Press as an introduction to an American edition of his short stories.

DOSTOJEWSKI—MIT MASSEN (DIE NEUE RUNDSCHAU, Stockholm, September, 1946)

DOSTOYEVSKY—WITH IN LIMITS (in THE THOMAS MANN READER. Selected, edited, and with an introduction by Joseph Angell New York: Alfred A. Knopf, 1950. 754 pp.)

About July 20, 1945

T.M. is working on Chapter XXVII of *Doctor Faustus.*

August 6, 1945

The first atomic bomb is exploded on Nagasaki. "I had just concluded Chapter XXVII with Adrian's voyage into the depths of the ocean and 'up among the stars' . . . when news came of 'the first attack upon Japan with bombs in which the forces of the fissioned uranium atom are released.'" [*The Story of a Novel*]

August 8, 1945

In an open letter, Walter von Molo makes an appeal to T.M. to return to Germany. It is published in several German newspapers (the *Allgemeine Zeitung*, Berlin, and the *Hessische Post*, et al.). T.M. receives the letter through the Office of War Information.

August 13, 1945

There is a private memorial meeting for Bruno Frank; at the wish of the widow, it is held in T.M.'s home. "And so we invited some twenty persons, among them the Feuchtwangers and Bruno Walter, to foregather in our livingroom. From my little reading desk I spoke to them, saying that this was no hour for hanging our heads, but rather one for rejoicing in the magnificent legacy our departed friend had left behind." [*The Story of a Novel*]

T.M. reads Bruno Frank's novella *Die Monduhr (The Moon Clock)*, some poems by him, and some verses that Fontane had written in his old age.

August, 1945

"I finished Chapter XXVIII (the confusion of Baron von

Riedesel) in a mere ten days and began the following one, the marriage of Inez and Helmut Institoris." [*The Story of a Novel*]

T.M. attends musical evenings at the home of Adorno with Hanns Eisler and at the home of "hospitable Mrs. Wells" in Beverly Hills with the pianist Gimpel. The children from San Francisco come for a visit. "Frido is no longer so ideal, rather more like a boy, but he is comical and speaks English with a terribly Swiss accent." [Letter to Agnes E. Meyer, *Briefe II*]

August 26, 1945

T.M. has chamber music at his home. "Vandenburg, with American friends, played trios by Schubert, Mozart, and Beethoven." [*The Story of a Novel*]

The report of Franz Werfel's death comes during this evening.

August 29, 1945

T.M. attends Franz Werfel's funeral in Beverly Hills.

September 7, 1945

After a long hesitation, T.M. answers Walter von Molo's appeal to return to Germany. "I do not forget that you later went through much worse which I managed to forego, but you did not know the heartache of exile, the uprooting, the chill of homelessness." [*Warum ich nicht nach Deutschland zurückgehe*]

WARUM ICH NICHT NACH DEUTSCHLAND ZURÜCKGEHE (AUFBAU, New York, September 28, 1945)

"To my shame it took me no less than a full week to complete my answer. . . . But at last it was completed—in a humane spirit, so it seemed to me, in a spirit of reconciliation and, at the end, of heartening encouragement. . . . although I could predict that across the ocean what would be heard was chiefly the no." [*The Story of a Novel*]

A group of German writers calling themselves the Inner Emigration, headed by Frank Thiess, begin a campaign of hostility against T.M. "Now the armchair had collapsed around the armchair lookers-on, and for this they took great credit for themselves, were lavish with insults toward those who had breathed the cold winds of exile and whose lot had been, for the most part, misery and death." [*The Story of a Novel*]

Erika Mann is a correspondent in Germany.

September, 1945

"Worked hard at Chapter XXX . . . Not well at night:

chills, agitation, cold, disturbed sleep, feeling of approaching illness . . ." [*The Story of a Novel*]

September 29, 1945

There is a public memorial meeting for Bruno Frank at the Play House in Hollywood. "The big hall was filled, all of 'Germany in California' had foregathered. . . . I spoke last, before the concluding piano piece—spoke with strain, exhaustion, and from the bottom of my heart." [*The Story of a Novel*]

INDEFATIGABLE VIGILANCE (AUFBAU, New York, January 11, 1946)

October, 1945

T.M. is awarded an honorary doctorate by Hebrew Union College, Cincinnati, Ohio. The certificate is dated December 8, 1945. T.M. thanks President Julian Morgenstern.

Buddenbrooks appears in the Stockholmer Ausgabe of T.M.'s works (1,170,000 copies). In the same edition two more volumes appear: a volume of sixteen essays in literary criticism (*Adel des Geistes*) and a collection of stories (*Ausgewählte Erzählungen*).

ADEL DES GEISTES: SECHZEHN VERSUCHE ZUM PROBLEM DER HUMANITÄT (Stockholm: Bermann/ Fischer, 1945. 5,000 copies)

T.M. writes Erich von Kahler congratulations on his sixtieth birthday. "The true feat of his life—a feat which even now remains incomplete because of a rupture in his existence—is his grandiose work *Der deutsche Charakter in der Geschichte* [The German Character in History] charged with his enormous, carefully assimilated knowledge of history. This work, planned long ago in Germany, has had to remain a torso, but the first volume, which alone is a monument, appeared in Switzerland." [*Erich von Kahler*]

AUSGEWÄHLTE ERZÄHLUNGEN (Stockholm: Bermann/ Fischer, 1945. 5,000 copies.)

ERICH VON KAHLER (DEUTSCHE BLÄTTER, Santiago de Chile, November/ December, 1945)

October 25, 1945

He is writing on Chapter XXXI of *Doctor Faustus*. "At present I am moving happily forward with the novel again. Through the medium of the biographer, I have given a description full of memories from the outbreak of war in 1914. Now I am on a grotesque opera suite for the marionette theater which Leverkühn is composing and the plot of which he takes from the old book of fables and legends, the *Gesta Romanorum*. There are stories there, at least one, which I should like best to take away from him and make an interesting novella from it myself." [Letter to Agnes E. Meyer, *Briefe II*] This is the first mention of plans for *The Holy Sinner*.

November 9, 1945
He begins working on Chapter XXXII, the conversation between Inez and Zeitblom, and finishes it in twenty days.

November 25, 1945
At the home of the composer Hanns Eisler, T.M. meets Charlie Chaplin. "I laughed for three hours long at his imitations, scenes, and clownings and was still wiping my eyes as we got into the car." [Letter to Fritz Strich, *Briefe II*]

End of November, 1945
T.M.'s health becomes worse with infection of the trachea and bronchial tubes, low blood pressure, and loss of weight. He consults a physician.

Beginning of December, 1945
"And so back to the novel, equipped with fat red vitamin capsules to swallow three times daily, which I did with great difficulty." [*The Story of a Novel*] Chapter XXXIII is finished on December 27.

During this time, T.M. performs many social duties and makes public appearances. He gives a lecture on Dostoyevsky and Nietzsche in Royce Hall at the University of California in Westwood. Delegates from the Russian consulate are present. He writes the foreword for a prison newspaper for German prisoners of war. He gives a speech at a dinner of the Independent Citizens Committee, "a very fine and all too necessary antifascist organization, of which I have become a member out of fear for the situation of democracy in this country." [Letter to Agnes E. Meyer, *Briefe II*]

WESTZIVILISATION (in the prison newspaper for German prisoners of war in Papagos Park, Arizona, December, 1945)

He is in occasional social touch with his neighbors Count and Countess Ostheim. "He was a 'red' prince who detested the Kaiser, Prussia, and the military and was early divested of his inheritance . . . But one still notices something of his earlier life about him, and he has at least as much of Hohenzollern blood as he has of liberalism." [Letter to Agnes E. Meyer, *Briefe II*]

Christmas, 1945
"On Christmas Eve and for a few days longer, we shall have the little ones from San Francisco with us, especially enchanting little Frido, in whom I take delight. Otherwise, our young seed leave us in the lurch, and one cannot blame them." [Letter to Agnes E. Meyer, *Briefe II*]

Released from military service, Klaus Mann remains in Rome, "where his interests in films are keeping him." Golo is working with the American Intelligence Service in Bad Nauheim. Erika is a reporter of the Nuremberg trials.

December 30, 1945

T.M. requests the help of Adorno for presenting Leverkühn's main work *Apocalipsis cum figuris*. "The problem is to imagine, realize, graphically describe a work of art (which I regard as a highly German product, as an oratorio with orchestra, choruses, soloists, and a narrator). . . . What I need are a few concrete details which will help with characterization and contriving a sense of reality (one can make do with little), which will give the reader a plausible, in fact a convincing, picture of the opus. . . . What I have vaguely in mind is something satanically religious, diabolically pious, seeming at one and the same time strictly bound by form and criminally irresponsible, frequently a mockery of art itself; and also something that goes back to primitive, elementary levels of music (memories of Kretschmar's Beissel lectures), abandoning the division into bars, even the ordering of notes (trombone glissandi); furthermore, something which could hardly be executed in practice: old church modes, *a cappella* choruses which have to be sung in untempered tuning, so that scarcely a note or an interval occurs of the piano— etc." [Letter to Theodor W. Adorno, *Briefe II* (also in *The Story of a Novel*)]

". . . but he [Adorno] assured me that he was thinking about the matter, that he already had all sorts of ideas stirring inside him, and that he would shortly be ready to assist me." [*The Story of a Novel*]

January, 1946

During the first half of the month, T.M. makes frequent visits "with notebook and pencil" to Adorno. "Fully cognizant as he was of the intentions of the whole and of this particular section, he aimed his suggestions and recommendations precisely at the essential point, namely to make the opus open simultaneously to the criticism of bloody barbarism and to the criticism of bloodless intellectualism." [*The Story of a Novel*]

Mid-January, 1946

In spite of interruptions for other duties, such as writing the speech *In Defense of Academic Freedom* and a speech on the radio at Roosevelt's sixty-fourth birthday, T.M. finishes the description of the oratorio in six weeks.

ÜBER AKADEMISCHE FREIHEIT (in GESAMMELTE WERKE IN ZWÖLF BÄNDEN. Frankfurt on Main: S. Fischer, 1960. Vol. XI)

RADIO-ANSPRACHE ZU ROOSEVELT'S 64. GEBURTSTAG (unpublished)

February 2, 1946

He attends a concert by Bronislav Hubermann at the Philharmonic Hall in Los Angeles. "We did not allow ourselves to be disheartened by the long ride, but went to hear the ugly little wizard who had always had so much of the demonic fiddler about him. He played Beethoven, Bach (a *chaconne* in the course of which he extracted from his violin strange organ effects), a charming sonata by César Franck, and some gypsy-like encores. Afterwards we presented ourselves in the crowded green room to him. He cried out with delight when he caught sight of us." [*The Story of a Novel*]

February 5, 1946

Hubermann dines with T.M., and they discuss a European tour, about which Dr. Hohenberg, a Brussels agent, has approached T.M.

February 6, 1946

T.M. writes *Bericht über meinen Bruder* for Heinrich Mann's seventy-fifth birthday. "But he remains in his little first-floor apartment on South Swall Street, from where he can do his shopping on foot and in which the memory of his deceased wife remains . . . In the morning at seven, after he has drunk his strong coffee, he writes; he produces unerringly in his usual audacity and self-consciousness, borne forward by that belief in the mission of literature, which he has confessed so often in words of proud beauty. His writing is of current interest, as he covers page after page with his clear and well-formed Roman script—certainly not without pains, for the good is always difficult, yet with the trained facility of a great toiler." [*Bericht über meinen Bruder*]

BERICHT ÜBER MEINEN BRUDER (FREIES DEUTSCHLAND, Mexico City, March, 1946)

February, 1946

The Canadian photographer Karsh visits T.M. to take a series of photographs. "Several of these, in their successes as likenesses and their graphic lighting effects, represent the utmost in perfection that I have ever seen in photographs, not just in those of myself." [*The Story of a Novel*]

Beginning of March, 1946

T.M. attends an evening of recitations by Ernst Deutsch at the Warner Studio in Los Angeles.

He becomes ill with a grippe. Earlier x-ray photographs have shown shadows on his lungs. This is the beginning of a serious lung ailment. "I had for some time been having slightly higher temperatures afternoons and evenings, although I only half admitted this to myself. I had another such mild fever in the evening of the day I completed the oratorio section. That evening I went with my brother to a recitation given by Ernst Deutsch in the Warner Studio. . . . I enjoyed the evening greatly, in that somewhat faraway, at once weak and elevated, state into which we are cast by a moderate fever. It was late before I went to bed—and for several days thereafter I did not leave it, having come down with a grippy illness that brought about fevers of 102° every afternoon. . . . I slept a great deal, by day also, and read considerably, chiefly Nietzsche, for the lecture on him seemed to be the most pressing item on my program of work." [*The Story of a Novel*]

March 21, 1946

Heinrich Mann's seventy-fifth birthday is celebrated with a small party in the evening.

Dr. Frederick Rosenthal takes over the treatment of T.M. After calling in a specialist and after a bronchoscopy, it is decided that an operation is necessary. T.M. has to give up immediate plans for a lecture tour.

April, 1946

"The vigorous fashion in which matters henceforth proceeded, and fortunately so, was due solely to my wife, the only one of all of us who knew what she wanted and who took the necessary steps. . . . She got in touch with our daughter Elisabeth Borgese in Chicago, and Elisabeth in turn with the university's Billings Hospital. Here one of the foremost surgeons in America, Dr. William Elias Adams, works; he is especially noted as a pneumotomist. . . . before I knew it I found myself outside our front door, under the troubled eyes of our Japanese couple, Vattaru and Koto, for I was lying on a stretcher which was slid into an ambulance." [*The Story of a Novel*]

Mid-April to May 28, 1946

T.M. has a lung operation in Chicago after his arrival at Billings Hospital. ". . . the doctors who were to treat me came *in corpore* to pay me a welcoming visit, at their head the surgeon himself. Dr. Adams was a man of unpretentious amiability and kindliness . . . with him his medical adviser, specialist in internal medicine and university professor, Dr. Bloch—tall, brown-haired, born in Fürth near Nuremberg . . . and a considerable white-jacketed entourage in addition." [*The Story of a Novel*]

Erika Mann flies in from Europe.

During the time of preparing for the operation, T.M. reads Golo Mann's *Friedrich von Gentz* [The Story of a European Statesman]. "Gentz occupied and entertained me for a whole week, which, by the way, was the time dedicated to preparation for my operation. I must say that even in translation . . . it is an outstanding gratifyingly shrewd, intellectually original, fascinating book, which does great honor to its author and will certainly bring him practical recognition and advancement also." [Letter to Golo Mann, *Briefe II*]

April 24, 1946

"It was a beautiful morning; everyone had slept so splendidly that they were all hale and in good spirits, first of all Dr. Adams, who worked with his customary mastery, never hurrying, the tempo precisely calculated, but saving time nevertheless by the precision of each stroke. . . . That, combined with advanced medical technique, produced an almost sensational clinical success. For days afterwards, I heard, medical circles in New York and Chicago discussed this 'most elegant operation.'" [*The Story of a Novel*]

"There was an abscess in my lung, which was confirmed by the bronchoscopic examination and which was about to deteriorate beyond help. Now I am cleansed of it." [Letter to Agnes E. Meyer, *Briefe II*]

He convalesces without complications, reads Nietzsche's writings and Gottfried Keller's *Der grüne Heinrich* [*Green Henry*], "which strangely, indeed scandalously, had remained virtually unknown to me until this moment." He receives visits from Gottfried Bermann Fischer, Martin Gumpert, Bruno Walter, Caroline Newton. "And there was never any lack of flowers. If they ever threatened to give out, Erika would come in bearing fresh roses." [*The Story of a Novel*]

May 14, 1946

"Today in the sunny weather, I was out in the open for the

first time, still with the help of a wheelchair, although at intervals I am walking quite unchecked and need only take care that I do not run out of breath from moving too quickly." [Letter to Frederick Rosenthal, *Briefe II*]

May 20, 1946

T.M. leaves the hospital and moves for a few days to the Hotel Windermere. At his departure from the hospital, he gives a short press conference in the social and smoking room. He wants to "sing the praises of the institution, the doctors, and the glorious deeds they had performed upon me," but is not allowed to do so, since the hospital refuses to have any publicity.

May 25, 1946

He returns to Los Angeles on the *Santa Fe Chief*. "The return trip took place in the most comfortable circumstances; we had a drawing room with private meals." [*The Story of a Novel*]

May 28, 1946

He arrives at Pacific Palisades. "It was the loveliest time of the year. The garden had been beautifully looked after by Vattaru, and every stroll amidst its rich display of flowers, every view over valley and hills to the clearly outlined chain of the Sierra and over the tops of the palm trees on the other side to Catalina and the ocean—all these paradisaical scenes and colors enraptured me. I was happy to have kept my hold upon the natural world, to have passed *cum laude* a rigorous test." [*The Story of a Novel*]

May 30, 1946

He again takes up work on *Doctor Faustus*. ". . . lying on cushions, I am improving earlier parts of the novel." [Letter to Agnes E. Meyer, *Briefe II*]

June 6, 1946

On T.M.'s seventy-first birthday, he writes concerning the recent death of Gerhart Hauptmann. "My thoughts turned frequently to this departed colleague, to our many meetings, which occasionally, in Bolzano and at Hiddensee, involved our living together under the same roof. I thought of that unique, partly farcical but always moving, engaging personality, toward whom one always felt affection and reverence." [*The Story of a Novel*]

June, 1946

"The middle of June had not yet arrived when I began writing Chapter XXXV, the fate of poor Clarissa—freely following life, the actuality of my own sister's suicide. Twelve days later it was completed . . ." [*The Story of a Novel*]

The writer Richard Schweizer from Zürich visits T.M. They discuss the differing versions of Gottfried Keller's *Green Henry*. After returning to Zürich, Schweizer sends T.M. the eight-volume edition of the novel edited by Jonas Fränkel and containing the two versions.

In Weimar at the Goethe-Haus, a series of lectures is held on *The Beloved Returns*, "under Russian sponsorship."

ZWEI ROMAN-FRAGMENTE DER VATER and OPUS III (DIE NEUE RUNDSCHAU, Stockholm, June, 1946)

End of June to mid-July, 1946

T.M. writes Chapter XXXVI, "recalling the atmosphere of the twenties in Germany and introducing the invisible friend, that model of deepest discretion. I amused myself describing her gift of the ring." [*The Story of a Novel*]

Mid-July, 1946

He prepares and writes Chapter XXXVII. "I had long had in mind the character of the international impresario, had long ago conceived of the symbolic temptation from solitude exerted by the 'world.' As for the idea of doing the scene as a long monologue by the amusing tempter, with the reactions of his hearers merely hinted at—that came to me at once, as soon as I had assembled the materials for the conversation." [*The Story of a Novel*]

He interrupts his writing on the novel to prepare a greeting for Bruno Walter on his seventieth birthday, September 15.

AN BRUNO WALTER (AUFBAU, New York, September 13, 1946)
TO BRUNO WALTER ON HIS SEVENTIETH BIRTHDAY (THE MUSICAL QUARTERLY, October, 1946)

Mid-August, 1946

T.M. finishes the Fitelberg chapter. "It provides a refreshing episode amid all the gloom and makes very effective reading aloud, since the character has something of the gay equivocation and theatrical dash of a Riccaut de la Marlinière." [*The Story of a Novel*]

While working on Chapter XXXVIII, "dealing with the violin sonata and the conversation at Bullinger's," T.M. holds "editorial sessions" with Erika, who is determined to free the chapter of "draggingly long sections" and "burdensome pedantries." "Finally, after many a going-over of this shrewd counselor, the manuscript had been lightened by some forty pages—and precisely the right ones." [*The Story of a Novel*]

Elisabeth Borgese comes from Chicago for a visit along with her two daughters. "The elder girl is a charming little Mediterranean princess with a delightful intelligence; Domenica, the little one, even more like her father, with the face of a Sicilian peasant child, droll, possesses a curious sense of dignity such as is rarely found in children." [*The Story of a Novel*]

Professor Bloch and his wife come from Chicago for a visit. "He checked over the scar and the healing processes, and found me in the most satisfactory condition." [*The Story of a Novel*]

Beginning of September, 1946

T.M. becomes ill with a skin ailment, like that earlier one in Zürich. ". . . an extremely tormenting, itching, and inflamed skin disease which wrought havoc with my sleep. . . . dragged on deep into October." [*The Story of a Novel*]

September 8, 1946

He sends a greeting to Hedwig Fischer on her seventy-fifth birthday. "You belong to that time which has suffered great loss in personalities and color. In these days, I think often back to the time—it must be half a century ago—when I first made the acquaintance of you and your husband. You were a young woman, and I was so cordially received by you and your dazzling Berlin circle." [Letter to Hedwig Fischer, *Briefe II*]

September 13, 1946

Chapter XXXVIII is finished. ". . . and two days after completing it I began the next; opening in Zürich, it introduces Marie Godeau into our story, which from now on grows more and more novelistic, that is to say, dramatic." [*The Story of a Novel*]

In the evening T.M. attends the celebration of Bruno Walter's birthday at the home of Alma Mahler-Werfel, along with Professor Gustave Arlt and his wife, Fritzi Massary, and Oskar Karlweis. T.M. reads the German version of the birthday greeting to the guests and presents Bruno Walter with the manuscript. "Dear Friend, it is very annoying. After a rigorous test period of thirty-four years, we have just agreed to say '*Du*' to each other henceforth, and now I have to write you a birthday letter in which this handsome innovation won't count at all, since in this damnably over-civilized English one addresses even one's dog as 'you.' [*To Bruno Walter on His Seventieth Birthday*]

End of September, 1946

"With my skin troubles, from which I had to endure absurd torments, I finally landed at the office of a Russian Jewess doctor named Segetz—truly a landing after a storm, for the wise lady cured me fully in the course of five visits . . ." [Letter to Frederick Rosenthal, *Briefe II*]

End of September to October 26, 1946

T.M. continues to work on *Doctor Faustus*. ". . . and even during the worst of it, the maddening malady was unable to affect the progress of the novel. . . . I told of Adrian's announcement of his desire to marry, of the wintry outing into the Bavarian mountains; I did the dialogue between Adrian and Schwerdtfeger in Pfeiffering (Chapter XLI) . . . I added the scenes between Rudi and Marie preceding the engagement, and after the middle of October finished with ease (how easy it is to deal with catastrophic happenings!) Chapter XLII, the shooting in the tram." [*The Story of a Novel*]

FOREWORD to Bohuš Beneš' GOD'S VILLAGE. A Novel. (London: Allen & Unwin, 1947)

September 22, 1946

In the midst of work on the novel he writes a "foreword . . . in the form of a letter" for Bohuš Beneš' novel *God's Village*. He talks with a student from an "association for the propagation of the World Government idea" about "establishing a world authority for the safeguarding of peace." T.M. writes a message "on peace as the supreme commandment." [*The Story of a Novel*]

LOTTE IN WEIMAR (Berlin: Suhrkamp, 1946. 6,000 copies)

LEIDEN AN DEUTSCHLAND TAGEBUCHBLÄTTER AUS DEN JAHREN 1933–1934 (Los Angeles: Pazifische Presse, 1946. Private printing of 500 copies)

He spends an evening with Arnold Schoenberg. "He told me about the new trio he had just completed, and about the experiences he had secretly woven into the composition . . ." [*The Story of a Novel*]

October, 1946

The Beloved Returns is printed again in Germany in a licensed edition—the first time since 1935.

Leiden an Deutschland appears in a private edition in the United States.

Beginning of October to October 25, 1946

While the grandchildren from San Francisco are visiting, T.M. spends much time with Frido. "The diary now contains several descriptions of the winsome child, already represented in a transfigured, disembodied manner, and with the adjective 'elfin.' . . . His hour was approaching." [*The Story of a Novel*]

October 26, 1946

Chapter XLII is finished. ". . . just now the unfortunate Inez has shot poor Rudi at the tram, the incident that closes the next to last part of our slender, abridged little book." [Letter to Erika Mann, *Briefe II*]

October 28, 1946

T.M. writes Dr. Frederick Rosenthal to inquire about the course of meningitis.

October 31, 1946

He begins the chapter on chamber music (XLIII).

Beginning of November, 1946

He works on the first Echo chapter (XLIV). "I described the frail little boy in all his elfin charm. I took the tenderness of my own heart and transformed it into something no longer entirely rational, endowing the child with a loveliness which was somehow divine, so that people felt him as a visitor from some high and faraway realm, an epiphany. . . . For Echo's evening prayers, whose source none of the characters in the novel can identify, I used sayings from Freidank's *Bescheidenheit (Wisdom)* (thirteenth century), which I adapted as prayers usually by rephrasing the third and fourth verses." [*The Story of a Novel*]

November, 1946

Even while writing the Echo chapter, T.M. makes preparations for the oratorio, *The Lamentation of Dr. Faustus*, by discussions with Theodor Adorno. "We passed on to the cantata. For this, the 'Privy Councillor,' as I was to call Adorno in the dedication I penned upon his copy of the book, had thought up many valuable ideas." [*The Story of a Novel*]

End of November, 1946

Klaus Pringsheim, Katja Mann's twin brother, conductor of the Tokyo imperial orchestra, comes with his son for a visit. Golo Mann, who is to become professor of history at Pomona College, and Monika, returning from Europe, are in Pacific Palisades.

Beginning of December, 1946
T.M. works on the second Echo chapter. ". . . on Echo's fatal disease, sorrowing. . . . The 'divine child' was to be snatched away from the man who was not permitted love, the man of 'coldness'; that had long ago been decided and was the inescapable necessity." [*The Story of a Novel*]

December 10, 1946
Hermann Hesse is awarded the Nobel Prize. ". . . the gentlemen in Stockholm are certainly to be praised for finally taking my ten-year-old suggestion." [Letter to Anna Jacobson, *Briefe II*]

December 11, 1946
The Echo chapter is finished. "I should, of course, also have liked to send you the parts just finished about Nepomuk Schneidewein and how he is 'taken,' but there would not be enough time for copying and correcting." [Letter to Erika Mann, *Briefe II*]

December 13, 1946
He reads this chapter in his family circle. "Yesterday evening I read two chapters to Monika, my brother-in-law and his little son, and Golo, about how the charming Nepomuk Schneidewein, a kind of Ariel, comes to Pfeiffering and there dies of meningitis, because nothing is permitted Adrian. The little one, an elfin, idealized Frido, is certainly the most beautiful thing in the whole book, and then the devil takes him. None of us was far from tears." [Letter to Elisabeth Mann-Borgese, *Briefe II*]

December 15, 1946
He finally begins work on Chapter XLVI about the cantata. "I am fighting the final battle for my novel. It cannot last more than thirty or forty days into next year." [Letter to Anna Jacobson, *Briefe II*]

Christmas, 1946
"This Christmas Eve we had to do without the grandchildren. We spoke by telephone with Erika and Klaus in New York, with the children in Mill Valley, with Frido. For our evening concert we listened to the Ninth Symphony—highly suitable to what I was engaged on." [*The Story of a Novel*]

End of December, 1946
During a visit from Hermann Rauschning and his wife, T.M.

discusses German politics with them. "In his opinion the Germans as a nation could no longer be tolerated; what would remain were the Germans as individuals." [*The Story of a Novel*]

December 30, 1946

"For my musician, I am just now imagining and composing the 'symphonic cantata,' with which he takes his departure from the spiritual life, *The Lamentation of Dr. Faustus* (after the chapbook), an ode to sadness, since it is obviously not to be the joy of the Ninth Symphony and is to take back Beethoven's annunciation." [Letter to Emil Preetorius, *Briefe II*]

December 31, 1946

"In the evening Golo came to visit, and brought young Eysoldt, the son of the actress Gertrud Eysoldt, who in my youth had made an ineradicable impression upon me in the part of Wedekind's Lulu under Reinhardt's direction. The young people asked for a reading, and I read about Adrian's doctors, and from his dialogue with the devil." [*The Story of a Novel*]

January 1, 1947

He finishes the "still not right" cantata chapter. In the evening he is at the home of the philosopher Dr. Weil, with the Chaplins, Dieterles, Feuchtwangers, and Hanns Eisler. "With Eisler I once again had one of those talks about Wagner which so amused me, compounded as they were of enthusiasm and malice." [*The Story of a Novel*]

January 2, 1947

He begins "Chapter XLVII, dealing with the gathering of friends and Adrian's confession." "I needed seventeen days for the next-to-last chapter—the last, really, for the end was conceived as an epilogue. Adrian's speech touched me deeply, and came from the heart. Only my old habit of giving political matters equal place beside creative and personal activities, of alternating between these realms, can explain the fact that I still took note of the events of the day . . ." [*The Story of a Novel*]

About January 25, 1947

The honorary doctoral diploma from the Philosophical Faculty of the University of Bonn is reissued to T.M., who thanks Professor Oertel in a letter of January 28. "If anything can dampen my joy and satisfaction, it is the thought of the horrible price which had to be paid before your famous institution could recall the previous forced move. Unfortunate Germany! Such wild ups and downs of history have probably never before been alloted to a land and a people." [Letter to the Dean of the Philosophical Faculty of the University of Bonn, *Briefe II*]

January 29, 1947

"On the morning of January 29 I wrote the last lines of *Doctor Faustus*, as I had had them framed in my mind for a long time—Zeitblom's silent, fervent prayer for his friend—and looked back over the three years and eight months during which I had lived under the tension of this work, from that May morning in the midst of the war when I had first taken up the pen to begin it. 'I am finished,' I said to my wife when she fetched me in the car from my usual walk toward the ocean. And she, who had stood by me through many a finishing, how heartily she congratulated me!" [*The Story of a Novel*]

He spends an additional week with the manuscript, "reflecting on it and making improvements."

NIETZSCHES PHILOSOPHIE IM LICHTE UNSERER ERFAHRUNG (DIE NEUE RUNDSCHAU, Stockholm, September, 1947)

NIETZSCHE'S PHILOSOPHY IN THE LIGHT OF RECENT HISTORY (Translated by Richard and Clara Winston. LAST ESSAYS. New York: Alfred A. Knopf, 1959. 218 pp.)

About February 7, 1947

The finishing of the novel is celebrated at the home of Alfred Neumann.

February 9, 1947

He prepares to write the Nietzsche essay.

February 17 to March 17, 1947

He writes the essay. "This took me approximately four weeks. It came to forty manuscript pages, about twenty pages too long for oral delivery, in both English and German. Erika accomplished a masterpiece of editorial work in preparing the essay for the lecture hall. By a hundred deletions of details, yet preserving all the essentials, she cut it exactly in half." [*The Story of a Novel*]

FÜR HERMANN HESSE (NEUE ZÜRCHER ZEITUNG, June 2, 1947)

April, 1947

He writes a greeting to Hermann Hesse on his seventieth birthday.

April 22 to September 14, 1947

He decides to take a trip to Europe, accompanied by his wife and daughter Erika.

April 22, 1947

He leaves Pacific Palisades and goes to Chicago to visit the Borgeses.

April 28–29, 1947

In Washington, D.C. he is the guest of Eugene and Agnes E. Meyer.

April 29, 1947

He gives *Nietzsche's Philosophy in the Light of Contemporary Events* [first title] in Coolidge Auditorium of the Library of Congress.

April 30 to May 11, 1947

He stays in New York City, where he gives the Nietzsche lecture at Hunter College.

May 11, 1947

He boards the *Queen Elizabeth* for the trip to Europe.

May 16, 1947

He arrives in Southampton. "The trip over on the giant ship was disturbed by a rolling caused by the ship's being built so tall. One cannot be relaxed. The arrival in Southampton with two thousand people and their mass of luggage was confused to the point of catastrophe." [Letter to Heinrich Mann, *Briefe II*]

On board the *Queen Elizabeth*, T.M. gives a Reuter correspondent an interview alarming to the German press. "To look at Germany today is to look at Europe as a whole. Germany has suffered during the war, but sufferings are equally endured by France, Italy, Poland, Greece and other European countries. Germans appear full of self-pity, unable to see the chaos in the neighboring countries. Only when Europe recovers as a whole, will Germany recover . . ." [Reuter's text]

"My interviews have, in part, been reported in a garbled fashion and with loss of proportion." [Letter to Arnold Bauer, *Briefe II*]

May 16–24, 1947

In London at the Savoy Hotel. "The first days here I had a struggle with a stomach and intestinal infection, in spite of which I bore everything: interviews, press conferences, receptions, broadcasts, and, in the midst of a great crowd, the lecture at London University. The Nietzsche lecture, simple as it is, stood the test here as in Washington and New York." [Letter to Heinrich Mann, *Briefe II*]

May 20, 1947
He gives the Nietzsche lecture at King's College, London.
May 21, 1947
He has an interview at the radio building of the B.B.C.
May 23, 1947
T.M. writes a message to the German people, which establishes his intention not to visit Germany. "I am fully aware of the extraordinarily difficult and sorrowful position in which Germany finds herself today and as a German deeply sympathize with it. One must, however, say that it cannot be expected a mere two years after so fearful a catastrophe as Germany has suffered to see Germany recovered again. But I hope and believe that after two, three, or five years, the horizon again will be brighter and that, thanks to that inborn industry and energy, Germany will not need to despair about the future." [*Botschaft an das deutsche Volk*]

BOTSCHAFT AN DAS DEUTSCHE VOLK (FRANKFURTER NEUE PRESSE, May 24, 1947)

May 24, 1947
He flies from London to Zürich.
May 28, 1947
His message to the German people causes a vigorous and, for the most part, hostile press campaign in Germany. Manfred Hausmann, for example, in his article in the *Weser Zeitung, Thomas Mann sollte schweigen*, throws suspicion on the writer. Hausmann supposedly made an effort in a letter to persuade T.M. to return to Germany in 1933.
May 24 to June 21, 1947
He stays in Zürich at the Hotel Baur au Lac. He goes to the Swiss border and meets Viktor Mann and his wife; both return with him to Zürich. "The protection of a French border official made it possible." [Letter to Kitty and Alfred Neumann, *Briefe II*]
May 30, 1947
He visits the publishing house Winterthur in Winterthur, where *Doctor Faustus* is being printed.
June 3–4, 1947
The fourteenth International PEN Congress takes place in Zürich.
June 3, 1947
The PEN Congress opens with words of greeting from the President of Switzerland Etter and the general secretary of the International PEN Congress Hermann Ould and an opening speech by the president of the Swiss PEN Club,

Professor Robert Faesi. Finally, T.M. gives his Nietzsche lecture.

June 4, 1947

In a discussion on the formation of a German group for the PEN Club, T.M. suggests Ricarda Huch for president and stands up for the German writers who are present: Johannes R. Becher, Erich Kästner, and Ernst Wiechert.

June 8, 1947

In the Zürich Schauspielhaus, T.M. reads from *Doctor Faustus* (the Fitelberg chapter and *Opus III*). "One June morning—and it was like a dream—I sat on the stage of the Schauspielhaus in Zürich, where eight years ago I had bidden farewell to Europe by reading from *The Beloved Returns*. Happy and animated by the reunion with this dear city, I performed Fitelberg's Riccaut scene for an audience that helped me celebrate the occasion in the friendliest fashion." [*The Story of a Novel*]

June 10, 1947

He gives a speech before Zürich students and afterwards a reading in the Auditorium Maximum of the Federal Technical Hochschule. "I believe that below and above the bloody wars and upheavals of this time a new love, a new belief, is preparing itself in the depths of the heart and in the heights of the spirit—a new feeling for humanity, indeed a new humanism, which needs in no way to be the optimistic, idyllic love of mankind, to which the eighteenth century dedicated its gentle tears—in no way a humanism of naiveté or sentimentality. It could and should be a manly, knowing, and deepened humanism which has broadly experienced all new explorations into the human and has taken into account all the lower and demonic elements in its respect for the human mystery." [*Ansprache an die Zürcher Studentenschaft*]

ANSPRACHE GEHALTEN AM 10. JUNI 1947, ANLÄSSLICH EINER VORLESUNG AUS DOCTOR FAUSTUS VOR ZÜRICHER STUDENTEN (ZÜRCHER STUDENT, No. 3, 1947)

About June 12, 1947

In Bern, he gives the Nietzsche lecture twice. In St. Gall, he gives a reading from *Doctor Faustus* for the benefit of the Munich orphanage.

June 14, 1947

He attends a performance of *Götterdämmerung* at the Zürich Stadttheater.

June 16, 1947

In Basel, he gives the Nietzsche lecture.

June 20 to July 20, 1947

He goes for a rest to Flims, Graubünden, at the Waldhaus Grandhotel Surselva. "Here it is very pretty and comforting after all the hustle and bustle: splendid silent forests of firs with rocks and gorges just like Doré's, and the view of the walls, rocky crags, and high alpine meadows of the surrounding mountains are something quite different after the eternal Pacific." [Letter to Kitty and Alfred Neumann, *Briefe II*]

June 25, 1947

T.M. answers Hausmann's attack. "Why he attacks me from behind with the senseless denunciation, which I did not deserve from him, what I have done to injure him—this I do not know. Is he so angry because today I do not want to do now what then I could not do?" T.M.'s letter to the German Ministry of the Interior mentioned by Hausmann is found and published with T.M.'s permission. It is only his effort in the spring of 1934 to have his confiscated property returned to him.

BRIEFE IN DIE NACHT (NEUE ZEITUNG, Munich, July 7, 1947)

BRIEF AN DAS REICHS-INNENMINISTERIUM (NEUE ZEITUNG, Munich, August 8, 1947)

T.M. prepares the selections for the Goethe reader to be printed by the Dial Press.

July 20, 1947

He returns to Zürich, at the Hotel Neues Schloss.

July 23, 1947

He travels to Lucerne for a meeting with Hermann Hesse and his wife at the Hotel National. "It was good to be together, and we shall think back on it the whole year." [Letter to Hermann Hesse, *Briefe II*]

July 24–25, 1947

There is a "family visit from Germany."

July 30 to August 3, 1947

He spends four days at Meina on Lake Maggiore at the home of his Italian publisher Mondadori. He has a press conference with Italian and German journalists.

August 3–10, 1947

He is back in Zürich at the Hotel Baur au Lac.

August 5, 1947

In Amriswil, at the invitation of the editor of the *Internationale Bodensee-Zeitschrift*, Dino Larese, he gives a reading from *Doctor Faustus*. "In Amriswil I gave a reading to the smallest group to which I have ever read. But in the cultivated, obliging receptivity of the audience, this town can vie with any great and famous city or center of culture." [Letter to Dino Larese, *Internationale Bodensee-Zeitschrift*, September, 1955]

The Uttwil painter, Ernst E. Schlatter does a drawing of T.M. (the original is in the Thomas Mann Archives, Zürich).

August 7 or 8, 1947

He visits Robert Faesi at his country house "Neugut" above Wäddenswil. He reads the devil's conversation from *Doctor Faustus* to a small circle of friends.

August 10, 1947

He flies from Zürich to Amsterdam.

August 10–18, 1947

At the Hotel Amstel, "In Amsterdam the same hubbub of press conferences, receptions, and lectures has again begun a little." [Letter to Robert Faesi, *Thomas Mann/Robert Faesi, Briefwechsel*. Zürich: Atlantis Verlag, 1962]

August 18–28, 1947

While resting at Huis ter Duin in Nordwijk aan Zee, T.M. writes a eulogy on Menno ter Braak, who committed suicide when the German troops marched into Holland in 1940. "It is good to see the free Netherlands once again after the fall of the enemy, but a shadow falls across this return, this happy sojourn: the thought of him who, when Hitler came, decided to meet a tragic end. With my last visit here in 1939, it was he among others, but above all others, who introduced me to the public. Who then could more legitimately be the mediator between my work and the Dutch friends of literature?" [*In memoriam Menno ter Braak*]

IN MEMORIAM MENNO TER BRAAK (HET PAROOL, Amsterdam, August 28, 1947)

T.M. writes an introduction to *Jeunesse* by Frans Masereel, who had visited him in Zürich.

DER HOLZSCHNEIDER MASEREEL (NEUE ZEITUNG, Munich, March 14, 1948)

August 29, 1947

He returns to America on the Holland-American steamer, *Westerdam*.

September 4, 1947

On the ship T.M. writes a letter to Hans Reisiger, which contains an explanation of *Doctor Faustus*. The letter is printed privately along with a note forbidding its publication.

September 8, 1947

He arrives in New York.

September 14, 1947
He is back in Pacific Palisades.

September, 1947
Klaus Mann is back in New York after a trip through France. While in Paris he had visited Jean Cocteau.

With the help of Klaus, T.M. prepares the Goethe reader. "I have sent to the Dial Press a complete arrangement of the contents as I should like it to be, along with lengthy comment in which I discuss our examination of the present translations . . . What is primarily to be determined is whether the poems and sayings we intend to use are to be left untranslated or whether they are to be put into new translations, so that I can go to Auden, Spender, or Prokosch about definite projects . . . The whole affair will certainly cost many troubles and headaches, more than the two thousand dollars will pay for. But if I have to do it at all, I must do the whole thing." [Letter to Klaus Mann, *Briefe II*]

THE PERMANENT GOETHE, Edited, selected and with an Introduction by Thomas Mann. (New York: The Dial Press, 1948)

Erika Mann is back at home after a trip through Poland and Czechslovakia.

October 5, 1947
T.M. is chosen as a member of the Accademia Lincei in Rome.

October 6 to November 23, 1947
He writes the introduction to the Goethe reader. "While writing a *Fantasy on Goethe* (for 1949), slowly and somewhat distractedly, I am awaiting tensely as never before the 'reaction,' if one can speak of such a thing, to Echo in the German edition of *Doctor Faustus*." [Letter to Ida Herz, *Briefe II*]

October 9, 1947
He attends the film *The Best Years of our Lives* and defends it forcefully against a disparaging criticism by Agnes E. Meyer. ". . . it belongs to the most outstanding work that I have seen in this area—of an incomparable naturalness, basically respectable in its sentiments, excellently played, and full of genuine American life." [Letter to Agnes E. Meyer, *Briefe II*]

October 10, 1947
He has new writing plans. "In more lively hours I go over all sorts of plans for work: a medieval legend-novella which

could form *Trois contes* along with *The Transposed Heads* and the Moses tale, the shaping of the Felix Krull fragment into a modern picaresque novel taking place in the period of affluence. The comic, laughter, humor appear to me more and more as a balm for my soul . . ." [Letter to Agnes E. Meyer, *Briefe II*]

Autumn, 1947

He gives the Nietzsche lecture in San Francisco.

October 17, 1947

Doctor Faustus appears in the *Stockholmer Gesamtausgabe*. To protect the American original rights, a mimeographed edition of fifty copies is put together in the United States. ". . . As Bermann cables me, the first Swiss reviews are out; the earliest, like that of Rychner's in the Zürich *Tat*, are supposedly enthusiastic. Well, there will be no lack of kill-joys and rebuffs." [Letter to Ida Herz, *Briefe II*]

DOKTOR FAUSTUS: DAS LEBEN DES DEUTSCHEN TONSETZERS ADRIAN LEVERKÜHN, ERZÄHLT VON EINEM FREUNDE (Stockholm: Bermann/ Fischer, 1947. 14,000 copies.) *DOCTOR FAUSTUS:* THE LIFE OF THE GERMAN COMPOSER, ADRIAN LEVERKÜHN, AS TOLD BY A FRIEND (New York: Alfred A. Knopf, 1948. 510 pp.)

November 10, 1947

He sends a greeting to Martin Gumpert on his fiftieth birthday. ". . . to my younger friend and my children's older friend, in whom I have ever found friendliness, comfort, and encouragement, and to whom I, for my part, have always been friendly, let me offer congratulation from my heart and renew the respect and sympathy that I hold for you. You will surely receive signs of affection and esteem from many corners on this day, to the physician, the writer, and the man." [Letter to Martin Gumpert, *Briefe II*]

November 25, 1947

"At the time I am not doing anything really, only probing inwardly here and there, and keeping watch on *Doctor Faustus*, which has just entered the European world (what would you say if I formed the Felix Krull fragment into a proper picaresque novel for entertainment in my old age?)." [Letter to Hermann Hesse, *Briefe II*]

December, 1947

He writes the foreword to *The Masters of Buddenbrooks* which is to appear in the anthology *The World's Best* published by The Dial Press. "It is a meaningful coincidence and perhaps more than a coincidence, what one might call a fitting event, when a part of that melancholy work of my youth, in which the conflict with the idea of the middle class is resolved with music, appears in an excellent anthol-

DER "FESTE PUNKT" IM MENSCHEN (Foreword to a chapter from Buddenbrooks. THEMA, Gauting near Munich, 1949)

ogy at the same time as a novel of my old age, which is so strongly shaken by the horrors of this epoch. Thus are the two books brothers . . . After fifty years of wandering through space and time, my way opens once again to familiar old German cities and things, to German music . . ." [*Der 'feste Punkt' im Menschen*]

December 21, 1947

T.M. decides to write *The Holy Sinner*.

Christmas, 1947

"Now we shall have children, grandchildren, uproar, and parties." [Letter to Theodor W. Adorno, *Briefe II*]

December 31, 1947

"Now comes the end of a year which, to me personally, has not been poor in experiences. The completion of *Doctor Faustus*, the trip to Europe, the appearance of the novel and a response to it in Switzerland—I am looking back over it all thankfully." [Letter to Agnes E. Meyer, *Briefe II*]

January, 1948

"This year we want to remain calm and not travel, but in the spring of 1949, if we are living and events of world history permit, we shall come back." [Letter to Robert Faesi, *Thomas Mann/Robert Faesi, Briefwechsel*. Zürich: Atlantis Verlag, 1962]

January 4, 1948

T.M. refuses the invitation to come to Frankfurt and give a speech at St. Paul's Church at a reception in the Garden of Palms. "I respectfully refused an invitation to Frankfurt as a speaker at St. Paul's. About this coming year I could only speak stiffly and without true belief." [Unpublished letter to Lavinia Mazzucchetti]

BRIEF AN DEN OBERBÜRGERMEISTER DER STADT FRANKFURT (NEUE ZEITUNG, Munich, February 5, 1948)

January 21, 1948

He writes the first lines of *The Holy Sinner*.

February 17, 1948

"Now I am reading a great deal of Middle High German (Hartmann von Aue) and informing myself of the church in Rome of the ninth and tenth centuries. I want to retell an often-told saint's legend of the Middle Ages, *Gregorius on the Rock*, in modern prose—a variation on the Oedipus story, which recounts the choosing by God himself of a fearfully incestuous sinner to be the Roman pope. It is a religious grotesque, which I must laugh about as I conceive it but which is actually to be about mercy." [Unpublished letter to Samuel Singer]

End of February, 1948

Nietzsche's Philosophy in the Light of Recent History appears. T.M. breaks his left collar bone in a fall at the house of his friend Max Horkheimer. He soon overcomes the difficulty in writing.

March 25, 1948

T.M. protests against the decision of the United States to withdraw its approval of the establishing of a Jewish state in Palestine. "The little Jewish state in Palestine would have been a democracy of people willing to work and to build up their own culture. This state would naturally have had to find the sympathy of a land with the American tradition. Why are we cursed to support everywhere the evil, the filthy reaction that is hated by the people—in this case the feudalism of the Arabian oil magnates—and to destroy democracy when we pretend to defend it?" [*Gespenster von 1938*]

March, 1948

He writes a foreword to the one-volume American edition of the Joseph novels. "Here then is the whole work in a single binding, in Helen Lowe-Porter's admirable translation—an achievement of loyalty and devotion which this woman would not have been able to accomplish without faith in the worthiness of her task. May I share this faith? How will posterity regard this work? Will it soon become a dust-covered curio for antiquarians, the easy prey of fleeting time? Or will its pleasantries cheer those who come after us, its pathos touch them? Or will it perhaps be numbered among the great books?" [Foreword to *Joseph and His Brothers*]

April, 1948

T.M. withdraws from The Authors' League of America.

May 24, 1948

"I have written fifty pages of the novel *The Holy Sinner.*" [Unpublished letter to Alfred Neumann]

June, 1948

The collection of essays, *Neue Studien*, appears with the dedication, "This little book, which appears in a year of painfully great historical memory, I dedicate to the city of Frankfurt on Main, in which the spirit of St. Paul's Church

NIETZSCHES PHILOSOPHIE IM LICHTE UNSERER ERFAHRUNG (Berlin: Suhrkamp, formerly S. Fischer, 1948. 20,000 copies. The licenced edition of Bermann/ Fischer, Stockholm.)

GESPENSTER VON 1938 (AUFBAU, New York, March 26, 1948)

SECHZEHN JAHRE (NEUE SCHWEIZER RUNDSCHAU, Zürich, March, 1948)

FOREWORD to JOSEPH AND HIS BROTHERS (New York: Alfred A. Knopf, 1948. 1,216 pages.)

NEUE STUDIEN (Stockholm: Bermann/ Fischer, 1948. 7,000 copies. Simultaneously a licensed edition in Germany: Berlin: Suhrkamp Verlag. 11,000 copies)

never died and which will carry this spirit into the future of Germany." [*Neue Studien*]

June 3, 1948

For T.M.'s seventy-third birthday, *Fiorenza* is broadcast as a radio play by the group *Rot-Weiss-Rot*.

June 6, 1948

He gives a speech in Hollywood to the Peace Group. "I have to prepare something political, a speech, which I am giving at an important peace conference. One must support these movements, which are working for a reasonable settlement with Soviet Russia and which are opposed to a highly ill-advised toying with thoughts of war in this country." [Unpublished letter to Ida Herz]

Summer, 1948

The Permanent Goethe appears. The introduction is entitled *Phantasie über Goethe* and is published in *Neue Studien*.

July 21, 1948

He interrupts work on *The Holy Sinner* to write the first lines of *The Story of a Novel*.

September, 1948

A licenced edition of the collection of stories *Ausgewählte Erzählungen* appears in Germany.

Autumn, 1948

T.M. edits a volume of Schopenhauer, a shortened version of *Die Welt als Wille und Vorstellung* [*The World as Will and Representation*]. The introduction, which is the Schopenhauer essay of 1938, is also shortened.

October 9, 1948

"A few weeks ago, I wrote a statement about August Strindberg." [Unpublished letter to K. R. Gierow] "Experiencing Strindberg's monstrously challenging work, going almost beyond the human in its inward and outward extent, and his often grotesque, often repulsive humanity, which, however, was bathed in a noble and touching beauty, was an essential part of my youthful development, and my feelings have not changed in the thirty-six years since his death." [*August Strindberg*]

October 21, 1948

He finishes writing *The Story of a Novel*. "Recently I have written something strange, the story of *Doctor Faustus* during the troubled years of 1943–1946. I used my notebooks on

PHANTASIE ÜBER GOETHE (in NEUE STUDIEN)
FANTASY ON GOETHE (in LAST ESSAYS)

AUSGEWÄHLTE ERZÄHLUNGEN (Frankfurt on Main: S. Fischer Bibliothek, Suhrkamp Verlag, 1948. 30,000 copies)
SCHOPENHAUER (Zürich: Werner Classen Verlag, 1948)
HYLLNING TILL AUGUST STRINDBERG (SVENSKA DAGBLADET, Stockholm, December 27, 1948)

DIE ENTSTEHUNG DES DOKTOR FAUSTUS. Chapters I–VII (DIE NEUE RUNDSCHAU, Amsterdam, Winter, 1949)

a background of world events, with even the clinical interlude and everything. It is actually only something for friends, and I do not know at all yet in what form I shall have it published." [Unpublished letter to Viktor Mann]

October, 1948

With the immediately available funds from the publication of his books in Germany, T.M. establishes a foundation for preserving the Lübeck altar by Memling and for the rebuilding of St. Mary's Church in Lübeck.

November, 1948

Doctor Faustus is chosen by the Book-of-the-Month Club for November and appears in a printing of over a hundred thousand copies.

End of 1948

"The winter months of 1948/49 were primarily dedicated to *The Holy Sinner*. Along with this, Thomas Mann had to work out the lecture for the Goethe Year (*Goethe and Democracy*)." [Hans Wysling in *Euphorion*, 1963]

February 24, 1949

T.M. is elected honorary chairman of the Literary Section of the Bavarian Academy of Fine Arts by a large majority of the votes. Thereupon, Leopold Ziegler withdraws from the Academy as a protest against T.M.'s speech *Germany and the Germans*.

April 21, 1949

Viktor Mann, T.M.'s brother and author of *Wir waren fünf*, dies in Munich. He lived through the years of the Third Reich in Germany.

April, 1949

T.M. is awarded the Medal of Service of the American Academy of Arts and Letters, which makes this award to a writer every five years.

April, 1949

The German version of *The Story of a Novel* appears.

May 2, 1949

He gives *Goethe and Democracy* in Coolidge Auditorium of the Library of Congress.

May 3–10, 1949

He stays for a while in New York at the St. Regis before his departure for Europe. He gives *Goethe and Democracy* at Hunter College.

THE STORY OF A NOVEL: THE GENESIS OF DOCTOR FAUSTUS. (New York: Alfred A. Knopf, 1961. 256 pp.)

DIE ENTSTEHUNG DES DOKTOR FAUSTUS: ROMAN EINES ROMANS. (Amsterdam: Bermann/ Fischer/ Querido, 1949. 10,000 copies. Simultaneously a licensed edition in Germany: Berlin: Suhrkamp Verlag. 10,000 copies)

GOETHE UND DIE DEMOKRATIE (DIE NEUE RUNDSCHAU, Amsterdam, Summer, 1949)

GOETHE AND DEMOCRACY (Washington: Library of Congress, 1950. 29 pp.)

May 10, 1949
He leaves from La Guardia Airport flying via British Eastern Airways to London. This is his first flight across the Atlantic.

May 11–18, 1949
He stays at the Savoy Hotel in London and spends some time at Oxford.

May 13, 1949
T.M. is awarded an honorary doctorate by Oxford. Since he cannot be present for the honors convocation, a private ceremony is held in the lecture hall of the School of Divinity. After a dinner there is an official reception at the invitation of the Vice-Chancellor. Then T.M. gives *Goethe and Democracy* in German in an overcrowded lecture hall of the Taylorian Institute. The lecture appears several months later in German as the Taylorian Lecture.

GOETHE UND DIE DEMOKRATIE (Oxford: Clarendon Press, 1949. 23 pp.)

May 14, 1949
T.M. gives a speech at a joint meeting of the PEN Club of German Authors Abroad and the Thomas Mann-Gruppe in London.

May 16, 1949
He gives *Goethe and Democracy* at the Senate House of London University sponsored by the English Goethe Society. Established in 1886, it is the oldest Goethe society except for Vienna's.

May 18, 1949
In the Wiener Library in London, T.M. gives a speech in answer to a speech greeting him by L.G. Montefiore. "These books are a means of remembering this time [the Third Reich]. One should not forget this time; the Germans have a tendency to forget it, to suppress it. Already in Germany they do not want to hear anymore about it, I have permitted myself to say. To remember the crimes of twelve years is to be tactless and unpatriotic. But the Germans should remember, and from this memory they should create the drive to make good again that which they did wrong." [*Thomas Mann's Rede in der Wiener Library*] [The Wiener Library, founded in London by Dr. Alfred Wiener, emigrated from Berlin via Amsterdam to London, contains all literature about, against, and for National Socialism, and is an indispensable source, and the most important one, for all

THOMAS MANN'S REDE IN DER WIENER LIBRARY (MITTEILUNGSBLATT DES *PEN*-CLUBS DEUTSCHER AUTOREN IM AUSLAND, London, September, 1949)

scholarly investigation of the Nazi period, beginning in the early 1920's.]

May 19–31, 1949

T.M. travels to Sweden and Denmark.

May 21, 1949

Klaus Mann commits suicide in Cannes.

May 24, 1949

Sponsored by the Swedish Academy, T.M. gives his *Goethe and Democracy* lecture in the great hall of the Stockholm stock exchange.

May 25, 1949

He delivers the same lecture at the University of Copenhagen.

May 31, 1949

In the cathedral of the University of Lund, T.M. is awarded an honorary doctorate and presented with an engraved ring of ducat gold.

June, 1949

The B.B.C. broadcasts the speech *Goethe, the German Miracle*, which T.M. had recorded while in London.

GOETHE, DAS DEUTSCHE WUNDER (DER MONAT, Berlin, August, 1949)

June 1–26, 1949

T.M. is in Zürich, staying at the Hotel Baur au Lac.

June 7, 1949

He gives *Goethe and Democracy* as the main address at the opening of the June festival week of the Zürich, Schauspielhaus.

June 14, 1949

He gives a reading from *The Holy Sinner* in Küsnacht.

June, 1949

He gives the *Goethe and Democracy* lecture in Bern and reads portions of *The Holy Sinner* to students in Zürich.

June 24, 1949

He gives a reading from *The Holy Sinner* in the music hall of the Basel city casino, under the sponsorship of the student body the University of Basel.

June 25 to July 18, 1949

He goes to Vulpera/Schuls in the Engadine Valley, stopping at the Hotel Schweizerhof, for a rest.

July 19–22, 1949

He returns to Zürich, where he stays at Hotel Baur au Lac.

July 23 to August 8, 1949

He travels through Germany—his first visit in sixteen years. "My speech *Germany and the Germans*, and even more my novel about Doctor Faustus, should convince all understanding people that my heart has remained with Germany and that I have suffered for the fate of Germany as only a German could . . . As an American citizen, I have remained a German writer, true to the German language, which I consider my true cultural home." [*Botschaft für das deutsche Volk*]

BOTSCHAFT FÜR DAS DEUTSCHE VOLK (HEUTE, Munich, July, 1949)

He visits in Frankfurt, Weimar, and Munich, and spends brief periods of time in Stuttgart and Nuremberg.

July 24, 1949

He arrives in Frankfurt and is received at the train station by Mayor Kolb, City Councillor Reinert, and the publishers Gottfried Bermann Fischer and Peter Suhrkamp. As a guest of the city of Frankfurt, T.M. lives in the guesthouse in Schönberg.

July 25, 1949

At a press conference in the club house of the Society for Trade, Industry, and Science, Dr. Siegfried Horstmann, an official in the Lübeck schools and trustee of the Thomas Mann Archives, is present as a representative of Lübeck.

ANSPRACHE IM GOETHEJAHR (NEUE ZEITUNG, Munich, July 26, 1949)

For the Goethe celebration in St. Paul's Church, T.M. gives the principal address, which he also will give in Weimar at the invitation of the Councillor of State of the German Democratic Republic. "I recognize no zones. My visit is to Germany itself, Germany as a whole, and to no occupied zone. Who should vouch for and proclaim the unity of Germany if not an independent writer whose true cultural home, as I have said, is free language, untouched by occupations?" [*Ansprache im Goethejahr*]

July 26, 1949

In response to many protests in the Federal Republic against his visit to Weimar, T.M. writes an explanation, particularly about the request of the Society to Combat Inhumanity, which has asked to visit Buchenwald in connection with his trip. T.M. refuses to protest against the refusal of the German Democratic Republic to allow the visit of the Society to Buchenwald as a part of his visit. He states that it is his

ERKLÄRUNG ZU DER AUFFORDERUNG DER GESELLSCHAFT ZUR BEKÄMPFUNG DER UNMENSCHLICHKEIT, BUCHENWALD ZU BESUCHEN (FRANKFURTER RUNDSCHAU, July 28, 1949)

wish that his visit pertain to all of Germany. "I have repeatedly argued my reasons for determining also to visit Weimar during this trip to Germany for the Goethe Year . . . The essential point is that my visit is to the fatherland as a whole, and it seems to me ungracious not to visit the people of the East Zone, to give them, so to speak, a cold shoulder. To make demands . . . that the German officials inviting me cannot fulfill is out of the question, and the society making the request knows this as well as I." [*Erklärung zu der Aufforderung der Gesellschaft zur Bekämpfung der Unmenschlichkeit, Buchenwald zu besuchen*]

July 27, 1949

At a reception in the Prince Karl Palace in Munich, sponsored by the Bavarian Academy of Fine Arts, T.M. is greeted by Ernst Penzoldt and makes a speech of thanks.

July 29, 1949

In the morning there is a press reception in the council room of the city hall. Afterwards the city of Munich holds an official banquet in the city hall for a small group of members of the Bavarian government, representatives of the American occupation, some members of the parties in the Bundestag, and a few of T.M.'s old friends. In the great hall of the Ministry of Economics, T.M. gives the lecture *Goethe and Democracy*.

July 30, 1949

On the way to Weimar, T.M. is accompanied from Bayreuth across the border into the East Zone by the President of the Cultural Union for Democratic Renewal of the German Democratic Republic, Johannes R. Becher. On the way, they have lunch in Plauen/Vogtland.

August 1, 1949

T.M. has breakfast in Weimar with General Tulpanov, the Soviet commandant of the city of Berlin. At the Nationaltheater in Weimar, T.M. gives his *Ansprache im Goethe Jahr* and is awarded the Goethe Prize. With the prize, twenty-thousand East German marks, T.M. establishes a fund for the rebuilding of Herder's church in Weimar. "It is a fact, which one should not minimize but rather recognize in its auspicious meaningfulness, that Eastern and Western Germany over and above all differences in governmental organization, all ideological, political, and economic con-

ANSPRACHE IN WEIMAR (FRANKFURTER RUNDSCHAU, August 2, 1949)

trasts, have found a common cultural ground and awarded their Goethe Prizes in this particularly festive year to one and the same writer." [*Ansprache in Weimar*]

August 6, 1949

In Munich, T.M. is awarded honorary membership in the Vereinigung der Verfolgten des Naziregimes [Society of Those Persecuted by the Nazi Regime]. He is named honorary chairman of the Schutzverband der Deutschen Schriftsteller [Union of German Writers], which he had helped to establish a decade before.

August 5, 1949

He boards the steamer *Nieuw Amsterdam* in La Havre for his return to New York.

August 20, 1949

He writes a letter to the mayor of Frankfurt, which is read publicly by Mayor Kolb at the Goethe celebration on August 28. "Being back in the peace of our home for twenty-four hours, after four months of turmoil, both my wife and I feel a need in our hearts to express once again our thanks for the wonderful care and refreshing hospitality which we enjoyed in Frankfurt . . . My memory of our visit to Frankfurt is without a shadow. None of the dissonances of which I was warned by some overcareful people spoiled the memory of my stay, and your letter of the eighth of the month confirms in the most gratifying way that my speech of July 25, prepared for so cleverly and winningly by your introduction, hit the mark. One could say that it was not at all easy to hit it, and yet in order to do so, I had only to follow my feelings, . . . since I have always said and done, my whole life through, just what seemed natural for me . . ." [*Brief an den Oberbürgermeister der Stadt Frankfurt*]

BRIEF AN DEN OBERBÜRGERMEISTER DER STADT FRANKFURT (in Emrich's DIE TRÄGER DES GOETHEPREISES DER STADT FRANKFURT)

August 27, 1949

He writes a letter to the Swedish journalist Paul Olberg justifying his trip to Weimar.

BRIEF AN DEN SCHWEDISCHEN JOURNALISTEN PAUL OLBERG (DAS VOLKSRECHT, Zürich, September 9, 1949)

August 28, 1949

He is awarded the Goethe Prize of the city of Frankfurt in his absence. The prize amounts to ten thousand marks. He is made an honorary citizen of Weimar. "In memory of its classical tradition, which must continue as a lively concern for our generation, the city of Weimar honors the famous defender and augmenter of German language and literature and, at the same time, the worthiest representative of humanism in our time." [From the certificate of honorary citizenship]

August, 1949

T.M.'s speech in Frankfurt and Weimar appears as a brochure simultaneously in both cities.

ANSPRACHE IM GOETHE-JAHR 1949 (Frankfurt on Main: Suhrkamp Verlag, 1949. Weimar: Thüringer Volksverlag, 1949)

September 20, 1949

He writes a letter of thanks to the mayor of Weimar, Dr. Buchterkirchen. ". . . the single steps of our sojourn—the beautiful celebration in the Nationaltheater, seeing once again the Goethe places, the visit to the Liszt House with the masterful lecture on Beethoven's Opus 111, the farewell banquet at the hotel with the many good speeches, and especially the touching homage paid us on the journey back through Thuringia—all this will remain unforgettable for us, and we shall always think back on it with gratitude." [*Thomas Mann dankt*]

THOMAS MANN DANKT (TÄGLICHE RUNDSCHAU, Berlin, September 21, 1949)

October 10, 1949

He gives the Frankfurt and Weimar speech as an official memorial address on the university campus at Berkeley.

November, 1949

In San Francisco, he has a one-hour conversation with Jawaharlal Nehru. "At his request (how otherwise could I have done it?) I made him a visit in San Francisco, and I do not consider the hour spent with him as wasted. A highly attractive, intelligent man." [Unpublished letter to Agnes E. Meyer]

December, 1949

He writes a report of his trip through both Germanies in the Goethe Year. "I made the visit as a crowning end to my European trip, which gave me colorful experiences and, at the same time, the most painfully violent emotions but was nevertheless of great value." [*Reisebericht*]

REISEBERICHT (NEUE SCHWEIZER RUNDSCHAU, Zürich, December, 1949)

January 12, 1950

He gives a speech to the assembly of the National Council of Arts, Science, and Professions in Beverly Hills and is given an award.

March 14, 1950

Shortly before Heinrich Mann plans to return to Berlin, he dies in Santa Monica. "The fact that this man, who has now reached his home, was one of the greatest writers of the

German language will be grasped sooner or later by the conflicting consciousness of the Germans . . . Now he rests in peace after a full life, whose memory will depart this earth, I believe, only when culture itself and man's self-respect have disappeared." [*Ein Brief über Heinrich Mann*]

EIN BRIEF ÜBER HEINRICH MANN (GERMANIC REVIEW, December, 1950. Later under the title BRIEF ÜBER DAS HINSCHEIDEN MEINES BRUDERS. In NEUES)

March, 1950

T.M. interrupts work on *The Holy Sinner* to write the lecture *Meine Zeit*. "At the moment I am working out a lecture which is to be called *The Years of My life*, or something similar, and will present a kind of condensed autobiography, which will have less to do with my own life than with the epoch I have lived through." [Unpublished letter to Benno Lee]

MEINE ZEIT (Frankfurt on Main: S Fischer, 1950) *THE YEARS OF MY LIFE* (Translated by Heinz and Ruth Norden. HARPER'S, October, 1950)

March 28, 1950

He writes an article in memory of his son Klaus. ". . . I seriously believe that he belonged to the most gifted of his generation and was perhaps the most gifted of all . . . But a constantly growing, passive desire to do away with himself—overcoming his good intentions and nourished by disappointments—was mixed in him with the general intellectual despair of and for this era, as he described it in his last essay, *Die Heimsuchung des Europäischen Geistes* . . ." [*Mein Sohn Klaus*]

MEIN SOHN KLAUS (DIE WELT, Hamburg, May 20, 1950)

April 19, 1950

He gives *The Years of My Life* lecture at the University of Chicago.

April, 1950

His lecture to be given April 25 in the Library of Congress is cancelled by the Library on account of the unfavorable feelings towards him in the United States after his visit to Eastern Germany in 1949. ". . . as matters lie now, there is nothing more reasonable than to keep silent my thoughts about the lecture before a loud protest begins. Except for my words at the end about peace, my lecture closes with a decided and solid denunciation of communism, but I see now that I deceived myself in thinking it possible to present my confession in the Library." [Letter to Agnes E. Meyer, *Briefe III*]

"I hope that America—great and good, only overexcited—will not misunderstand me. I am very fond of her and have heartily good intentions towards her. I tell no one that I was not permitted to speak in Washington and stress only that I did speak in Chicago and New York." [Letter to Agnes E. Meyer, *Briefe III*]

April 26–30, 1950

He is in New York.

April 26, 1950

He gives *The Years of My Life* lecture in New York at Kaufmann Auditorium on Lexington Avenue in German, sponsored by the German language periodical *Aufbau.*

May 3, 1950

Three chapters of *The Holy Sinner* are published.

DREI KAPITEL AUS DER ERWÄHLTE DIE HOCHZEIT JESCHUTE DER ABSCHIED (DIE NEUE RUNDSCHAU, Amsterdam, April, 1950)

May 1, 1950

T.M. flies from New York to Stockholm.

May 3, 1950

At a reception in the stock exchange Hall of the Swedish Academy, at the invitation of Prince Wilhelm of Sweden and the Swedish PEN Club, T.M. gives the lecture *The Years of My Life*.

May, 1950

He gives the same lecture in Lund. Going on to Paris and staying at the Hotel Regina, he is given a reception sponsored by the French publisher Albin Michel on the occasion of the appearance of the French edition of *Doctor Faustus*. He gives *The Years of My Life* at the Sorbonne.

May 16–23, 1950

He is in Zürich at Hotel Baur au Lac.

May 24–30, 1950

He is in Lugano at the Palasthotel. He visits Hermann Hesse in Montagnola.

May 31 to June 23, 1950

He returns to Hotel Baur au Lac in Zürich.

End of May, 1950

From Lugano he sends a message to the Germans. "I greet my old homeland quite cordially in the midst of my eighth decade. What does it matter whether I am there in the flesh? Even thus, as fate has ordained, is the contact closer than one thinks, and my concern, hopes, and wishes are always with my homeland." [*Eine Botschaft an die Deutschen*]

EINE BOTSCHAFT AN DIE DEUTSCHEN (RHEIN-NECKAR-ZEITUNG, Heidelberg, June 3/4, 1950)

He writes a preface to Heinrich Eduard Jacob's *Joseph Haydn*. ". . . here Haydn is rediscovered, quite as himself and by himself. This is a book, as far as I know, like no

PREFACE (In Heinrich Eduard Jacob's JOSEPH HAYDN. Paris: Corrêa, 1950)

other concerning him, with such art of presentation, written, as it is, so well, vividly, attractively, and entertainingly."

June 5, 1950

He gives *The Years of My Life* at the Zürich Schauspielhaus on the eve of his seventy-fifth birthday. Afterwards, at a reception by the International PEN Club and the Schauspielhaus, he is presented with an award by the president of the city of Zürich, Dr. Emil Landolt, with the inscription, "To the great German writer and thinker." There are speeches by Fritz Strich, Carl Helbling, and J. R. von Salis.

June 6, 1950

For the celebration of his birthday, Richard Schweizer and Georges Motschan invite a group of close friends to a dinner at the Zunfthaus zu Saffran. Besides the family, among those present are the publisher Dr. Emil Oprecht and his wife; Kurt Hirschfeld; the director of the Schauspielhaus, Professor Fritz Strich; T.M.'s cousin, Heinrich Marty; and Senator Hans Ewers from Lübeck.

June 9 to July 13, 1950

After an operation, Katja Mann is in the Hirslanden Clinic in Zürich.

June 10, 1950

In Basel, T.M. gives *The Years of My Life* at the Stadttheater.

June 15, 1950

The South German Radio broadcasts *The Years of My Life*, which was recorded in Zürich. T.M. reads from *The Holy Sinner* at the Zürich Schauspielhaus.

End of June, 1950

During the Zürich Festival in June, he attends a performance of *The Marriage of Figaro* conducted by Fritz Busch. In an interview during the Zürich *Weltwoche* of June 23, T.M. describes his reaction to the performance. "He praised highly and heartily the Figaro production at the Stadttheater. 'One notices,' he says, with the free and easy, measured manner peculiar to him, 'that Mozart was also slyly political.' He could not praise enough the accomplishment of Professor Fritz Busch's conducting. Busch, in turn, praised Thomas Mann in an interview."

An exhibition opens at Yale University Library presenting fifty-seven years of the life and work of T.M. and ranging from the student publication, *Der Frühlingssturm*, which he edited in 1893 and which contained some of his own poems, to the April issue of the *Neue Rundschau* with its three chapters from *The Holy Sinner*. The December issue of the *Germanic Review* appears as a special seventy-fifth birthday number with numerous articles of homage and *Ein Brief über Heinrich Mann*, written by T.M. at the time of Heinrich's death.

June 23 to July 14, 1950

He is in Zürich at the Grandhotel Dolder.

July 15 to August 8, 1950

In St. Mortiz at Hotel Suvrettahaus, he writes an essay on the poetry of Michelangelo for a new German–Italian edition of the poems in German translation by Hans Mühlestein. He is made a member of the American Academy of Art and Literature and is awarded the Pegasus Medallion.

MICHELANGELO IN SEINEN DICHTUNGEN (DU, Zürich, October, 1950. Later under the title DIE EROTIK MICHELANGELOS in ALTES UND NEUES)

August 11–17, 1950

He is back in Zürich at the Hotel Baur au Lac.

August 17, 1950

He flies to London on an unofficial visit.

August 17–20, 1950

He stays at the Savoy Hotel.

August 20, 1950

On returning to New York by plane, he spends two days at the St. Regis Hotel.

August 23, 1950

He visits the Thomas Mann Exhibition at Yale and has a press conference. "From New York we paid a visit to New Haven and the Yale Library, which has brought together an astonishing birthday exhibit of documents from my life as a writer and has organized it all really very meaningfully and clearly . . . Thornton Wilder, a charming man, declared that a living author has never before been honored with such an exhibit." [Unpublished letter to Georges Motschan]

August 29, 1950

He returns to Pacific Palisades.

October 26, 1950

He completes *The Holy Sinner*.

October, 1950

The Magic Mountain appears in the first single-volume edition in German since the war.

December 21, 1950
"The proper way to publish *Die Erotik Michelangelos* in book form is still to be found. In the meantime, several other essays have come into existence: a radio lecture on Shaw, an essay on some unknown letters of Wagner, which have just appeared here in English, and a New Year's letter to a great Tokyo newspaper. Sometimes I think of bringing these out altogether under a discreet title, like 'Four (or Three) Little Works.' Bermann is now publishing *The Holy Sinner*, and thus it is time to think of other things." [Letter to Hans Mühlestein, *Briefe III*] This plan is never realized.

January 8, 1951
T.M. again takes up work on *Felix Krull*. "While in Frankfurt they are thinking of fabricating a book from what I have put aside, I have set myself to writing again on the *Confessions of Felix Krull*, a work which I deserted forty years ago. In a certain way, I am enjoying it—describing a curve over all the time and work lying in between. In that interim I have done quite a bit, and Felix grows strong from Joseph. I must see whether this work continues to suit my taste." [Letter to Otto Basler, *Briefe von Thomas Mann*, contributed by Otto Basler. *Blätter der Thomas Mann-Gesellschaft*, Zürich, No. 5, 1965]

BERNARD SHAW (The Listener, London, January 18, 1951)

BRIEFE RICHARD WAGNERS (Neue Schweizer Rundschau, Zürich, January, 1951)

January, 1951
He was Mankind's Friend, T.M.'s eulogy to Bernard Shaw, is broadcast twice on the B.B.C.'s Third Program.

January, 1951
T.M. writes a review of the *Letters of Richard Wagner* from the Mary Burrell Collection, edited by Professor John N. Burk. The review appears also in the *New York Times Book Review* and the London *Observer*.

ERINNERUNGEN AN DAS RESIDENZ THEATER (In Festschrift zur Eröffnung am 28. January 1951. Ed. Alois Johannes Lippl, Munich, 1951)

January, 1951
He writes a letter to the Intendant of the Munich Residenztheater at its formal opening.

February, 1951
He reads from *The Holy Sinner* before the Jewish Club of 1933 in Los Angeles.

March, 1951
The Holy Sinner appears. "*The Holy Sinner* is a late work in every sense, not only according to the years of the author but also as a product of a late time, a product which has to do

with venerable things, with a long tradition. Much travesty —not unlovingly—is mixed in. The courtly epic, Wolfram's *Parzival*, old songs to the Virgin, the *Lay of the Nibelungs* are slightly parodied—monuments of a late period in which culture and parody were closely related concepts. Amor fati—I have little against being a late comer, one of the last, a finisher, and I do not believe that this story and the Joseph stories will ever be told again after me." [*Alter und Neues*]

DER ERWÄHLTE (New York and Frankfurt on Main: S. Fischer, 1951)
THE HOLY SINNER (New York: Alfred A. Knopf, 1951. 336 pp.)
BEMERKUNGEN ZU DEM ROMAN DER ERWÄHLTE (In ALTES UND NEUES. Frankfurt on Main: S. Fischer, 1953)

March 11, 1951

He continues work on *Felix Krull*. "Excuse me if I fall into Krull's style. His is now once again my language (how many other's languages have I spoken!), and every morning I seek distraction in this merriment . . ." [Letter to Alfred Neumann, *Briefe III*]

March 25, 1951

He also has other plans. "I am now quite differently occupied—with the continuation of the Krull memoirs, which I have left lying for forty years. Perhaps it is only mischief, but it gives me pleasure, and I still have something to do for a while. When I no longer have anything to do, I should like to write a proper Conrad Ferdinand Meyer novella about Erasmus, Luther, and Hutten. Thus is this old head still full of plans." [Letter to Otto Basler, *Briefe von Thomas Mann*, contributed by Otto Basler. *Blätter der Thomas Mann-Gesellschaft*, Zürich, No. 5, 1965]

April, 1951

He has a controversy with the editor of the periodical *Freeman*, Eugene Tillinger, who has accused T.M. of procommunist tendencies. "I am not a communist and have never been one . . . At this opportunity, however, it should be stated that the hysterical, irrational, and blind hate of communism presents a danger for this country, whose citizenship was an honor and a joy for me. This danger is far more terrible than communism itself; indeed, this insanity and persecution mania into which America has fallen and to which the people seem to be giving themselves over tooth and nail—all this can lead not only to nothing good but even to the most evil consequences unless the people come to their senses very soon." [*Ich stelle fest*]

ICH STELLE FEST (AUFBAU, New York, April 13, 1951)

He considers for the first time a return to Europe.

April, 1951

An edition of *Buddenbrooks* appears to commemorate the fiftieth anniversary of its publication.

May 10, 1951

T.M. writes an article on the dedication of the rebuilt Goethehaus in Frankfurt. "What more could one wish than that in the German people the spirit of its best son, of the Prince of Peace, and of morality find ever firmer and deeper roots!" [*Glückwunsch zur Einweihung des wiedererrichteten Goethehauses in Frankfurt/Main am 10. Mai 1951*]

GLÜCKWUNSCH ZUR EINWEIHUNG DES WIEDERERRICHTETEN GOETHEHAUSES IN FRANKFURT AM 10. MAI 1951 (FRANKFURTER NEUE PRESSE, May 11, 1951)

May 14, 1951

He has dealings concerning the sale of the Thomas Mann manuscripts *in toto* to the Yale Library for $40,000. The transaction does not take place.

June 18, 1951

Attacks appear against T.M. in the periodical *New Leader* for his writing a birthday greeting to Johannes R. Becher, Minister of Education in the German Democratic Republic. "Even more . . . than I love and honor the poet and writer Johannes R. Becher, I love and honor the man—this urgently troubled heart driven by inner impulses, a heart which I have felt beat with mine at so many occasions, but especially in Weimar in 1949." [*Johannes R. Becher zum Gruss*]

JOHANNES R. BECHER ZUM GRUSS (AUFBAU, New York, May 1951)

July 4, 1951

T.M. starts out for Europe, spending first several days in Chicago and one day in New York.

July 10, 1951

In New York, he boards the steamer *De Grasse*.

July 19, 1951

On arriving in Le Havre, he is met by Erika Mann, and they travel by car to Zürich.

July 21–26, 1951

He is in Zürich at the Hotel Baur au Lac.

August, 1951

While spending some time at the Grandhotel in Strobl on the Wolfgangsee, he writes a review of Albert J. Guérard's book on André Gide. ". . . this spirit sways and plays constantly between order, which it most deeply desires, and anarchy, to which it is likewise born, until he makes this condition of oscillation itself the basis of a new ethic." [*Zu Albert J. Guérards André Gide*]

ZU ALBERT J. GUÉRARDS ANDRÉ GIDE (NEUE SCHWEIZER RUNDSCHAU, Zürich, November, 1951)

August 14, 1951
In Salzburg, T.M. gives a reading from *Felix Krull* in the *Aula Academica.*

August 19 to September 9, 1951
He spends three weeks taking the cure in Bad Gastein, the first two days at the Hotel Kaiserhof, then at Haus Gerke. He has arthritic-rheumatic pains in his hip and arm.

End of August, 1951
He writes an article for the seven hundredth anniversary of St. Mary's Church in Lübeck. "Down from the chancel of St. Mary's—the church in the shadow of which my grandparents' house stood, whose bells rang through my youthful days, and in which I was confirmed—from this chancel always came much talk of death and resurrection. In the thirteenth century, it was the rich citizens who turned their means to the erection of this splendid building in honor of God and their city. Today, even the poorest, as you write, makes his contribution, so that out of the sad state in which the earthquakes of the time have placed it, the church may be resurrected in its old honor and beauty." [*Thomas Mann grüsst St. Marien*]

THOMAS MANN GRÜSST ST. MARIEN (LÜBECKER NACHRICHTEN, September 2, 1951)

September 8–13, 1951
He is in Lugano at Villa Castagnola.

September 13–29, 1951
He is in Zürich at Hotel Waldhaus Dolder.

September 24, 1951
He makes a speech at the Zürich Schauspielhaus expressing hopes for its preservation and gives a reading from *Felix Krull.*

ANSPRACHE THOMAS MANNS (In the program notes of the Zürich Schauspielhaus for Christopher Fry's THE LADY IS NOT FOR BURNING, September 27, 1951)

September, 1951
T.M. writes about Wagner's *Meistersinger* at the time of its production in the Basel Stadttheater. ". . . for the *Meistersinger* is a marvelous work, a festival opera if there ever was one, a poem in which wisdom and boldness paint the venerable and revolutionary, tradition and the future, in a magnificently bright manner that awakens a deep enthusiasm for life and art." [*Brief an den Intendanten des Stadttheaters Basel*]

BRIEF AN DEN INTENDANTEN DES STADTTHEATERS BASEL (THEATERZEITUNG DES STADTTHEATERS BASEL, September 17, 1951)

The Holy Sinner is chosen by the Book-of-the-Month Club for September and is printed in an edition of at least one hundred thousand copies.

September 29, 1951

From Zürich's Kloten Airport, T.M. returns to the United States and spends one day in New York. For three days he visits his youngest daughter Elisabeth Mann-Borgese in Chicago, where he spends some time in the Museum of Natural History, which plays a part in *Felix Krull*. "Chicago has an outstanding museum of natural history, which we visited not once but, at my wish, twice. It contains quite graphic displays of the beginnings of organic life—in the sea, when the earth was still without form and void—the whole animal kingdom, the likeness and life of early man (reconstructed on the basis of discovered skeletons). I shall never forget the group of Neanderthal men (whose type marks the end of a line of development) in their caves and the devout, crouching, primeval artists who, using paints made from plants, cover the cliff walls with animal pictures, probably for magical purposes. I was completely fascinated. There is a peculiar sympathy that warms and enchants one on seeing these faces." [Letter to Hermann Hesse, *Briefe III*]

October 9, 1951

He is again at home in Pacific Palisades.

October 12, 1951

He writes a letter to Erich Auerbach, professor of Romance Languages at the Institute of Advanced Studies in Princeton, concerning the sources for *The Holy Sinner*.

BRIEF AN ERICH AUERBACH (GERMANIC REVIEW, April, 1952)

November 20, 1951

Two chapters of *Felix Krull* are published in the *Neue Rundschau*. "It says something that the two pieces of the Krull memoirs in the *Neue Rundschau* have entertained you. I only released them because Bermann wanted them after I read them in the Zürich Schauspielhaus. The end is a great way off. I often doubt whether I shall be able to dredge up the necessary mood to carry through with the book." [Unpublished letter to Hermann Kesten]

BEKENNTNISSE DES HOCHSTAPLERS FELIX KRULL: ZWEI NEUE ROMAN-FRAGMENTE: REISE UND ANKUNFT, CIRKUS (DIE NEUE RUNDSCHAU, Frankfurt on Main, November, 1951)

November 30, 1951

T.M. is formally accepted into the Academy of Arts and Letters in New York. "America has just accepted me into its Academy of Arts and Letters with great publicity as one of its fifty immortals, 'as a creative artist whose works are likely to achieve a permanent place in the nation's culture.'" [Unpublished letter to Ida Herz]

THE RETURN TO EUROPE

February 22, 1952

At the tenth anniversary of the death of Stefan Zweig, T.M. writes, "It is true that even this world, which has caused his death, could hold nothing against his enormous insight into man. His literary fame reaches to the farthest corner of the earth—a remarkable matter considering the limited popularity that German literature enjoys in comparison to French and English. There has perhaps been no writer since the days of Erasmus (about whom he has written brilliantly) so famous as Stefan Zweig. But never has world fame been borne with deeper wisdom, finer modesty, or more unaffected humility." [*Stefan Zweig zum sehnten Todestag*]

STEFAN ZWEIG ZUM 10. TODESTAG (In ALTES UND NEUES. Frankfurt on Main: S. Fischer, 1953)

March 11, 1952

Along with *Felix Krull*, T.M. has other work to do. ". . . there is a half-hour program to be written for the B.B.C.—*The Artist and Society* (!); a collection of essays, material from five decades, which I must prepare for the press and for which I must write a foreword; with this and the demands of my reading and the letters I owe, I often no longer know what I am doing." [Letter to Emil Preetorius, *Briefe III*]

May 16, 1952

He interrupts work on *Felix Krull* after finishing Chapter Five of Book Three, the conversation with Professor Kuckuck, and begins writing *The Black Swan*. "At the time I am quite tired but am working steadily, not just now on the Krull manuscript but rather on a novella, which, I think, will pleasantly interrupt the lengthy work. I should like to be finished with something again." [Unpublished letter to Ida Herz]

May 28 and 30, 1952

The B.B.C. broadcasts *The Artist and Society* on its Third Program.

THE ARTIST AND SOCIETY (THE LISTENER, London, June 5, 1952)

June 12, 1952

He is awarded the Italian literary prize of Antonio Feltrinelli by the Accademia Nazionale dei Lincei, Rome. "In the official document, which was written by Professor Francesco Flora (Milan), it states that not only my 'powerful' literary work is to be honored but rather quite particularly also 'the rare example of a man who has attained a vital humanism, which overreaches spiritually the cleavages of our time and thus offers direction to all creative spirits." [Letter to Agnes E. Meyer, *Briefe III*]

June 14, 1952

He writes a greeting to Hermann Hesse on his seventy-fifth birthday. "That I heartily admire you and am fond of you, I know. But everyone knows that, and so do you. Let me simply say it once again on your seventy-fifth birthday and with happiness to the blessed, joy-bestowing life which you have lead. Let me wish happiness, peace, and cheerfulness also for the still rewarding evening of life which remains precious to both of us." [*Brief an Hermann Hesse*]

BRIEF AN HERMANN HESSE (NEUE SCHWEIZER RUNDSCHAU, Zürich, July, 1952)

June 24, 1952

T.M. leaves Pacific Palisades.

June 24–29, 1952

He makes his last sojourn to Chicago and New York. In New York he stays at the Hotel St. Regis.

June 29, 1952

He flies from New York via Amsterdam to Zürich, traveling only with his briefcase and hand luggage. He departs the United States never to return. His last visitors before he leaves the hotel are Professor Klaus W. Jonas and his wife. Jonas is professor of German languages and literature at the University of Pittsburgh and writer of the bibliography *Fifty Years of Thomas Mann Studies*. T.M.'s desire to live in Europe again and his disappointment with political developments in the United States brought on by the McCarthy group are the causes for his giving up residence in California. "Nevertheless, it is a spiritual fact that the longer I lived there the more I became conscious of being a European, and in spite of the most comfortable living conditions, my already far-advanced age made always more pressing the almost anxious desire to return to the old earth in which I wanted someday to rest . . . I only want to admit that, as in 1933, political matters were not excluded from my considerations. In that land so smiled upon, yet grown too powerful, an unfortunate world constellation has brought forth changes in the atmosphere, which can be perceived as depressing and alarming." [*Comprendre*]

COMPRENDRE (in NACHLESE. Frankfurt on Main: S. Fischer, 1956)

June 30, 1952

He arrives at Kloten Airport in Zürich.

July, 1952

He writes *Lob der Vergänglichkeit* for a radio broadcast in the Columbia Broadcasting System's series *This I Believe*.

LOB DER VERGÄNG-LICHKEIT (ECKART, Witten, July–September, 1952)

From the middle to the end of July, 1952

He goes for a rest to Kandersteg, Hotel Regina-Waldrand.

July 30 to August 8, 1952

He is in Zürich at Hotel Baur au Lac.

August 9–12, 1952

He is in Salzburg.

August 10, 1952

At the Mozarteum in Salzburg, he gives *The Artist and Society* for the benefit of the Mozart Foundation.

DER KÜNSTLER UND DIE GESELLSCHAFT (Edited under the Austrian UNESCO Commission with a foreword by the editor. Vienna: Wilhelm Frick, 1953)

August 12–19, 1952

He is at the Pension Appesbach in St. Wolfgang in northern Austria.

August 19, 1952

In Salzburg, he attends the opera *Danae* by Richard Strauss. "It is not a truly auspicious work, as you indicate in your image of the legs of unequal length, and will hardly conquer the world. Gregor has written bad poetry, and Hofmannsthal would glance hastily at his fingernails. Naturally there is much beauty and charm in the music but too much kettledrum, too much pomp and emptiness also. Your scenery is, of course, simply incomparable, a constant treat for the eyes. And the gilding scene, beginning with the little Pompeian vase is also technically quite excellent." [Letter to Emil Preetorius, *Briefe III*]

From August 20, 1952

T.M. spends three weeks in Bad Gastein at the Haus Gerke. "I should be grateful if you would not ask me about new plans. I want to enjoy Europe in peace. With increasing age, one is urged toward his place of origin. One returns to where one started." [From a conversation]

September, 1952

He gives *The Artist and Society* at a UNESCO congress in Venice.

September 11 to December 24, 1952

During his stay at the Waldhaus Dolder in Zürich, T.M. takes several short trips.

September 17, 1952

He gives a reading from *Felix Krull*, sponsored by the Gutenberg Bookguild, in the small Tonhalle-Saal.

September 29, 1952
He gives *The Artist and Society* in the Zürich Schauspielhaus.

September 30, 1952
During the Berlin premiere of Christopher Fry's *The First Born*, the translator, Hans Feist, dies. He was also the translator of Jules Romains and Benedetto Croce. Feist was a friend of the Mann family.

HANS FEIST ZUM GEDÄCHTNIS (In GESAMMELTE WERKE IN ZWÖLF BÄNDEN, Volume X. Frankfurt on Main: S. Fischer, 1960)

October 3, 1952
Alfred Neumann dies. Hermann Kesten reads T.M.'s eulogy at the memorial meeting in the Munich Kammerspiele on October 24. "I was very, very fond of him in his discreet gentleness, his fairness, his manly quietness and goodness, and I have admired him because he did not have a single enemy . . . Matters were different with me . . . I have never heard a bad, unfavorable word about him from human mouth." [*Für Alfred Neumann*]

FÜR ALFRED NEUMANN (NEUE ZEITUNG, Munich, October 25/26, 1952)

October, 1952
T.M. is with Katja and Erika Mann in Munich, where there is a reception for him given by the director of the night studio of the Bavarian Radio, Dr. Gerhard Szczesny. Here T.M. meets the writer Ernst Penzoldt and the publisher Kurt Desch.

October 13, 1952
T.M. gives a eulogy of his publisher and friend Dr. Emil Oprecht at the crematorium in Zürich. ". . . My finest memory of him is on New Year's Eve, 1936, in one of the rooms of his office, when I read to him the letter I had just written to Bonn, the polemic against the destroyers of Germany. That letter, thanks to his initiative, made its way around the world." [*Abschied von Emil Oprecht*]

ABSCHIED VON EMIL OPRECHT (WELTWOCHE, Zürich, October 17, 1952)

October 19, 1952
He gives a reading from *Felix Krull* at the Munich Kammerspiele.

November 4, 1952
Dwight D. Eisenhower is elected president of the United States.

November 9, 1952
T.M. gives a speech on Gerhart Hauptmann's ninetieth birthday in the presence of Hauptmann's widow Margarete, his son Benvenuto, the Hessian minister of education Metz-

HAUPTMANN, DER GROSSE GÜTIGE FREUND (NEUE ZEITUNG, Munich, November 15/16, 1952)

ger, and the mayor of Frankfurt Walter Kolb. T.M. is introduced by the Frankfurt theater director Buckwitz.

November 10, 1952
He gives a reading from *Felix Krull* at Frankfurt University. "An exciting liveliness streamed from the hardly graying man of seventy-seven, the liveliness of an alert spirit, emphasized by the movement of his hand, his shoulders, his heavy dark eyebrows." [Rolf Schroers]

November 17–26, 1952
He is in Vienna.

November 18, 1952
After a press conference, T.M. gives his *The Artist and Society* lecture in the Mozartsaal of the Vienna Konzerthaus. He is invited to Vienna by the Austrian PEN Club.

December 2, 1952
T.M. rents a house in Erlenbach near Zürich, Glärnischstrasse 12. "In Erlenbach, high above the Zürcher See, we have rented a little house and hope to be able to move in by the middle of the month. We are again taking up the form of life from 1933–1938, which, during the fifteen American years, I have actually always wished for. In my request for permission to settle (settle is also meant in its generous sense), I have given as my purpose 'to spend the evening of my life and to write.' That is nice, isn't it?" [Letter to Robert Faesi, *Thomas Mann/Robert Faesi, Briefwechsel.* Zürich: Atlantis Verlag, 1962]

December 4, 1952
T.M.'s son-in-law and friend, Professor Guiseppe Antonio Borgese, dies in Fiesole.

December 16, 1952
The French government awards T.M. the Officer's Cross of the Legion of Honor with the words, "This distinction is a homage rendered by France to the exceptional valor and the worldwide importance of your literary works as well as the struggle which you have not ceased to maintain in the interest of liberty and human dignity."

December 26, 1952
"Truly a finer Christmas present could not have been given me. It is not simply a manner of speaking when I say that no other honor for my work from any other source has given me such great joy as this one, and I am particularly deeply

and happily touched by the words which the French government gave as its reason for offering me this high distinction." [Letter to Robert Schuman, *Briefe III*] At the beginning of January, 1953 in Erlenbach, Robert Schuman presents the order personally to T.M., who from that time always wears the little red rosette in his buttonhole.

December, 1952

T.M. clarifies the misunderstood remarks that he made at the Vienna press conference of November 18. "All my action and effort, all my books and writings, and all my being prove me to be constantly dedicated to contributing my powers to the great cultural heritage of the West—to spreading among my fellow men a little more joy, understanding, and serenity, to serving them and thus justifying my existence through my work. Can anyone who has really read one of my books deny that terror, force, lies, and injustice are to me a horror?" [*Bekenntnis zur westlichen Welt*]

THOMAS MANNS BEKENNTNIS ZUR WESTLICHEN WELT (AUFBAU, New York, December 19, 1952)

December, 1952/January, 1953

He is ill with a grippe from which he only slowly recovers. "After the trip in Germany and Austria, during which I contracted a serious case of bronchitis, there came the move from the hotel into the house, the arrival of our things from California, which are hard to squeeze into our much smaller dwelling—particularly the setting up of the library caused pointless effort—the endlessness of these matters, even now still unfinished, tormented me. Contributing to my nervousness are the pressing letters that I owe and the lack of energy that has made me falter in writing a story which up to a certain point was going quite well. In short, I am doing poorly . . . also the world situation and the odiousness that it brings out in man have their effect. Often I am fed up with it all but am too healthy to find a death wish anything but humorous." [Letter to Karl Kerényi, *Thomas Mann/Karl Kerényi, Gespräch in Briefen.* Zürich: Rhein-Verlag, 1960]

February 3, 1953

T.M. receives a visit from Ignazio Silone in Erlenbach.

February 12, 1953

He attends the premiere of Shaw's *Pygmalion* at the Zürich Schauspielhaus.

DIE BETROGENE (MERKUR, Stuttgart, May–July, 1953)

March 13, 1953

In Zürich at the Zunfthaus zu Saffran, he gives a reading from *The Black Swan* sponsored by the PEN Club.

March 18, 1953
He finishes *The Black Swan.*

THE BLACK SWAN (Translated by Willard R. Trask. New York: Alfred A. Knopf, 1954. 141 pp.)

March, 1953
The collection of essays, *Altes und Neues*, appears. "But autobiography is everything, and the charm that the book has for me myself consists in its holding firmly to life, in its preserving through the written word situations that were endured to a considerable extent at great personal peril. I look back on these situations with the curious satisfaction one feels in recalling his life, a life completed." [Foreword to *Altes und Neues*]

ALTES UND NEUES: PROSA AUS FÜNF JAHRZEHNTEN (Frankfurt on Main: S. Fischer, 1953. 8,000 copies)

April, 1953
T.M. writes a foreword to Klaus W. Jonas' bibliography, *Fifty Years of Thomas Mann Studies.*

EIN WORT HIERZU (Foreword to Klaus W. Jonas' FIFTY YEARS OF THOMAS MANN STUDIES. Minneapolis: University of Minnesota Press, 1955.)

April 11, 1953
He writes further on Felix Krull. "That woman's story is finished, and now I am again sitting over the old material for *Krull*, reading what I last wrote, and seeking to find again the specific 'tone of voice.'" [Letter to Max Rychner, *Briefe III*]

April 20–30, 1953
He travels to Rome in order to thank the Accademia Nazionale dei Lincei officially for the international Antonio Feltrinelli Prize. The Academy gives a reception in honor of T.M. as well as the two Italian publishers of his books, Einaudi and Mondadori. T.M. has a private audience with Pope Pius XII. "I had already thought of visiting the Pope when I was in Rome. Although the space of time for requesting an audience was very short, it was, strangely enough, all arranged in a few days with the help of the Academy and a gentleman from the *Osservatore Romano*. After a slow advance through the antichambers, it was a conversation *tête à tête* for a brief quarter hour, yet for me it was a noteworthy and touching moment in my life to stand before the pale figure who brings so much to mind. He was utterly cordial . . . he speaks very good German . . . As a sign that it must come to an end (indeed, so many are waiting), he gives one a little silver medal with his likeness as a memento, and one then bows his knee again, which I succeeded in doing easily and naturally. I like to think back on the occasion and with a certain tenderness." [Letter to Gottfried Bermann Fischer, *Briefe III*]

After many years, T.M. visits the little Italian mountain town of Palestrina, where in 1896, he and his brother Heinrich "spent a long passionate Italian summer." The house at the steps in *Doctor Faustus* is brought to mind again. Here Adrian's meeting with the devil takes place.

June 2, 1953

He writes a foreword to a book of pictures of Zürich. "When, however, I thought and said 'Europe,' I always meant Switzerland—more exactly, 'the dear town,' which I have loved from an early time and in whose protection I lived happy and active for five years." [*Die liebe Züristadt*]

DIE LIEBE ZÜRISTADT . . . (In ZÜRICH. Zürich: Oprecht, 1953)

June 3, 1953

From the Zürich airport he flies via Swissair to London, and from there he travels to Cambridge University in a university car. Here T.M. and Katja are guests of Sir Charles Darwin, son of the natural scientist.

June 4, 1953

T.M. is awarded an honorary doctorate in the Senate House of the university along with nine others, among them Jawaharlal Nehru and Sir Frank Whittle, inventor of the jet airplane.

June 5, 1953

He returns to London to the Savoy Hotel.

June 5–7, 1953

He is in London without official duties.

June 7, 1953

He arrives in Hamburg at the invitation of the director of the North German Radio, Ernst Schnabel; rector of Hamburg University, Professor Bruno Snell; and the chairman of the Goethe Society in Hamburg, the publisher Christian Wegner. T.M. stays in an apartment of the guest house of the city of Hamburg.

June 8, 1953

He gives a speech and reading from *Felix Krull* before students of the University of Hamburg.

ANSPRACHE VOR HAMBURGER STUDENTEN (NEBELHORN, Hamburg, June 12, 1953)

June 9, 1953

He reads from *Felix Krull* in the Hamburg Musikhalle at the invitation of the Hamburg Goethe Society. Professor Hans Pyritz makes the introduction.

June 10, 1953

He receives an invitation to visit Lübeck, brought to him by the bishop of Lübeck Pautke, from former Senator Ewers and the Senator for Education Frau Dr. Klinsmann.

June 11, 1953

He makes a short trip to Travemünde and Lübeck, his first since 1931. "I am so very happy to execute my decision—made long ago secretly—to see once again Travemünde and Lübeck on the occasion of my being in Hamburg. Heaven gave its blessing to the trip: it was a beautiful day in the midst of days of constantly bad weather. Particularly the thought of having breathed once again the air of Travemünde, the paradise of my childhood, 'sits smiling to my heart,' as it goes in *Hamlet*." [*Ein Brief Thomas Manns*]

EIN BRIEF THOMAS MANNS (LÜBECKER FREIE PRESSE, July 4, 1953)

July 24, 1953

In Zürich at the Hotel Eden au Lac, Katja Mann's seventieth birthday is celebrated. It is arranged by Richard Schweizer and Georges Motschan. Among those present are the orchestra leader Klaus Pringsheim, Katja's twin brother. T.M. gives a speech. "If any kind of afterlife is alloted to me, the essence of my being, and my work, she will live it with me, at my side. As long as men remember me, they will remember her. If the afterworld has a good word for me, it will be for her also, as a reward for her vivacity, her diligent faithfulness, endless patience and courage." [*Katja Mann zum siebzigsten Geburtstag*]

KATJA MANN ZUM SIEBZIGSTEN GEBURTSTAG (In NACHLESE. Frankfurt on Main: S. Fischer, 1956)

July, 1953

Since the house in Erlenbach is not large enough, particularly the study, T.M. looks for a new home. He considers moving to Lake Geneva but prefers settling on the Lake of Zürich.

September 6, 1953

He reports to Ida Herz on some of his reading. "Although much pours in, one does not get many good things to read. But I stay alert as well as I can and have even found some interesting German to read: the stories of Ilse Aichinger, *Der Gefesselte*, very gifted surrealistic sketches with a light flavor of Kafka and related to certain new American products in keeping with this generation . . . One must watch what one's green successors are doing. The safest way, of course, is to hold with the great old writers as I am at present devouring one Balzac after the other in the handy little Rowohlt edition given me by the publisher. For they are actually made for devouring: suspenseful, sensational, powerfully told, often unbearably romantic, though almost always talking of money, sentimental, even hypocritical, but with an enormous sense of the social, at the same time with adventurous sympathy for criminal revolt *against* society. In general they are of a wild grandeur which seems to me always to spring out of the pages. Also the style suits me quite well now in my *Krull* book . . ." [Letter to Ida Herz, *Briefe III*]

September, 1953

The Black Swan appears in book form. "*The Black Swan*, the first story I have written since being back in Europe? Well, it is a controversial thing, much scolded at, by some also heartily praised. I do not intend to dispute its value. I am indeed the first to admit that it is a problematic product . . . I did not think up the plot. It came to me as an anecdote from life, an incident about which I heard and which gripped me through the horrible demonic nature which was expressed in it, and since it perplexed me, it stimulated me to productivity." [*Rückkehr*]

DIE BETROGENE (Frankfurt on Main: S. Fischer, 1953. 15,000 copies.)

RÜCKKEHR (In NACHLESE. Frankfurt on Main: S. Fischer, 1956)

September 10–14, 1953

T.M. travels around Lake Geneva (Geneva, Lausanne, Vevey) to examine "fine dwellings which are within our means."

September 15–October 1, 1953

While in Lugano at the Villa Castagnola, he visits Hermann Hesse in Montagnola.

October 6, 1953

T.M. is made an honorary member of the Gerhart Hauptmann Society.

October 22, 1953

The Zürich Schriftstellerverein [a writers' society] celebrates Robert Faesi's seventieth birthday. T.M. is present.

December 18, 1953

He declines to take part in the Herder celebration in Weimar. "My health is no longer on a firm footing. Readjusting to the central European climate has been harder on my years than I had thought." [*Gruss an Weimar*]

THOMAS MANNS GRUSS AN WEIMAR (SONNTAG, Berlin, December 20, 1953)

December 27, 1953

Under the title *Sprache und Humor in meinem Werk*, T.M.'s discussion with Werner Weber and Carl Helbling, recorded under the direction of Oskar Jancke, is broadcast in September from Zürich by the South German Radio. "Well, let me say the following: you will have already noticed from private statements by me that I feel a bit bored when criticism defines my work absolutely and completely through the concept of irony and sees me as a thoroughly ironic writer without taking into consideration the concept of humor, which can and ought not to be entirely disregarded as it seems to be . . . I am always pleased when one sees in me less an ironic writer than a humorous one. I believe that it will not be difficult to demonstrate the humorous element in my work." [*Humor und Ironie*—from a radio discussion]

HUMOR UND IRONIE: BEITRAG ZU EINER RUNDFUNK DISKUSSION (In NACHLESE. Frankfurt on Main: S. Fischer, 1956)

January 4, 1954

Royal Highness, made into a radio play, is broadcast by the Southwest German Radio and the Swiss Rundspruchgesellschaft. T.M. writes a foreword to it, in which he indicates the meaning of the book and his own criticism. "And now Radio Basel, in connection with the Southwest German Radio, presents the story of Klaus Heinrich and Imma as a radio play in continued series. In this connection it is pleasant and noteworthy that for the first time a Swiss and German broadcasting system work thus arm in arm . . . Indeed, the story concerns the suggestive analysis of the Prince's existence as a formal, personal, suprapersonal one, in a word, an artistic existence. His Highness's salvation through love—below the superficiality and behind the foreground of the 'novel of court life'—is the real plot of the book. And also the story of the little lonely prince who is, in such a painful way, made husband, political economist, and benefactor of his people is not a realistic novel of manners from the court life at the beginning of the twentieth century but rather an allegorical fairytale." [*Vorwort zu dem Hörspiel Königliche Hoheit*]

VORWORT ZU DEM HÖRSPIEL KÖNIGLICHE HOHEIT (In NACHLESE. Frankfurt on Main: S. Fischer, 1956)

End of January, 1954

T.M. buys a house in Kilchberg on the Lake of Zürich, Alte Landstrasse 39. "After all the wandering and change that life has brought with it, this is definitely to be my last address." [*Rückkehr*]

January 17, 1954

At the Café ABC in Basel, the Literarischer Zirkel opens a Thomas Mann exhibit.

January 19, 1954

"I became tired long ago of writing the *Confessions of Felix Krull*. There is enough manuscript to cut it off as Part One. In case anyone finds these jests too heavy with my years, I shall begin something quite different. Again and again comes to my mind the completing of Goethe's *Achilleis* according to his psychological intentions. A counselor necessary for this undertaking would be on hand . . ." [Letter to Karl Kerényi, *Thomas Mann/Karl Kerényi, Gespräch in Briefen*. Zürich: Rhein-Verlag, 1960]

Kerényi, who in his answer calls the "indication of a possible, indeed, imminent Mann-*Achilleis* exciting" offers to cooperate in collecting the material, but the plan is never carried out.

NOCH EINMAL DER ALTE FONTANE (DIE WELTWOCHE, Zürich, February 5, 1954)

February, 1954

He writes a review of an edition of the letters of Theodor Fontane to Georg Friedländer. "I never knew old Fontane. I might have been able to meet him in Munich at the home of his defender Bernstein, but at that time I did not traffic there, being still too young. Did *Little Herr Friedemann* really appear during his life time? I should not have known that. In any case, it did not occur to me to send him a copy." [Letter to Henry Remak, *Briefe III*]

BEKENNTNISSE DES HOCHSTAPLERS FELIX KRULL: (DER MEMOIREN ERSTER TEIL (New York: S. Fischer, 1954. Mimeographed edition)

CONFESSIONS OF FELIX KRULL, CONFIDENCE MAN: THE EARLY YEARS (New York: Alfred A. Knopf, 1955. 384 pp.)

He finishes work on *Felix Krull* after forty-four years (begun in November, 1909). "It is a volume of four hundred and forty-odd pages, 'The First Part of the Memoirs,' which is to appear in September—a fragment still, but fragment the strange book will surely remain, even if time and mood might permit me to continue it for four hundred and forty pages further . . . The most characteristic description which I can make of it is that it will be broken off, stopped, but never finished. It belongs, by the way, to the type and tradition of the picaresque, the adventure novel, whose German archetype is *Simplicius Simplicissimus*." [*Rückkehr*]

February 4 to the beginning of March, 1954

T.M. makes a trip to Sicily.

February 4–5, 1954

He is in Rome.

February 6–21, 1954

In Taomina, Sicily, at the Hotel San Domenico Palace, he becomes feverishly ill with bronchitis.

February 22 to the end of the month, 1954
On his return, he makes a stop in Rome and in Florence visits with Elisabeth Mann-Borgese.

Beginning of March, 1954
He is back in Zürich.

March, 1954
T.M. writes a foreword to a book in Italian of the letters written by members of the European resistance condemned to die. The book appears in German in 1955 under the title *Und die Flamme soll Euch nicht versengen.*

INTRODUZIONE (to LETTERE DI CONDANNATI A MORTE DELLA RESISTENZA EUROPEA. ed. Piero Malvezzi, Giovanni Pirelli. Torino: Einaudi, 1954)

March 25 to April 15, 1954
The house in Erlenbach is given up, and T.M. and Katja move to the Hotel Waldhaus Dolder.

April, 1954
T.M. writes Lion Feuchtwanger a greeting on his seventieth birthday.

FREUND FEUCHTWANGER (AUFBAU, Berlin, July, 1954)

April 15, 1954
T.M. and Katja move into the new house in Kilchberg.

Mid-April to the end of August, 1954
He makes corrections in *Felix Krull.*

April 18, 1954
"We are happy to live in our own house again. It lies charmingly above the lake, spacious and comfortable. In the study I again have my California sofa, which could not be got into my former study, and in the corner of which I wrote large portions of *Doctor Faustus* and *The Holy Sinner*. On it now, I am reading the proof sheets of *Krull, The First Part of the Memoirs*. In three books." [Unpublished letter to Kuno Fiedler]

May, 1954
He works on the essay *Heinrich von Kleist and his Short Stories* written as an introduction to an American edition of Kleist's short stories.

HEINRICH VON KLEIST UND SEINE ERZÄHLUNGEN (In GESAMMELTE WERKE IN ZWÖLF Bänden, Volume IX. Frankfurt on Main: S. Fischer, 1960)

He writes an article on the meaning of the film. "I can indeed speak from my own experience, for the splendid color film which was made from my novel *Royal Highness* . . . is truly an enjoyable presentation, and I understand perfectly the applause and popularity that it has found in many German and Austrian cities." [*Unterhaltungsmacht Film*]

UNTERHALTUNGSMACHT FILM (In FILMFESTTAGE IN BERLIN. FESTSCHRIFT DER 4. INTERNATIONALEN FILMFESTSPIELE. ed. Fritz Frank and Felix Henseleit. Berlin, 1954)

June 6, 1954
T.M. celebrates his seventy-ninth birthday in Kilchberg. "To

my dismay, my seventy-ninth birthday has been remembered in so many places on the earth by so many amiable greetings that I am unable to express my gratitude for them except in this summary form. I beg every single one of you to take my thanks as quite personally and most cordially directed to you particularly." [*An die Geburtstagsgratulanten, Briefe III*]

June 7, 1954
In a letter to Erika Mann, T.M. sketches his plans for future work. "Something is in my mind like a little character gallery of the epoch of the Reformation, miniatures of Luther, Hutten, Erasmus, Charles V, Leo X, Zwingli, Münzer, Tilman Riemenschneider—how those things that bound the contemporaries together and the complete difference in standpoints and viewpoints of each individual destiny stood opposed to each other to the point of being comical." [Letter to Erika Mann, *Briefe III*] The plans subside, and T.M. occupies himself up to his death with a play entitled *Luthers Hochzeit* [*Luther's Wedding*], of which there are 46 handwritten octavo pages with notes.

LUTHERS HOCHZEIT (Unpublished notes)

End of July, 1954
He receives an invitation from the president of the Federal Republic of Germany, Theodor Heuss, to give the main address at the Schiller celebration to be held in Stuttgart in May, 1955.

August, 1954
While staying for several weeks in the Waldhaus Sils Maria, he meets Hermann Hesse and his wife, who are living in the same hotel. In the mornings, T.M. works on the essay *Chekhov.*

VERSUCH ÜBER TSCHE-CHOW (SINN UND FORM, Berlin, September/December, 1954) *CHEKHOV* (Translated by Tania and James Stern. LAST ESSAYS)

End of August, 1954
For the first time after more than 20 years, he travels into the Rhineland.

August 24, 1954
There is a reception for him at the Domhotel in Cologne. As arranged by Professor Wilhelm Emrich, T.M. reads from *Felix Krull* to those taking part in the international summer course at the University of Cologne. He has his last visit with Ernst Bertram living in Cologne-Marienburg.

August 25, 1954
He travels on to Düsseldorf and stays at Hotel Briedenbacher Hof.
August 26, 1954
In the morning he visits the Schrobsdorff Book Shop and views an exhibition of his works, among which are many first editions from the collection of Hans-Otto Mayer. "You have many more than I still possess. My editions were stolen from my house in Nidden during the Third Reich." [From a conversation]
In the evening, at the invitation of the labor union of cultural organizations, he reads from *Felix Krull* in the Schumann Hall. The General Director Gustav Lindemann makes the introduction. Afterwards there is a reception in the historic Malkasten.
August 27, 1954
He attends an exhibition of masterpieces from São Paulo in the Düsseldorf Kunstverein. Afterwards, accompanied by the North Rhine-Westphalian minister of education Werner Schütz, he visits the Benrath palace and park, the scene of *The Black Swan*.
He returns to Kilchberg tired and disinclined to work.
September 6, 1954
"Joking aside, my condition is not the best. A tormenting lack of energy has control of me, and my productive powers seem used up. After all, it is psychological, and I should give in to it as Hesse has done and settle myself to rest . . . But I cannot understand this and do not know how to spend the day without working, struggling to accomplish something without being able to muster the vigor necessary to realize it. A tormenting situation . . . And thus I am publishing the fragment grown into a novel, *Felix Krull*, as 'The First Part of the Memoirs' and act as though the continuation of this jest were already under way, while not one word has been put on paper, and I know deep down that I shall never bring this absurdity to conclusion. I should actually like to do something quite different, more respectable, and in keeping with my years . . ." [Letter to Emil Preetorius, *Briefe III*]
Mid-September to the end of December, 1954
T.M. manages to overcome his fatigue. He takes up work on

the Schiller speech and continues intensively. "The writing of *On Schiller* went further, or rather it was the preparations which occupied my father and from which he would not tear himself so soon. He read, made excerpts, became absorbed with true passion—not only with everything Schiller had ever written, studied, and planned but also with all things that had occupied him or that were related to him. In the end my father might have written several books. . . . months passed. When he realized that he was writing his last work, he struggled with the mass of material. 'Oh,' he sighed from the depths of his heart, 'this work is causing me such worry . . . At the same time,' he added giving a tender smile and as though apologizing, 'at the same time, work is my only joy.'" [*Das letzte Jahr* by Erika Mann]

VERSUCH ÜBER SCHILLER (Frankfurt on Main: S. Fischer, 1955. 25,000 copies) *ON SCHILLER* (Translated by Richard and Clara Winston. LAST ESSAYS)

End of September, 1954

The Confessions of Felix Krull, Confidence Man appears in Germany.

BEKENNTNISSE DES HOCHSTAPLERS FELIX KRULL (Frankfurt on Main: S. Fischer, 1954. 20,000 copies)

October 26, 1954

A Thomas Mann-Arbeitskreis, a literary study group, is formed in the German Kulturbund with its seat in Potsdam. Founders are Professor Hans Schlemmer and Georg Wenzel.

October, 1954

Gustav Seitz models a portrait bust of T.M. under contract with the German Democratic Republic. "I believe that Seitz has performed this matter excellently. My wife agrees with me that the somewhat larger-than-life bust bears a close resemblance and has really a rather monumentally immortalizing effect." [*Hans Reisiger*]

October, 1954

T.M. writes a greeting to his friend Hans Reisiger on his seventieth birthday. "My dear friend and the friend of my family for many years, Hans Reisiger, the poet and translator, distinguished in both occupations, has reached his seventieth birthday. Congratulating him on this high day, congratulating myself because life has lead him to me, I lay everything aside to remember his pleasant character, his service to German letters, his faithfulness, to which, in my heart, I have always responded to with sympathy, respect, and tenderness." [*Hans Reisiger*]

FESTGRUSS AN HANS REISIGER (STUTTGARTER ZEITUNG, October 16, 1954)

November, 1954

"*Krull* has been sold out now for several weeks. The forty

thousand copies are gone." [Unpublished letter to Anna Jacobson]

November 25, 1954

In Kilchberg, Marino Marini makes an agreement with T.M. for a special issue of the Swiss periodical, *Du*, on T.M.'s eightieth birthday.

November 30, 1954

At the invitation from the student body of the Zürich Technical Hochschule, T.M. gives *Kleist und seine Erzählungen* at the Auditorium Maximum.

Christmas, 1954

The manuscript of *On Schiller* is finished. Instead of twenty typed pages, which was the number required for the Schiller Year lecture, there are a hundred twenty. Erika Mann undertakes the necessary abridgement.

December, 1954

In Kilchberg, T.M. records *Chekhov* in an English translation for the B.B.C.

1955
THE LAST YEAR

January 18, 1955

He leaves Zürich and goes to the Hotel Excelsior in Arosa, for the cure.

January 20, 1955

He becomes ill with a serious virus infection.

January 27 to February 5, 1955

After a collapse, he is treated in the canton hospital in Chur. He returns to Kilchberg.

February 11, 1955

T.M. and Katja celebrate their golden wedding anniversary in Kilchberg with the closest members of the family.

February 27, 1955

The Chekhov lecture is broadcast in English by the B.B.C.

Beginning of March, 1955

An outline of the shortened Schiller lecture is sent to President Heuss and the president of the Schiller Society, who are also to speak at the celebration in Stuttgart. "Out of this festival speech, which was requested of me and which I intend to give in the two cities of Schiller, Stuttgart and Weimar, there has grown an extensive essay of which I could deliver hardly a fourth orally [in the time allotted]. This treatise attempts to praise the specific stature of the genius—a generous, soaring, flaming, upward-striving greatness, which Goethe's wiser majestic nature does not offer. Schiller's spirit is drunk with the universal, the pedagogical in matters of humanity and culture, manly in all to the highest degree, not at all lost in ecstasy, with strongly realistic lines, destined for the most exalted success and suited for this world, yet profoundly thirsting for the heavenly, for a release from this world, for transfiguration." [Letter to the editor of *Sonntag*, Berlin, *Briefe II*]

March 3, 1955

T.M. accepts honorary citizenship from the city of Lübeck. "I have heard with emotion how thoughtfully and kindly the city of my fathers thinks of me." [*An den Bürgermeister von Lübeck*]

THOMAS MANN AN DEN BÜRGERMEISTER VON LÜBECK (LÜBECKER FREIE PRESSE, March 11, 1955)

March 16, 1955

He works further on *Luthers Hochzeit*. "I cannot send you any news of *Krull*. On the continuation not one word has been put to paper. Between us, I have something quite different in mind: an actable work, *Luther's Wedding*, for which I am reading much and taking notes without being sure that I shall carry it out." [Letter to Agnes E. Meyer, *Briefe III*]

March 22, 1955

He reads *Chekhov* at the Hotel Elite in Zürich at the invitation of the Zürich Schriftstellerverein.

March 24, 1955

He is awarded honorary membership in the German Academy of Arts in Berlin.

April, 1955

He writes an introduction to Alexander M. Frey's novel, *Kleine Menagerie*.

LIEBENSWERTE MENAGERIE (In Alexander M. Frey's KLEINE MENAGERIE. Wiesbaden: Limes-Verlag, 1955)

April 16, 1955

The Thomas Mann Archives for the Preservation and Research of His Work is established as a department of the Institute for German Language and Literature by decision of the president of the German Academy of Sciences at Berlin.

April 18, 1955

Albert Einstein dies at Princeton. "Deeply shaken by the report of the death of Albert Einstein, I am at the moment able to say only that through the passing of this man, whose fame even during his lifetime had taken on a legendary character, a light has been quenched for me, which had been a comfort for many years in the dark confusion of our times." [*Zum Tode Albert Einsteins*]

ZUM TODE VON ALBERT EINSTEIN (NEUE ZÜRCHER ZEITUNG, April 19, 1955)

April, 1955

In Kilchberg, T.M. makes a tape recording of Tonio Kröger for the Northwest German Radio.

May 6, 1955

The unabridged and uninterrupted recording of *Tonio Kröger* is broadcast. "It lasted from sundown to midnight, and the listeners let us know that it was good." [Ernst Schnabel, Director of the North German Radio, in program notes for the broadcast as issued as a commercial recording.]

May 7, 1955

T.M., Katja, and Erika Mann depart by car from Zürich to go via Rottweil to Stuttgart. They stay at the Parkhotel. In the afternoon they meet President Heuss. In the evening they are with a small circle of friends including Hans Reisiger, Gottfried Bermann Fischer and his wife, and Rudolf Hirsch.

May 8, 1955

The Schiller celebration takes place at eleven o'clock in the large auditorium of the Stuttgart Landestheater. T.M. gives the main address, and there are speeches by President Heuss, Minister Gebhard Müller, and the president of the Schiller Society, W. Hoffmann. "One noticed with what proud joy Thomas Mann had transformed this commission, asked of him as a favor, into an inner duty. The free, expressive, and undisguised homage to the poetic genius, the moralist and thinker, the masterful creator and director of historical political events was in its undercurrents something quite different from the esthetic and intellectual praise of one writer for another, of a living writer for one whose works still have meaning. Thomas Mann's speech was a concerned admonition to his own time, to this German people of his own era." [Theodor Heuss writing in the *Neue Rundschau*, 1956]

In the evening T.M. attends a festival performance of *Maria Stuart*.

May 9, 1955
He visits the Schiller National Museum in Marbach on the Neckar.

May 10–13, 1955
He is in Bad Kissingen. "We are resting here a few days. In Stuttgart I was put to it like a Swiss soldier. But the Schiller speech pleased. At the end the audience rose from its seats." [Letter to Robert Faesi, *Thomas Mann/Robert Faesi, Briefwechsel.* Zürich: Atlantis Verlag, 1962]

May 13, 1955
He travels on to Weimar. A reception is given him in Wartha by the minister of education Johannes R. Becher.

May 14, 1955
The Schiller celebration takes place in the Weimar Nationaltheater. T.M. gives the main address after being introduced by Johannes R. Becher. In the evening he attends a festival performance of Schiller's *Maid of Orleans.*

May 15, 1955
He is awarded an honorary doctorate by the Friedrich Schiller University of Jena in the White Hall of the Weimar Palace with a *laudatio* by Professor Müller, and T.M. expresses his thanks. He is also named honorary president of the German Schiller Society in Weimar. He goes on to Göttingen.

ANSPRACHE NACH DER VERLEIHUNG DER EHRENDOKTORWÜRDE (Wissenschaftliche Annalen, Berlin, September, 1956)

May 16–21, 1955
He is in Lübeck and Travemünde.

May 19, 1955
He attends a concert of ancient instruments at the Possehlhaus in Travemünde.

May 20, 1955
At eleven o'clock in the Lübeck city hall, he is awarded honorary citizenship and expresses his thanks.

ANSPRACHE GEHALTEN IM RATHAUS ZU LÜBECK (Lübecker Nachrichten, May 21, 1955)

May 21, 1955
At the Lübeck Stadttheater, he reads from *Tonio Kröger, The Coat of Many Colours* (in *Young Joseph*), and the circus chapter of *Felix Krull.* At his request, T.M.'s share of the ticket sales goes to the Holy Spirit Hospital, a home for the aged.

June 4, 1955
The Zürich city council sponsors a noontime celebration of T.M.'s coming birthday in the Muraltengut. The president of

the city, Dr. Emil Landolt, greets T.M. in the city's behalf. That afternoon, a celebration is held in Kilchberg at the Conrad Ferdinand Meyer Haus, with a speech by the President of Switzerland, Dr. Max Petitpierre. T.M. is given a diploma of Doctor of Natural Sciences from the Zürich Technical Hochschule by its rector, Professor Karl Schmid. Then there is a dinner at the restaurant Löwen, in Kilchberg, with the President of Switzerland and other guests.

June 5, 1955

A birthday celebration is held at the Zürich Schauspielhaus. Bruno Walter, who has made a surprise trip to Zürich in honor of his old friend, conducts Mozart's *Eine kleine Nachtmusik*. Maria Becker, Therese Giehse, Gustav Knuth, Erwin Parker, and Hermann Wlach give readings from T.M.'s works. There are speeches by Richard Schweizer and Fritz Strich. T.M. speaks a brief word of thanks and reads from *Felix Krull*. Afterwards, at a reception and dinner given by Gottfried Bermann Fischer and his wife at the Zunfthaus zum Rüden, there are about a hundred guests—painters, writers, musicians, actors, journalists—and speeches by Fischer and Albrecht Goes.

June 6, 1955

On the morning of T.M.'s birthday, a reception is held in his home in Kilchberg. There are greetings and gifts from all over the world. "Every half hour the postman brought piles of telegrams." Gustav Seitz presents T.M. with the portrait bust done by Seitz himself. Senator Dehnkamp of Bremen, president of the Standing Conference of West-German Ministers of Education, brings T.M. a certificate from the representatives of the German states that confirms a donation of fifty thousand marks to the Thomas Mann Fund for the support of ill and needy writers. He is also given the Aufbau Verlag twelve-volume edition of his works by that publishing firm. The S. Fischer Verlag presents him with the drawings done by Gunther Böhmer for the novella *A Man and His Dog*. As a special birthday edition, five hundred copies of *The Confessions of Felix Krull, Confidence Man* are bound in calf leather, numbered, and signed by the author.

With the document *Hommage de la France*, about two hundred leading figures in French intellectual and political life honor T.M. on his eightieth birthday. Among the congratulants are the President of the Republic, Vincent Auriol; the honorary president of the national assembly, Édouard Herriot; the foreign minister, Robert Schuman; the former French ambassador in Berlin, André François-Poncet; as well as Albert Camus, André Malraux, Roger Martin Du Gard, Pablo Picasso, Albert Schweitzer, and Marguerite Yourcenar. "During the transition, Thomas Mann has maintained intact the glory of the German genius. His life does honor to his work. His greatness is not confined merely to his writings. In the time of subjection, he was able to remain a liberal spirit. He has preserved the honor of Germany." [François Mauriac]

The German Academy of Language and Poetry in Darmstadt awards T.M. honorary membership.

Following the birthday reception at the Kilchberg house, T.M.'s American publisher, Alfred A. Knopf, gives a lunch for him.

In the evening T.M. dines at the Hotel Baur au Lac in Zürich with his friends Richard Schweizer and Georges Motschan, at the invitation of Emmie Oprecht.

June 7, 1955

ALLGEMEINE DANKSAGUNG (In Erika Mann's DAS LETZTE JAHR. Frankfurt on Main: S. Fischer, 1956)

"I have many to thank, so many that it is not physically possible for me to thank each person with my own hand. In these days as I complete my eightieth year, from all over the world come expressions of good will, touching remarks about my character, my work, and the effect of my work in the form of letters, telegrams, beautiful flowers and gifts in such unbelievable quantity that I still have not had time to open them all. I am confused, ashamed, and overjoyed that I must use this summary means of expressing to everyone who has sent me greetings my joy at having gained through my work and efforts for the good and the just so many friends." [*Allgemeine Danksagung*]

June, 1955

The Schiller essay appears in a single edition.

June 12, 1955

ERNST PENZOLDT ZUM ABSCHIED (SCHWÄBISCHE LANDESZEITUNG, Augsburg, June 14, 1955)

A memorial meeting is held for the writer Ernst Penzoldt in the Munich Residenztheater. T.M.'s speech is read by the state theater director Kurt Horwitz.

June 18, 1955
T.M. gives a memorial speech on the tenth anniversary of Bruno Frank's death.

IN MEMORIAM BRUNO FRANK (DIE WELT, Hamburg, June 18, 1955)

June 30, 1955
He departs from Zürich for Amsterdam.

July 1, 1955
He holds a press conference at the Amstelhotel in Amsterdam. In the evening he gives the Schiller lecture at the university. On this occasion he is introduced by Professor D. N. A. Donkersloot and is awarded the Cross of Orange-Nassau in the name of the Queen by Foreign Minister J. W. Beyen. "To receive an honor from a land that has suffered so much without bowing down is a high honor indeed, which to the end of my life will be a joy and a pride." [*Ansprache nach der Verleihung des Ordenkreuzes von Oranje-Nassau*]

ANSPRACHE NACH DER VERLEIHUNG DES ORDENKREUZES VON ORANJE-NASSAU (In Erika Mann's DAS LETZTE JAHR. Frankfurt on Main: S. Fischer, 1956)

July 2–4, 1955
He stays in The Hague (at the Hôtel des Indes) and attends a dinner and reception at the home of German Ambassador Mühlefeld. He also attends the La Scala production of Rossini's *Italian in Algiers*.

July 4, 1955
He gives the Schiller lecture sponsored by the Holland Festival.

July 5–23, 1955
He stays at Huis ter Duin in Nordwijk aan Zee.

July 8, 1955
T.M. and Katja attend the Dutch premiere of the film *Royal Highness*.

July 11, 1955
He has an audience with the Queen of Holland at her summer place, the Soestdijk Palace in the Province of Utrecht.

July, 1955
He writes an article on a new production of *Fiorenza* in Bremen.

THOMAS MANN SCHREIBT ÜBER FIORENZA (WESER-KURIER, Bremen, July 23, 1955)

July 12, 1955
He writes an article in answer to a forum question about the film and the novel.

FILM EN ROMAN (DE KIM, LITERAIR PAMFLET, Amsterdam, May, 1956)

July, 1955
T.M.'s last work is an article to be published in the anthology entitled *Die schönsten Erzählungen der Welt (The Most*

Beautiful Stories in the World). "This is a book the like of which I have never seen before. I am writing a foreword to it out of plain astonishment at the breadth of its horizon, out of honest pleasure in its universality . . . Not that this does not hold true for every story of this collection, but clearly Melville's *Billy Budd* is one of the most beautiful stories in the world!" [Foreword to *Die schönsten Erzählungen der Welt*]

DAS LETZTE MANUSKRIPT (DIE GEGENWART, Frankfurt on Main, August 27, 1955)

July 18, 1955

Pains in his left leg are the first signs of his final illness.

July 20, 1955

He is visited by the painter Paul Citroen, who does a charcoal drawing of T.M.—the last portrait before his death.

July 21, 1955

Professor Mulder of Leyden gives T.M. a physical examination and finds a blood clot. Absolute rest is prescribed.

July 23, 1955

Since clinical treatment seems necessary and the flight to Zürich possible, T.M. undertakes the trip to Kloten Airport accompanied by his wife. He enters the Zürich Canton Hospital under the private care of Professor Löffler.

July 23 to August 12, 1955

He is in the hospital. After the thrombosis subsides, his general condition improves only gradually because of a complete loss of appetite. He is visited by his friends Erich Katzenstein and Richard Schweizer, he writes some letters, he listens to some favorite phonograph records (especially the fifteenth Beethoven string quartette in A-minor, opus 132), "but my nerves cannot take much of it at all, and I do much better reading Alfred Einstein's book about Mozart, which is quite good . . ." This is the last book that T.M. is to read.

August, 1955

In Israel, near Jerusalem, a "Thomas Mann Grove" is planted from the Jewish National Fund in honor of T.M.'s eightieth birthday. The dignitaries present are Pinhas F. Rosen, at that time Israel's Minister of Justice, Elias Auerbach of Haifa, and Erich Bloch of Naharia.

August 10, 1955

T.M. is elected to the Peace Class of the order, "Pour le Mérite." He is told of this in a wire from the Hessian Minister of Education Arno Hennig.

T.M. writes his last letter to Lavinia Mazzucchetti, the translator and editor of his works in Italian. "My head is empty. My stomach is heavy as though I had eaten too much, but there is almost nothing there of what I have eaten. But this weakness . . . is only a secondary symptom of the main trouble—this obstruction in my leg, which is constantly improving, so that hope of return to my normal existence moves nearer."

LETZTER BRIEF (In ALMANACH, DAS 77. JAHR. Frankfurt on Main: S. Fischer, 1963

The Parisian publisher and bookdealer Martin Flinker is one of the last visitors to the hospital. T.M., sitting in an armchair, says that nothing has made him so happy as *Hommage de la France à Thomas Mann*, edited by Flinker.

August 11, 1955

Toward evening T.M. goes into a decline.

August 12, 1955

By morning his situation has become very serious. His blood pressure can no longer be measured. A blood transfusion, injections to stimulate him, and all other efforts fail. He is conscious the whole day, however, and before going to sleep he asks for his glasses. He sleeps, breathing freely, calm, and without pain.

At eight that evening his heart stops, but this is unnoticed by his wife sitting beside his bed.

The cause of death is heavy calcification of the large leg artery. Owing to abrasion, a small vein is torn from which blood seeps into the vegetative system, preventing it from functioning.

August 13–15, 1955

T.M.'s body lies in state at the clinic.

August 16, 1955

He is buried in the cemetary at Kilchberg not far from the grave of Konrad Ferdinand Meyer. At the family's request, only a small group is to attend the funeral, but many hundreds of people come. The Swiss Minister of the Interior, Dr. Etter, represents his government. The Ambassador from the Federal Republic, Dr. Holzapfel, and the Minister of Education from the German Democratic Republic, Johannes R. Becher, are present, as well as the rectors of many German universities, directors of German theaters, a delegation from Lübeck, and many of T.M.'s friends. The sermon and burial are performed by Pastor Schweingruber of Kilchberg.

At the request of the family, T.M.'s friend Richard Schweizer gives the eulogy. "Our pain is great, but what a grand conclusion has this life reached! In the last few months, Thomas Mann was able to celebrate his golden wedding anniversary and his eightieth birthday. He held his last great lecture to the honor of Schiller, and he was permitted to breathe once again the air of the North Sea, so familiar to him in his youth . . . Let us imagine the deep peace which this ever restlessly active man has found . . . Each of his creations shows indescribable care. His words of relief on completing *Doctor Faustus*, which are expressed in *The Story of a Novel*, are unforgettable: 'I am finished . . . In truth I did not have the feeling of having finished simply because of having written the words "the end."' This sentence, it seems to me, has a special meaning today. Does not Thomas Mann's having written 'the end' even during his life have the meaning that everything is completed? His spirit is present here and now. Who among us does not feel him with us?"

Carl Zuckmayer's *Worte des Abschieds*: "The voice of today lies silent in this coffin. A life has been fulfilled that could have been dedicated to only one purpose—to perpetuate the German language and the European spirit . . . It is said that one carries his native land along with him on his soles. Thomas Mann carried it like a burden next to his heart, as though he had to bear it anew. Painful often to the point of being unbearable was this writer's struggle in exile from a sorely tried, violently shaken and torn Germany. His memory and the gift of his great work have become the enduring possession of that indivisible Germany to which we all belong today and always and under whose sky are our homes also."

Hermann Hesse's farewell: "In deep sadness I bid farewell to Thomas Mann, my dear friend and great colleague, the master of German prose, a man misunderstood in spite of many honors and much success. His heart, fidelity, responsibleness, and capacity to love, which stand behind the irony and virtuosity, and which for decades went completely unrecognized by the great German public, will give to his work and memory a liveliness far beyond our disordered times."

INDEX OF PERSONS

Page numbers in italics indicate that the person is mentioned only as having received a letter from Thomas Mann.

INDEX OF PLACES

INDEX OF WORKS

For a complete bibliographical listing of works by the articles about Thomas Mann, see Hans Bürgin, *Das Werk Thomas Manns* (Frankfurt: S. Fischer Verlag, 1959).

Index of Works

Index of Works

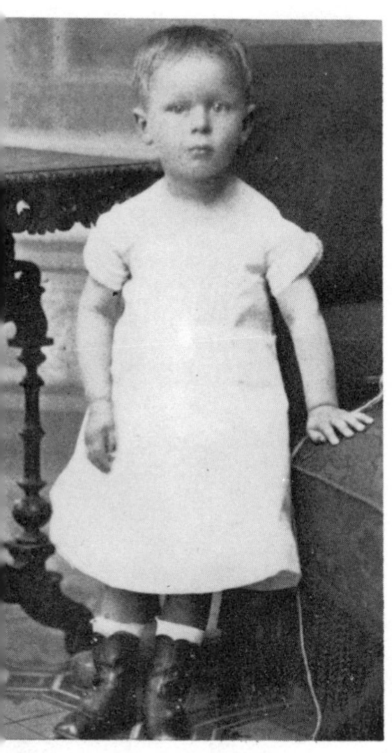

T.M. at about two and a half

2. T.M., at five, with his sister Carla

T.M. in 1906 or thereabouts

4. *Katja and T.M. with Erika, Klaus, and baby Golo at the country house in Bad Tölz, 1909*

5. *Katja Mann with Klaus, Erika, Golo, and Monika,* c. *1915*

T.M. with Samuel Fischer, Hans Reisiger, Annette Kolb, and Brigitte Fischer (Garmisch, 1915)

T.M. early in the 1930's, possibly in 1932 ("the Goethe year")

8. *T.M. and Albert Einstein in Princeton, N.J., shortly before World War II*

9. *T.M. at Pacific Palisades in 1944, when he was writing* Doctor Faustus

. T.M. with Bruno Walter and Arturo Toscanini, at the home of Stefan Zweig in Salzburg, 1935

. T.M. and Katja at Princeton, c. 1939

N.B.: T.M.'s favorite grandchild, Frid
lin, who appears in pictures 13, 1
15, and 16, served as model f
the Ariel-like character Nepom
Schneidewein in Doctor Faustus

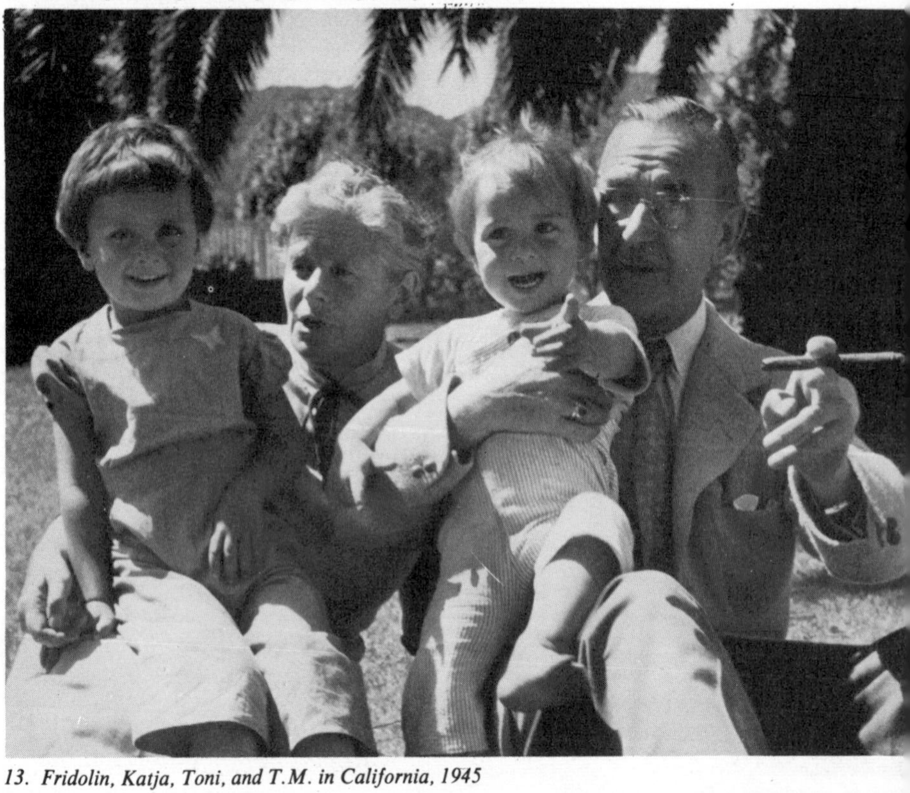

12. T.M.'s favorite photograph of himself (California, 1944)

13. Fridolin, Katja, Toni, and T.M. in California, 1945

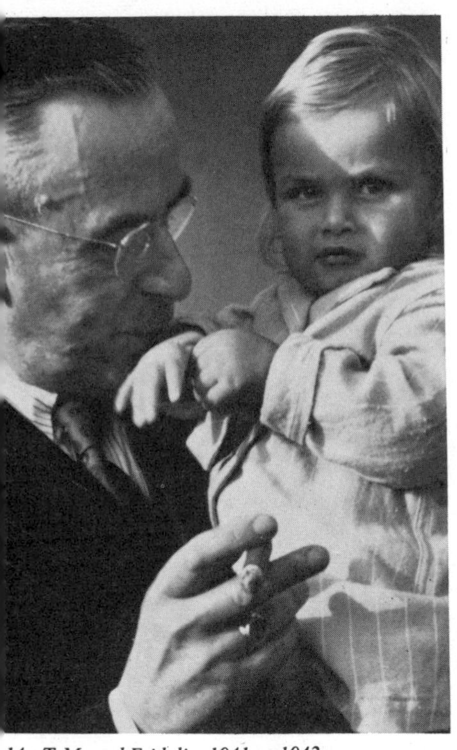

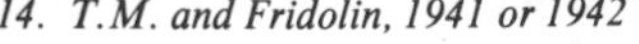

14. T.M. and Fridolin, 1941 or 1942

15. T.M. and Fridolin in Zürich, 1947

16. Fridolin, Toni, and T.M. in California, 1947

17. *T.M. in Pacific Palisades, 1947*

18. *T.M. as sketched by E. E. Sclatter, 1947*

19. *T.M. at home with Erika and Katja in Pacific Palisades, 1942*

T.M. returns to Europe, arriving at Kloten Airport in Zürich, June 30, 1952

21. Katja and T.M. visit the ruins of the Buddenbrooks house in Lübeck, 1953

unterhalten können. In dem Procuristen Herrn Marcus habe ich ja einen erfahrenen und bedächtigen Helfer. Wenn nur Krögers ihre Sachen ein wenig besser bei einander halten wollten; die Erbschaft wird für uns von so großer Wichtigkeit sein! ~~[illegible]~~

Ich bin mit geschäftlichen und städtischen Arbeiten außerordentlich überhäuft. ~~Ich~~ Nach Annahme des Bürgerschafts-Collegiums und hat man mich successive zum bürgerschaftlichen Deputierten für's Finanz-Departement, das Commerz-Collegium, die Rechnungs-Revisions-Deputation, das St. Annen-Armenhaus und zum Mitvorsteher des St. Jürgen Gotteshauses erwählt. Auch das ~~[illegible]~~ niederländische Consulat macht mir hinreichend zu schaffen.

Deine Mutter, Marie und Clothilde grüßen Dich herzlich. Auch haben mir an der Börse ~~werthen~~ Herren wie Senator Möllendorpf ~~und~~ & Consul Kistenmaker (beide im Comptoir per Marcus) Grüße an Dich, nahe Freunde und C. F. Köppen aufgetragen. Gottes Segen mit Dir, mein Sohn!

In treuer Liebe Dein Vater.

X

Hochwohlgeborenen Herrn Consul Johann Buddenbrook und Frau Gemahlin. xxx, Mengstraße No. 4.

Hamburg-Eimsbüttel d. 8. Oktober 1846.

Liebe und hochverehrte Eltern!

Unterzeichneter sieht sich in der angenehmen Lage, Sie von der, vor einer halben Stunde erfolgten, glücklichen Niederkunft Ihrer Tochter, meiner innig geliebten Gattin Antonie zu benachrichtigen. Es ist nach Gottes Willen ein Mädchen, und finde ich keine Worte, zu sagen, wie freudig bewegt ich bin. Das Befinden der theuren Wöchnerin sowie des Kindes ist ein ausgezeichnetes, auch hat das Kind, wie die Hebamme sagt, ... gewiß ... — und zeigt sich Dr. Klaassen völlig von dem Verlaufe der Sache befriedigt. Die Erregung zwingt mich, die Feder niederzulegen. Ich empfehle mich den würdigsten Eltern in hochachtungsvoller Zärtlichkeit.

B. Grünlich.

L. Papa! L. Mama! Ich schr. m. Bleist. weil ich ganz platt a. d. Rücken l. O wie bin ich glücklich. Wenn es ein Junge wäre so wüßte ich e. sehr hübsch. Namen. Jetzt ~~spreche~~ möchte ich sie Meta nennen, aber Gr. ist für Erika. Sie hat 2 × mit d. größten Anstand geniest.

Eure Tony.

22. *A page from the manuscript of* Buddenbrooks *(part IV, end of chapter 1)*

23. *T.M. at his desk in Kilchberg, 1954*

4. *Seated in the yard of his house in Kilchberg, the Lake of Zürich at his back, T.M. records a radio broadcast for America on the occasion of his eightieth birthday*

25. *T.M. reads selections from* Felix Krull *to students at the University of Hamburg, June 8, 1953*

26. In the yard of his home in Kilchberg, 1955

T.M. is made an honorary citizen of Lübeck, May 21, 1955

T.M. celebrates his 80th birthday in Zürich (also shown: G. B. Fischer and Emmie Oprecht)

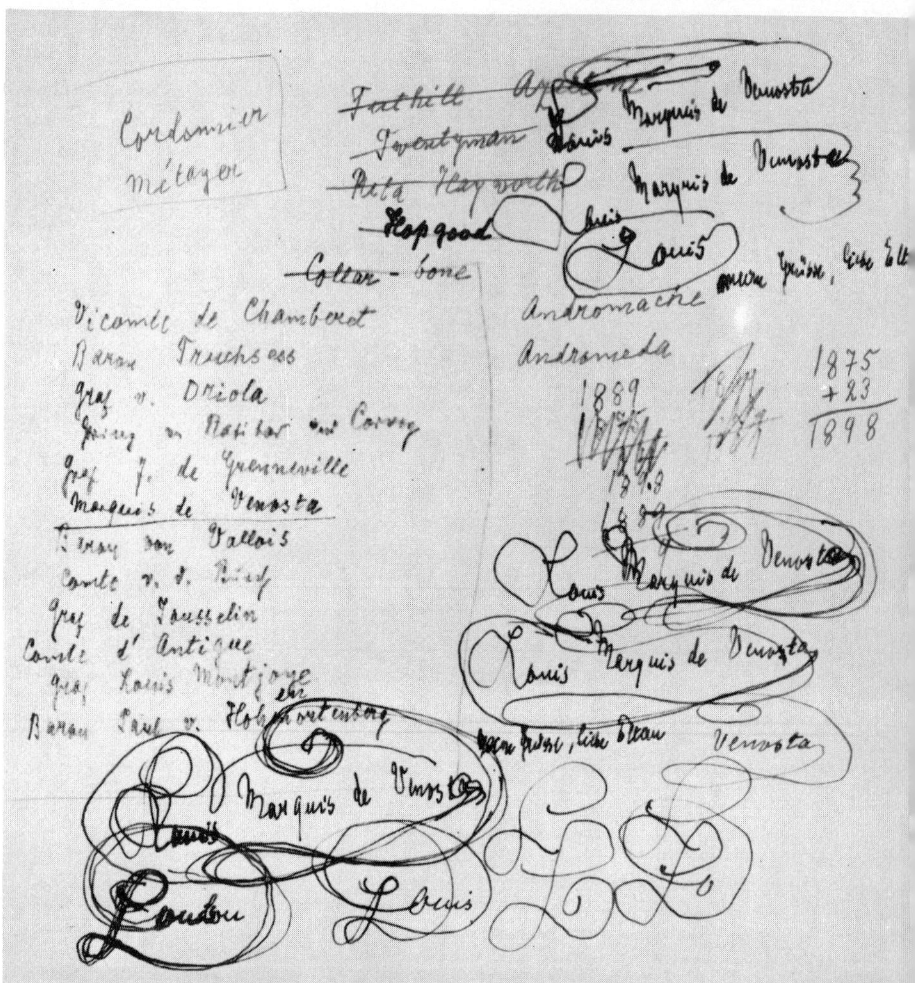

29. *T.M. works out the signature that the rogue Felix Krull will use in his impersonation of the Marqu de Venosta. "With the pen inclined steeply to the left, he [Venosta] wrote his signature and pushed across to me. Even seen upside down, it was very droll-looking. Dispensing with a flourish at the en it began with one instead. The artistically eleborated* L *swept off to the right in a wide loop whi returned and crossed the stem of the initial from the left; it proceeded from there in a tight backhar script within the oval thus described as* ouis Marquis de Venosta. *I could not repress a smile, b nodded to him approvingly." [*Confessions of Felix Krull, Confidence Man, *translated by* Denv *Lindley (New York: Alfred A. Knopf, Inc., 1955), Modern Library edition, 1965, p. 243]*